A SHEARWATER BOOK

Islands
at the Edge
of Time

ISLAND PRESS / Shearwater Books

Washington, D.C. · *Covelo, California*

Gunnar Hansen

Islands at the Edge of Time

A JOURNEY TO AMERICA'S

BARRIER ISLANDS

Foreword by Frank Stewart

A Shearwater Book
published by Island Press

Copyright © 1993 by Gunnar Hansen
Illustrations copyright © 1993 by Abigail Rorer

SHEARWATER BOOKS is a trademark of The Center for
Resource Economics.

The illustration on page 136 was based on a photo from the
Penn School Collection. Permission granted by Penn Center,
Inc., St. Helena Island, South Carolina.

Maps by George Ward
Composition by Wilsted & Taylor
Text design by David Bullen

Library of Congress Cataloging-in-Publication Data

Hansen, Gunnar.
    Islands at the edge of time : a journey to America's barrier
islands / Gunnar Hansen.
        p.   cm.
    "A Shearwater book."
    Includes bibliographical references (p.).
    ISBN 1-55963-251-8
    1. Barrier islands—Atlantic Coast (U.S.)   2. Barrier islands—
Gulf Coast (U.S.)   3. Atlantic Coast (U.S.)—Description and
travel.   4. Gulf Coast (U.S.)—Description and travel.   5. Natural
history—Atlantic Coast (U.S.)   6. Natural history—Gulf Coast
(U.S.)   I. Title.
F216.2.H36   1993
917.304'929'09142—dc20   93-24733
                                                      CIP

To my mother,
Sigrid Eva Hansen,
and my brother,
Kristinn Ingi Hansen

C o n t e n t s

A man may stand there and put all America
behind him.   HENRY THOREAU, *Cape Cod*

Nobody owns where the tide ebbs and flows.

DAN GARRISH, quoted in Ann Sebrell Ehringhaus,
Ocracoke Portrait

Islands have an unreasonable and tenacious hold on the human heart. As the geographer Yi-Fu Tuan reminds us in his book *Topophilia*, nearly every culture, including many surrounded entirely by land, seems to have a myth of the Blessed or Enchanted isles of imagination.

Easeful and self-contained, touched on all sides by the unpredictable sea, the islands of the mind are emblematic of a safe haven in the sometimes hostile natural world. Comforting us, they also remind us of our fears—the fear of being too long at sea, of being without landfall, of being without an oasis.

Living on islands most of my life, I've looked out at the sea nearly every morning. The line where the land is divided from the water is ephemeral and uncertain. The land grows and retreats hourly as the ocean shoulders into it. Pounding the shore with violent storms or caressing it tenderly, the sea's power is constantly reshaping where we are able to live.

Until recently, my experiences with islands had been mostly in the Pacific and along the Pacific Coast. Then several years ago, flying south by small plane from Norfolk over Pamlico Sound, I passed across the Outer Banks, from Kitty Hawk to Hatteras, and over Cape Lookout. The barrier islands below turned a dark gold as the sun was setting, and the withdrawing light made the tenuous strands below seem all the more unreal and temporary, a lacework of sand and waves, barely recognizable as part of the continent. From 2,000 feet up, the narrow strips of earth seemed placid and hardly islands at all.

The next evening I was on Saint Helena, the sea island just north of Savannah, to visit a friend. His old house opens onto the array of brackish rivulets that separate Saint Helena from Ladies, Hunting, Coosaw, Cat, Datha, Pola Wana, and the several other small islands that crowd together. Their inner shores shelter a tangle of teeming salt marshes rich in wildlife.

Awake at dawn, I walked out onto the decaying dock that leans into the marsh. Two black ducks circled, uncertain where to land among the green and bronze *Spartina* grass. A red-throated loon floated low in the water in a kind of dark repose—its head like a compass needle aimed into the current. All around were stands of huge loblolly pines and palmetto. And in their shadows along the bank, a little blue heron combed down its slender shape with a dawn-gray bill. The heron's blue was a tone between the water in morning light and the feathery tussocks of the marsh grasses at its back, brightening as the sun rose.

In the afternoon, we drove to nearby Hunting, one of the barrier islands of the group whose eastern shores face the Atlantic. Here was none of the tender luminousness and wildlife of the shaded saltwater marshes. Enormous broken tree trunks lay across the wide gray beach. The light was tawny and harsh. At the high-water line, where a forest of pines seventy to eighty feet tall had stood, more trees were broken and collapsing, their roots undercut by the tidal surge and huge waves driven into them from Hurricane Hugo. As far down the beach as I could see, the monumental scale of the devastation was astonishing.

In a short time, I had seen only a few faces of the barrier and sea islands—the serene face of the comforting isles and the horrific face of a landscape battered and destroyed.

Gunnar Hansen's *Islands at the Edge of Time*, in its careful attention to environment and geology, renders far more faces than these. He explores aspects of the islands of the Southeast and Gulf Coast most Americans have never seen—the subtle and hidden faces, as well as dramatic and violent ones.

The islands, as he says, are not merely places but "forces made visible." They affect and are affected by waves and weather, but also by everything living that encounters them—the settlers, visitors, and real estate speculators as much as the flora and wildlife. He takes the reader by car and by foot to the graves of the lost souls of the islands, to the hideouts and the marginal areas. While he tells the stories of settlements, hurricanes, and shipwrecks, he also gives the reader the past and present voices of the islanders themselves.

These complex elements—geography, natural history, and human emotions—are all part of Hansen's search for something that endures despite the perpetual flux, some deeper spirit of these fearsome and blessed islands. Through his vivid writing, we get closer to understanding that spirit, and perhaps the spirit of all islands, both real and imagined.

Frank Stewart

P r e f a c e

One day while flying from Boston to Miami I looked out the window and saw Fire Island along Long Island's southern shore. The surf breaking against it was clearly visible, even from some two miles in the air. I was struck by its narrowness, as well as its beauty from such a distance. As we flew south, we passed the barrier islands and marshes of the Jersey shore and then the Delmarva Peninsula. I noticed the obvious—America's coast is one long series of barrier islands. What, I wondered, are they like? And so this book was born.

Since that day I have fallen in love with these islands: with the heat and sun and loneliness of Padre Island; the quiet self-containment of Saint Helena and its surrounding barriers; the silence of the abandoned and vulnerable village of Portsmouth. These islands are some of the loveliest places I have ever been. On them I saw dense stands of live oaks draped with Spanish moss; flights of brown pelicans riding the onshore wind; thirty-foot sand hills covered with delicate evening primrose; lagoonal salt flats shimmering in the heat; solitary deer feeding in the golden-green marsh grasses; great thunderclouds marching in from the sea, so overpowering that the small sand where I stood was as nothing. I also saw days so placid and graceful that the light glittered blue across the lagoon waters as if nothing could ever disturb them. I had never imagined I would see such sights, never imagined I deserved to see them.

In a way, this book started in the middle, when I joined the coastal geologist Orrin Pilkey in Beaufort, North Carolina, and accompanied him to some of the Carolina Banks. Pilkey seems to have a profound grasp of what surrounds him as he strides down a beach or picks his way across a marsh. At the same time, to watch him with details, to observe him stop and peer down and brush away a bit of sand, is like being with someone who is seeing such a place for the first time. I began to view barrier islands not as sand, but as an expression of the processes that make them—forces made visible.

From Beaufort I traveled on, stopping at Saint Helena and the Sea Islands south of it in South Carolina and Georgia to get the lay of the land and to see the great marshes of Glynn, which as a youngster I had read verses about. (Such was the result of a southern education, to suffer through the poet Sidney Lanier.) I recited them to myself: "How ample, the marsh and the sea and the sky! A league and a league of marsh-grass, waist-high, broad in the blade . . ." I stopped on Jekyll Island, across these marshes, where at the turn of the century the rich had come to hide from the outside world. Today it is covered with golf courses and vacationing Americans whose bumper stickers cheerfully announce that they are spending their children's inheritance.

Then I drove west along the Gulf Coast through Alabama and Mississippi and across the deep swamplands of Louisiana to Texas. Here was Galveston where, fresh out of high school, I had first tried to surf (the waves were too small, I was too ungainly). Here was where my grandfather had been born and where he had survived a hurricane. Long before I reached arid Padre Island, deep on the lower reaches of the Texas coast, this scouting trip had told me that there was much along America's barrier islands to talk about. I knew I wanted to write this book.

Originally my intention was to travel all the way from south Texas to Long Island's South Shore. And I did so; during my return north on this first trip, I did explore north of Ocracoke and Portsmouth, North Carolina, where this book now ends.

I saw the Hatteras Light, where the National Park Service (with various geologists, engineers, preservationists, and promoters allied on one side or the other) was trying to decide what to do with the lighthouse. It stood in danger of falling into the sea as the island moved out from under it—which is what barrier islands do. Some wanted to build a wall around the light to protect it from the encroaching sea. Others wanted to move the light back from the shore, where it would be safe for another century or so, at least till the moving shoreline caught up with it again. Here was the entire issue of barrier island development: do we tough it out and try to control Nature, or do we back off and admit we are overpowered? Eventually the park service sided with those who wanted to withdraw. The light would be moved.

I crossed over Oregon Inlet, which separates Hatteras and Bodie islands and is considered by some the most dangerous channel on the Atlantic Coast (particularly by those fishermen who have to pass through it every day). Here another struggle: the Army Corps of Engineers wanted to build a jetty to supposedly stabilize the inlet, though such hard structures are illegal in North Carolina. I did not wait to see who won; I feared the worst.

I went north along the Delmarva Peninsula, past Assateague Island with its famous horses and remnant hunting camps. I passed through heavily developed Ocean City, Maryland. One geologist, speaking of overdevelopment and environmental skullduggery, claims that it is here that "the bodies are buried."

I traveled along the Jersey shore, from the wistful and fading Cape May along all those islands now paved, braced by seawalls, and stripped of their beaches. Here lay the true meaning of the geological neologism "newjerseyization." I passed through Atlantic City, an island where people came and dreamed of being somewhere else. I saw this part of the journey as my Descent into Hell, where all values had been lost, perhaps, but where I still had a chance to revive mine and escape back into the world with a new vision.

Finally I traveled out to Long Island. Passing Fire Island, where the park service was struggling with the issue of island development, I went east along the South Shore. Looking out from Shinnecock Inlet, I imagined I saw the sand draining away from the barrier island, carried by the littoral drift deep into the sea. This, I thought, would be a fitting place to end my book.

But that was not to be. I realized as I traveled and thought about what I was seeing, that I actually had two books—one about the nature of these islands and the experience of those who live on them, and another about the disturbing question of barrier island development. A book focused solely on development, I decided, would wait till a later time. For now I would make the less concrete journey. And so, when I got to Portsmouth, I knew I had found what I was looking for and I had said what I had to say. This book would end there.

One image in particular has stayed with me. I was leaving the islands for the last time and had driven north along Ocracoke late in the day to catch the ferry to Hatteras. Offshore the sea was wild and the winds strong, though the weather was easing. The ferry moved slowly north along the back side of the island. Between it and Ocracoke a sand ridge extended some distance. The water was shallow out to the ridge, and I saw two men wading across, shining their flashlights into the water, netting fish. The daylight was almost completely gone; only some blue remnants lingered in the western sky, enough to reveal the dark shape of the ridge against the brighter water. The sky was clearing. Saturn, massive and bright, was already visible.

Here is what stayed with me: The two fishermen casting their lights back and forth at their feet seemed to be walking on the water.

Islands
at the Edge
of Time

Boca Chica

Boca Chica, Texas, in March. The sun near the horizon, the air filtered through a petroleum-blue haze. Three days earlier, the biggest solar flare ever seen had erupted from the surface of the sun. Though the x-rays and ultraviolet light had reached the earth in eight minutes, the second stream of radiation—the solar wind of electrons, protons, and other atomic particles stripped from their atoms—was only now entering the earth's magnetic field. This evening, as the sun settled onto the horizon, I could see the cool spot on its northeast quadrant where the flare had blown off, a black mote three times the diameter of the earth. The air was thick and cloudless, and I looked directly at the undistorted solar disk as it approached the horizon.

The new moon floated directly above. It had come between the sun and the earth the day after the flare, and in much of western North America people had watched it eclipse part of the sun. Now two days old, it hung suspended, a thin silver scythe blade almost touching the sun, its horns pointing upward. The moon's dark side faced the earth, clearly visible.

I had come to the barrier beach at Boca Chica to begin an erratic journey along America's barrier islands. These islands run almost continuously from south Texas along the Gulf of Mexico to Florida, then up the Atlantic coast past the Sea Islands, past the Outer Banks, past the famed and hideous Jersey shore, past Fire Island to the small barriers of southern Maine—a twenty-seven-hundred-mile beach, the longest stretch of barrier islands in the world.

Even though we often think of the mainland shore as the coastline, these fragile offshore barrier islands are America's true coast. They serve as buffer to the mainland, protecting it against the direct attack of the sea. When the ocean hits it, a barrier island deflects the blow with its low angle to the water. And if that is not enough, if the water still slams too hard, then the island moves; it gives in a bit and accommodates the onrush. Barrier islands retreat when the sea rises; narrow when its energy increases or the sand supply diminishes; even spread out again when there is more sand.

These islands are small—most only a few feet above sea level, many only a mile, or even a few hundred yards, wide—and ephemeral—moving constantly, grain of sand by grain of sand, with the motion of the sea against them. From the air a barrier island appears to be a fine white band snaking along the mainland. From any distance at sea, it is nothing more than a thin dark line on the horizon.

I was taking this trip because I wanted to know about the geology and environment of these islands. But I had other, less concrete reasons for going. I was born on an island, and live on one now. I count myself blessed to have spent more than half my life surrounded by water. Since I became aware of islands as places in themselves, I have seen life on them as somehow different from life on the mainland. Now I wanted to know what made an island, particularly a barrier island, so different. What was the spirit of such a place?

I knew in a general sense: islands are separate from other places, with clear boundaries, not like the mainland, where one spot blends into the next. And so an island has a sense of definition and limits about it. It is *here*, and nothing else is *here*. I can travel only so far before I simply run out of island. On many an island, from some high spot I can see its entire world with a sweep of the eye. And with a sweep of my mind's eye, I can encompass any island.

Perhaps because of these physical characteristics, we islanders tend to have a deep sense of belonging to a community. We see ourselves, like our islands, as self-contained, free from the outside world. Yet there is an irony—in seeing ourselves and making ourselves separate from the rest of humanity, we are all the closer to those who share the island with us. We tend to think of our fellow islanders as family, and of those who do not live on the island as not. Often there is also a kind of contradiction among us (at least on those islands I have lived on or haunted); for all our wanting to stick together, islanders distinguish between natives and those who are newly arrived, between those who belong and those who wish to belong, between those whose island this is and those whose it is not.

I was setting off in search of something, a deeper understanding of the essence of barrier islands, something that would show me what they shared with each other and how these islands were unlike other places. That was the best way I could describe to myself what I was looking for—I hoped that "something" would become more clear as I looked. I wanted to know why I was so drawn. Maybe I was searching for the distinction between those who belonged to an island and those who did not.

I could not hope to visit all, or even most, of the three hundred or so barrier islands along the coast. I would go to certain islands because of their geology and because of their people. Serendipity too would lead me; I would go where my travels took me.

I would see much of the Texas coast. In addition to its geology, I was interested in its history. My grandfather was born in Galveston, a barrier island along eastern Texas, and had lived through a hurricane there. I would spend time in Louisiana. As one geologist told me, if I was going to write about barrier islands, I had better write about Louisiana; its sinking shoreline was a model for the disaster that would soon enough engulf the rest of the U.S. coast. I wanted to visit the Sea

Islands of Georgia and South Carolina, special kinds of hybrid barrier islands. And I wanted to go to the Outer Banks, particularly the islands of Ocracoke and Portsmouth—one the last surviving community of Bankers (as inhabitants of the Outer Banks were known), the other abandoned.

I would go in search of people as well. I once read about a man who had survived a hurricane on a small Mississippi barrier island by lashing himself to a tree; when friends in Beaufort, North Carolina, spoke of him, I knew I must learn what I could about him. As I traveled, others would make suggestions. A stranger in Columbia, South Carolina, said I should meet a man on Saint Helena who knitted casting nets (a skill brought here from Africa) and who could multiply and divide Roman numerals. That was enough for me; I remembered an elementary school teacher claiming that act was impossible—a reason, she contended, why the Roman Empire had collapsed.

I had prepared for this journey by spending time with the coastal geologist Orrin Pilkey, Jr. Already well respected internationally by his peers, he was becoming visible to the public as a strong voice among those who felt great concern about the development and use of the barrier islands. As such, he was also becoming a target for criticism; those involved with coastal issues seemed to either love him or hate him.

He has been described alternately as a giant elf and as a dwarf from a Wagnerian opera, descriptions based on his short stature, silvered beard, barrel chest, and, as one writer said, "whimsical disposition." I doubt that he cares much for these characterizations. He has also been called (in print) "the single most influential voice warning of the inevitably changing face of America's seacoast" and (not in print) "that pain in the ass." He probably likes these descriptions better.

Pilkey seems to conceive of barrier islands as living, conscious beings, and at times he even grants them will and thought. The only proper human approach to these islands, he says, is to leave them alone. That is an interesting idea to me. I like the notion of thinking of them as alive; it helps one see how to live with a place. Yet I find myself glad that people have lived on them.

Pilkey and I had walked the beaches of the Outer Banks as he talked geology and gave me a vision of Pilkey's True Faith. We would meet again when I returned to the Carolinas.

A friend's father, a sometime vacationer at Nags Head on the Outer Banks, had told me that the islands were all the same. Just sand and dunes and mosquitoes, he said. Sand and dunes and mosquitoes. He had chuckled to himself when he repeated it, as if he had come upon a new idea. Then he started to tell me a joke about two Outer Banks mosquitoes fighting over a tourist.

Even some Texans are not especially excited about their islands. One writer has said that none of the 624 miles of Texas tidewater coastline offers "anything spectacular in the way of scenery." What, I wonder, is she looking for?

The barrier islands *are* spectacular—moving, restless sand with life clinging onto it. There are plants: from the sea oats anchoring the dunes to the *Spartina* grasses of the back marshes, from small white morning glories in the beach sand to great maritime forests. And there is wildlife: pale ghost crabs picking their way out of their holes at night, countless gulls and terns drifting overhead or prowling the surf zone, delicate and rich protein life in the brackish bays between the islands and the mainland.

Some of these islands stand as much as twenty-five miles offshore, frighteningly thin, exposed sand ribbons. I have found myself on barrier islands so narrow and so far out to sea that standing atop a dune ten feet tall I could see both sides of the island and no other land. To the east the open North Atlantic beat against the beach, and to the west it might as well have been open ocean, for the mainland was too far away to see. It was a discomforting view, one that reminded me just how vulnerable these islands and their inhabitants are.

It is this vulnerability that has influenced the islanders most—both those who have held on for generations, living in careful harmony with the islands or in ignorance of their special nature, and those who have just arrived, tempted by the sea's lulling monotony to build their houses on the dunes or in front of them, forgetting that these islands move and that the sea is not always kindly. Almost three-quarters of America now lives within fifty miles of the shore. Those who do not live directly on the water seem to want to; many of them flock to the beaches in their free time.

Barrier islands are also places where lives have passed in isolation, tied to the sea and the weather, often in extreme circumstances. Life there is often marginal. These islands are less separate now with encroaching development, and the isolation will continue to diminish in coming years. But some of the lonely places survive. People had lived and died on these islands, and I wondered what that living and dying had meant to them.

In the eighth century the Venerable Bede wrote that our life on earth was like a sparrow that for a moment left the winter's storm, flashing in one door of the king's hall during his dinner and out another door at the opposite end. That life was seen for only a moment before it slipped away. Our life appears to be more or less like this, Bede wrote, and we are absolutely ignorant of what may follow or precede it.

For me barrier islands speak of our existence. Each island is small, specific, here, often at the edge, sometimes clearly seen, sometimes not. Whatever the island is, it is all we islanders have. And it is surrounded by the sea, the unknown and unknowable. Sometimes the sea is benign, sometimes it is dangerous; always it is indifferent. It is a notion that has always in some way been with me, maybe even as a child, when I would explore the shore and look out at the water, or when, visiting friends on other islands, I would stand in the boat and watch the approaching shoreline of a new place anchored in this blue uncertainty. Maybe the idea has not been articulated, but it has always been with me: these islands represent life.

I was starting my search for the definable and the undefinable at the mouth of the Rio Grande. And though Boca Chica is not an island, it is almost one—a narrow barrier spit connected to the mainland along a tenuous, shallow saltpan that threatens to flood at the slightest rising of the sea. The same processes that form barrier islands formed Boca Chica.

In preparation I had bolted a plywood box to the bed of my jeep to give me a secure place to store my gear. Unsure of what I would find, I took too many things. I filled the box with tent, sleeping bag, hot-weather and cold-weather clothes, small white-gas burner, cameras, field glasses, notebooks, and portable computer. Before I slammed it shut, I somehow managed to stuff in, too, a canvas bag of maps and books—ecology and geology guides, as well as local histories. I tied an ice-filled cooler on top and laced four five-gallon water jugs around the cooler.

Then I jammed a well-worn canvas hat on my head and started south through the poverty of south Texas, past the fabled and endless King Ranch, past the citrus groves and palms, toward Brownsville and the fertile Rio Grande Valley, and out onto Boca Chica. The warm air had the perfume of flowers; then, as I approached Boca Chica, it smelled of salt.

I drove out along the road on the saltpan and onto the barrier spit. The road came out through a small cluster of young foredunes and onto the beach, which rose barely a foot or two above sea level for a hundred yards. From there extended a low dune line maybe three feet high, with no vegetation—then a larger, grassy, more stable dune line farther back. The island was narrow, in places lacking any dunes between the beach and the back saltpan, and showing evidence of several overwashes, where storm waves had carried completely over the dune line and into the back marsh. The beach itself was eroding about ten feet per year, close to twenty feet near the mouth of the river.

Looking north, I could see the big condominiums and hotels built on the sands of South Padre Island a few miles away, across Brazos Santiago Pass. As high as ten or fifteen stories, they loomed up as if from the water. Just surf, some sand, and these buildings jutting out of nothingness.

Boca Chica, though, held no such development. There was only the sound of the sea's steady hiss from the lines of low breakers advancing on the shore. And the sound of cars and trucks as they cruised the hard sand of the forebeach. A light breeze blew in from the Gulf of Mexico. The temperature was in the midsixties. It was seventy-seven degrees in nearby Harlingen, on the mainland, and would be warmer tomorrow—late winter in south Texas.

Along the water, sanderlings ran ahead of the incoming swash, then followed the receding water back out, like children at play. The laughing gulls and herring gulls, though, stared like dreamy adults trying to remember something. Some waded into the water up to their bird-ankles. Several turned their heads toward me. A great blue heron flew off with slow strokes as I approached.

South toward the river, the foreshore narrowed to about fifty yards. Matted straw lay tossed up onto it. The beach was full of debris. Plastic milk jugs, shampoo bottles, six-pack rings, beer cans, pizza and sand-wich boxes, oil cans, glass bottles, antifreeze jugs, chlorine bottles, Styrofoam cups, rusty cans were everywhere. Masses of color from water jugs, detergent bottles, plastic excelsior punctuated the sand—white, yellow, blue, turquoise, green, pink. A broken chair sat for-lornly next to a yellow plastic hawser and an ancient oil drum. Even some logs had been thrown up on the shore. Much of this assortment had been dropped here. But much the sea had carried in. Throw trash into the Gulf of Mexico, and the currents will dump it on a Texas bar-rier island.

Alone in the midst of the wreckage stood a sandcastle, five feet from the water's edge. A wall six inches high connected two nine-inch tur-rets molded from foam cups. Shells decorated the sides; a foot-long stick served as a flagpole on one tower. It would not last.

At the southern tip of Boca Chica, the Rio Grande was some thirty yards across, with slow-moving and grayish brown-green water, not broad and brown as I had expected. On this shore stood two white Fords, each approaching twenty years old, each with a single fisher-man working out of an open trunk, a couple of poles stuck into the sand. On the Mexican shore two dozen people fished or leaned against their trucks in conversation; upstream, five men loaded tackle aboard a powerboat.

Behind the foredunes at the river, the island flattened out into a con-fusion of dunes. The backdune area looked as if it had been flooded a lot—from the front with ocean overwash, and from the rear by the river. Foot-deep gullies marked where water had run back into the marsh and the bay behind it. Bird tracks crisscrossed the wind-rippled surfaces. Back here the sand was clean—no debris, no castoffs, no shells—fine and golden and warm from the sun. I sifted it through my fingers, fistfuls sliding easily from my grip.

Two pickups stopped near me by the river's edge. Five men set up a single fishing pole, then stacked a large quantity of wood. When they lit it, it quickly came to a smoky roar. They stood there quietly chatting in Spanish, eating grapefruit.

The men in the boat came down the river. Instead of crossing the bar at its mouth, they ran parallel to the beach, testing the engine. They picked their way out along the surf and in a few minutes they were gone. I watched as they headed out. I imagined I could see the great lens of sand that lay below the water's surface, stretching far out into the Gulf. That sand had made this island. This was where it all came from, carried down on the Rio Grande when the river really was *grande* before the rainfall decrease of several thousand years ago. The river then had dumped its billions of tons of sand from the southwestern watershed into the Gulf and formed the Rio Grande headland. Now that sand lay out there somewhere, invisible under the featureless ocean. And the river was so small that I could have waded across.

I was disappointed. Boca Chica was not what I had expected. It was not pure and magical. It was used and dirty with human dirt.

I had to leave. With far to go, I started to make my way north along the beach.

The jeep's radio was describing a low-pressure area that had been tracking across the country for a week and now lingered on the East Coast. The storm threatened homes as far north as New Jersey. Tides were high on the Outer Banks. Beaches were eroding from Kill Devil Hills, North Carolina, to Vero Beach, Florida; twenty-eight houses had been damaged and three had fallen into the sea. Waves threatened to undermine sixty-one others. Much of the coast seemed to be melting away.

The sun fell toward the horizon and bloodied into a deeper red. The dunes began to glow, and the angular light showed off their forms— the long expanses of smooth surface with a knife-edge where the sand had slumped, unable to maintain its angle of repose; the ripples along the swollen dune lobe casting small shadows; mounds of sand that had become only lines against the dark blue water and the paler blue sky. The island became pure shape in these last moments before the sun slipped from view, leaving the horned moon to hang alone.

The solar flares continued throughout the following days, generating great magnetic storms. Trapped in earth's magnetic field, the ionized particles lit the sky and clouded radio transmissions with their static. Emergency phone lines filled with calls from those who wondered what was happening overhead. Red, blue, and gray lights streamed from the north, shaped like towering windblown curtains. As far south as Boca Chica, people watched as for a few hours the fire of the aurora blotted out the stars.

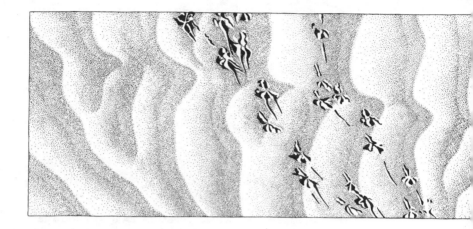

Sand

Let me explain a bit about barrier islands. They get their name because they serve as barriers, protecting the salt marshes and lagoons behind them, and of course the mainland itself. They are young, having formed since the Wisconsin glaciation, the most recent ice age, which ended twelve thousand to fourteen thousand years ago. They lie low: at five to ten feet above sea level, they are low enough so that more than 90 percent of American barrier islands are likely to flood during big storms. They move: they are dynamic, growing or eroding, always changing as sand supply, water volume, and energy conditions change. They are fragile: dynamic as they are, it takes little to disrupt their geologic or ecological balance.

Barrier island formation is the fastest of geologic events (except for catastrophic happenings such as volcanic eruptions or earthquakes), so fast that an island can grow or shrink or move significantly in a person's lifetime. Less than that: an island often will move as much as ten or twenty or even a hundred feet a year, enough for a person to notice if she pays attention—or builds a house at an island's retreating edge. In high-energy conditions such as a hurricane, an island can move hundreds of feet in a matter of days or hours. Or it can simply break up and disappear. In 1916, for instance, a hurricane completely removed the easternmost five miles of Dauphin Island, Alabama. It took twenty years for that breach to heal.

To see how dynamic these islands are in relation to geologic time, think about their age—roughly four thousand years. Some, in fact, are younger; some Louisiana barrier islands may be no more than three hundred years old. Then think of this: the earth is about four and a half *billion* years old, its oldest known rock formations about four and a third *billion* years old. These rocks are a million times older than the barrier islands. The islands are merely fast-forming juveniles. Babies.

Seen in geologic time, a barrier island would dance before the eye, a wisp of sand shaping and reshaping itself, rising, deflating, disintegrating; re-creating itself, coalescing, falling back against the sea—but always moving, and moving so quickly that it is almost not there.

Barrier islands are the product of a rising sea. The U.S. islands formed at the edge of the continental shelf as the sea began to rise at the end of the last glaciation, moving landward with the ongoing rise. The islands narrowed as they migrated, but once they stabilized as the rise slowed, they began to widen and even grow on their seaward sides.

If sea level were to drop, these islands would be stuck—they would not advance with the shore. Thus the Pleistocene barrier islands, dating from the geologic period just before today's postglaciation Holocene, sit inland, stranded as ocean water was lost to the glaciers of the last ice age. And so, when you stand at Aransas National Wildlife Refuge in Texas and look across Carlos Bay to a young, dynamic Saint Joseph Island, you are standing on an old, grounded barrier island frozen in time.

The rising and falling continue. Sea level oscillates, in a sort of geologic tide, between cool glacial periods and warmer eras, with the shoreline marching back and forth across the continental margin. In the last hundred thousand years, as many as three major glaciations have lowered sea level as they trapped water. In fact, when the last ice age ended, the sea was three hundred to four hundred feet lower than it is today; the Atlantic and Gulf of Mexico shorelines were twenty to seventy-five miles farther offshore. Sea level rose at three or three and a half feet feet per century until about four thousand years ago, when it stabilized at roughly its current level and with its current shorelines. The sea began to rise again some three hundred years ago; then, strangely, around 1930 the rate started to accelerate and the islands began to narrow again and move inland a bit faster. (This acceleration may come as a side effect of global warming. Conservative estimates put sea level in the year 2100 at four to seven feet above today's level, and some scientists predict a rise of as much as eleven feet. Indeed, there is enough water in the polar icecaps to raise sea level at least one hundred sixty-five feet above present levels.)

What exactly are barrier islands? Definitions vary, depending on whether the definer is looking at their structure or at the processes that shape them. Let's start by saying that barrier islands are long, narrow formations of loose sand, lying parallel to the shoreline and separated from the mainland by lagoons or marshes.

More specific definitions of barrier islands deal with their height and the ratio of length to width. Others examine their hydraulic regimes or depositional environments. But these discussions quickly enter the realm of geologic arcana. Enough to say that the island sand was delivered up by waves, currents, and wind.

How did the islands get there? Scientists have been thinking publicly about this question since the nineteenth century. Even so, they do not all agree. Three theories dominate: the upbuilding of once-submerged sandbars (theorized by De Beaumont in 1845); the growth of mainland spits later cut by inlets (Gilbert in 1885); and the separation of beach ridges from the mainland during sea level rise (McGee in 1890). Though more than a century has elapsed since the most recent of these, no new theories have replaced them.

Submarine bar upbuilding, the earliest explanation, sees waves and currents carrying material from the ocean bottom to form shoals that eventually emerge above sea level. Some Gulf Coast islands show evidence of this kind of activity, but many geologists argue that large barrier island chains probably could not form this way. Most coastal areas, they say, do not have enough sand to feed the process; at the same time the wave energy is too high for the bars to survive. Submarine upbuilding is not very popular these days with most coastal geologists. Only Ervin Otvos, at the Gulf Coast Research Laboratory in Ocean Springs, Mississippi, remains a strong advocate of the theory. These days he is a lonely man.

Most barrier islands along the northeastern coast of the United States seem to have formed by spit growth (or accretion by littoral drift, in geo-speak). Water carries sand from a source such as a sea cliff into open water. This spit grows till the sea breaches it, forming a barrier island. Jones Beach and the other barriers along the southern shore of Long Island probably are examples of this sort of formation.

The third theory argues that as sea level rose, dune ridges on the mainland shore were converted to barrier islands as the low-lying areas behind them flooded and formed lagoons. The Outer Banks of North Carolina may be the result of such a process, though there is some disagreement about their origins.

Barrier islands can also form against older islands, making a sea island, a kind of mixed-heritage barrier. The Georgia and South Carolina Sea Islands are Holocene barriers that have run into Pleistocene islands, themselves separated from the mainland by the rising sea. Thus the ocean-side part of a sea island such as Hilton Head, South Carolina, is a modern (to a geologist) load of sand sitting against an old core.

Of course, once a barrier island has formed, it immediately begins to change in response to variations in the sand supply and the nature of the energy supply. Islands short on sand tend to retreat toward the mainland. (These islands are called *transgressive*.) Conversely, islands with lots of sand tend to grow seaward (*regressive*). But these conditions are not constant. In fact, throughout the Holocene some barrier islands have alternated between the two conditions, depending both on rapid fluctuations in sea level and on rates of sediment supply. The energy supply comes from either tidal action or wave movement. Areas with a low tide range, below six feet, tend to have high wave energy. Those with higher tide range, six to twelve feet, tend to have lower wave energy. (Above twelve feet, the energy conditions generally do not allow barrier islands to form.)

Most of the U.S. coast's barrier islands are wave dominated. Islands such as those of the Texas and North Carolina coasts tend to be long and narrow; with a small tide range, little water transfers between an island's ocean side and its lagoon. Thus, large lagoonal areas need few inlets for transfer of water. Padre Island, for example, with a mean tide range of less than two feet, is more than a hundred miles long, with no natural inlets along that entire length (though the man-made Mansfield Channel lops off about a third of it). Along these coasts the currents running along the shore, and not through the inlets, dominate sediment dispersal, further helping to create long, continuous islands (and making it difficult to keep Padre's Mansfield Channel open). These currents also keep the ebb-tidal deltas, on the ocean side of inlets, small because waves disperse their sediment quickly. At the same time, the sediment moved by tidal currents accumulates in large back-barrier flood-tidal deltas, where it is sheltered from wave dispersal.

Because of the lack of inlets, these barriers and their lagoons have a problem when water level changes rapidly: the water has nowhere to go. When a storm hits, water flowing into or out of the lagoon will often cut apart a wave-dominated island. Most storm-generated inlets disappear fast, in a few months or years. Other such inlets may survive for long periods, but they will move with the littoral drift, the direction in which the island's sand supply is moving.

Tide-dominated barrier islands are relatively short and wide, because of the numerous tidal inlets needed to accommodate the large volumes of water passing between lagoon and ocean. The mean tide range along the Georgia coast, for example, is about six and a half feet. The mean breaker height is only one foot, so the energy comes mainly from tidal movement, not from wave action. Tidal inlets there tend to be much more stable than those of wave-dominated islands. The ebb-tidal deltas are also large, since stronger tidal currents can maintain them against the destruction of wave action.

A barrier island is made up of parts—beach, dune, flat, and marsh, though the relationship is more subtle than a mere four-part progression. In fact, because barrier islands are an interconnected dynamic system, we should also consider the nearshore environment (below water on the sea side), lagoon (between island and mainland), and inlets (between islands) as part of the system.

The nearshore extends to a depth of thirty feet, where waves can move significant amounts of sand. As the waves hit the beach at an angle, they generate a longshore current (the littoral drift) in the same direction. This nearshore environment includes the offshore bars (always submerged) and ridges (exposed at low tide). Ridges often move inshore till they become part of the beach. Similarly, bars become ridges and their sand also feeds the beach. Often it is ignorance of—or willingness to ignore—this dynamic relationship between littoral drift and sand that gets people into trouble when they deal with a barrier island, especially when they try to stabilize its beaches.

The beach, between the outermost breakers and the innermost limit of wave action, is quite unstable, for it changes shape constantly with energy conditions. It can be seen as two parts, the foreshore, the part sloping toward the ocean, and the backshore, the flatter part from the berm back to the dunes. The berm, the point at which the beach slope changes, dissipates waves during storms and in nonstorm conditions easily loses sand to the wind (which geologists, in their passion for the Greek lexicon, call aeolian transport).

Waves breaking on the beach become thin sheets of water— swash—that flow over the beach face. The sand-loaded swash loses energy, and thereby some of its sand, as it flows up the beach face. This growing sediment creates the berm. Some beaches have more than one berm, whereas others have none, depending on sand supply and wave energy. A storm, for instance, will quickly remove the berm and flatten the beach. Waves often dump the stolen sand into the offshore bars, which become the sand reserves for the beach. Lower-energy waves will later return this sand.

Dunes form mainly by wind action. Once the sea drops the sand, the wind carries it either inland or back out to sea. Where prevailing winds blow alongshore or offshore, the dunes tend to be small and open. With onshore winds, though, large dunes form quickly. If the wind is strong enough to carry sand over the tops of dunes, then they can move inland. On Padre Island, in fact, the wind marches the dunes right across the island and into Laguna Madre behind it. From there the sand continues to move onto the mainland. Traveling south on Highway 77 toward Boca Chica, perhaps twenty miles inland, you encounter dunes made of Padre Island sand that started as part of an offshore bar, then joined the beach, and eventually was taken up by the wind.

Even though dunes tend to form in ridges behind an island's beach, these ridges are not uniform and do not offer a solid face to the wind. If the wind is channeled, it can blow a hole in the sand—what is known as a blowout. Dune ridges protect the inner island from storm waves, yet the surge will often break through weak spots in the line, such as these blowouts, and carry sand back into the island. If the island is narrow enough, an overwash can clear it and dump sand in the lagoon itself, moving the island's lagoonal edge significantly landward.

Vegetation, mainly American beach grass in the Northeast and sea oats in the Southeast and Gulf of Mexico, stabilizes the dunes and helps them grow. The leaves of these salt-tolerant plants slow wind movement over the dune. The wind drops its sand, not only reducing the amount of dune sand carried back onto the island, but also increasing the sand supply of the dune itself. Eventually other plants arrive to further stabilize the dune and develop its soil.

Barrier flats, between the dunes and the back marsh, generally lie five feet or less above sea level. They are often created by washovers, which flatten the backdune area. Sometimes there are no flats at all, or they are small. Myrtles, elders, reed grass, and particularly salt meadow cordgrass (*Spartina patens*), which can grow quickly through new deposits of sand, cover flats that suffer overwash. As overwashes decrease, the flats support thickets and eventually maritime forests. These dense, beautiful stands of live oak cannot tolerate salt well and cannot grow in narrow, unstable islands with frequent overwashes. Because they thrive in stable, high areas, historically they have marked the safest places to build.

Sand, clay, and organic materials carried through tidal inlets or across the island form the base for its salt marshes. As the lagoon becomes shallow, marsh grass—particularly salt marsh cordgrass (*Spar-*

tina alterniflora)—spreads out and stabilizes the mud flats. This salt-tolerant grass thrives from sea level to high tide and dominates the low marsh. Where tides are large, it forms extensive marshlands, such as those bordering the sea islands of Georgia and South Carolina. Salt meadow cordgrass, which is less salt tolerant, dominates the high marsh, the area above high tide that floods only occasionally, usually during storms and on spring tides.

Behind the marsh the lagoon cannot exchange water freely with the open ocean. And so, often fed by streams and rainfall, it is less salty than the sea. The salinity of any given lagoon varies with recent conditions (a diluting rainstorm, for instance); some lagoons, such as Laguna Madre, which loses fresh water by evaporation more quickly than rainfall and streams can replace it, are actually supersaline. But such saltiness is rare.

Inlets are critical in a lagoon's ability to maintain its plant and animal life. Of course, they supply the salt water that maintains the lagoon's brackishness. More important, they are the primary way to move sand landward across a migrating barrier island system; sand carried through the inlet is eventually distributed along the lagoonal marshes. Aside from its channel through the island, the inlet is made up of two deltas. Seaward, the ebb-tidal delta is formed from sand dropped by currents flowing out of the lagoon during the ebbing tide. The delta is often visible as a large area of surf breaking offshore. The flood-tidal delta, in the lagoon, is made of sand carried into the inlet by a rising tide.

Inlets open and close as conditions change, and they may move long distances. Some systems, of course, such as the Sea Islands, tend to have far more stable inlets than others, such as the Outer Banks. An inlet may become stable if the currents that carry sand out of the channel (and thereby clear it) balance with the littoral drift (which tends to close it). Even so, these factors change constantly with the supply of sand and energy in the system. So an inlet changes constantly, even if in small ways, and the areas adjacent to it, particularly the beaches, are the least stable parts of any barrier island.

All these parts of barrier islands are interconnected in a complex dynamic of sand supply and movement, organic growth, wave and tidal action, and water supply, to say nothing of wild cards such as hurricanes. And each barrier island is itself only a link in a larger chain of islands, inlets, and lagoons. Because of this interdependence, when we disturb one part of the system, we disrupt some other part too. If we build jetties at the mouth of an inlet to stabilize it, we are very likely to disrupt the littoral drift and accelerate the loss of sand—the erosion—on the island downdrift of the inlet. The sand-laden longshore current has a problem getting past the jetties.

Barrier islands are, in fact, almost more process than substance. They certainly do not stand still, which is contrary to the way we think of land as behaving. At times it is hard to think of them as geologic at all.

Padre Island

The big emptiness. That is what I thought when I stood on Padre Island: *I see the big emptiness.* My feeling was one of exposure, like what had overwhelmed me the first time I drove onto the Outer Banks. It had been late in a winter day when I had crossed Oregon Inlet, dusk when I had reached Cape Hatteras Light. The wind had been blowing hard, the seas roaring across Diamond Shoals, just offshore. The houses had been empty, the island narrow and far out to sea—an uncomfortable feeling of vulnerability, of lack of shelter.

The feeling was similar here; this place was open. Yet on the face of it, Padre was different. It was wider than the Outer Banks and relatively close to the mainland. And I was here in broad daylight, in good weather. The wind was hot and steady, an astringent ninety-five degrees blowing in off the ocean, small waves breaking, no great crashing from the offshore shoals. Even so, I was edgy. When I stood on a dune and looked out to sea or down the beach, I was in the middle of the big emptiness. There were no hills, no buildings, no large trees, no obstructions, no last object on the horizon. The prospect kept going till it petered out. The far horizon was a shimmering dark line, more refracted light than real image, looming right at the edge of the earth's curve. The great emptiness.

The archaeologist Herman Smith had warned me about Padre. But about other things—about the danger if I were to travel too far down the beach. Once past the shrimpers' shacks, past the clusters of fancy-named condos, convenience stores, and gas stations at the north end of the island, down the thirteen miles of uninhabited road to the beginning of the National Seashore, things changed. After the visitor center the road ended, spilling you onto the beach. From there on, it was legal to travel only on the beach—no climbing the dunes, no walking down the interior flats, no crossing to the back dunes at the lagoon. Only the first four miles of beach were passable to ordinary vehicles. After that you were on your own. And you'd better have four-wheel drive, tow rope, winch, plenty of water, fuel, and time, and some degree of self-sufficiency. From there to the Port Mansfield ship channel, at the sixty-mile mark, there was nothing—no gas, no buildings, no people, no help. Rangers patrolled infrequently.

I had planned to stop somewhere down the beach where the island narrowed to about a mile and then, ignoring the law, hike across to Laguna Madre. Maybe I would even wade out a mile or two into the lagoon, since it averages less than three feet deep. I canceled that plan when a friend told me I would not make it across the island. Walking through the sand was almost impossible, and the heat would finish me quickly; I could not carry the weight of water I would need to keep myself going. If that did not stop me, the snakes would. Padre, like most Texas islands, was infested with rattlesnakes and I was sure to get bitten. He exaggerated, but these were reasons enough for me.

It had not been these conditions that Smith warned me about; he was concerned about people. *Coyotes* from Mexico brought illegal aliens north by boat and dropped them on the southern end of the island, he said, to be picked up later. And so-called fishermen set up on the isolated beaches, threw baitless hooks into the surf, and waited till dark to begin their real (and illegal) fishing—searching for shipwreck treasure with magnetometers. Drug runners came by boat and dropped cargoes to be carried north later. Smith wanted to excavate a site near the Mansfield Channel jetties, but did not dare. For that, he said, he would need accordion wire and security to protect his crew. These people, he claimed, carried machine guns, and the outgunned rangers weren't about to get in their way. Travel down the beach, but *come back*. Don't camp too far out.

So I was warned. A sign stood at the end of the conventional-vehicle zone: "You're on your own for the next 60 miles."

Ten miles down the beach, though, I did meet a man. He was walking north, striding urgently, shirtless, tanned dark from years in the sun, shiny with sweat. He had been fishing down the beach with his wife, and now they were having engine trouble. We drove south two miles, where his wife and their red jeep waited. It started easily with a jump from my battery.

As I got ready to leave, the man told me to be careful going down the beach. Two hundred aliens, his wife said, were recently caught right around here—hiding in the dunes, waiting to be picked up. "The travel is rough between the ten- and twenty-mile posts," he added. "My brother has been to the twenty. But this is as far as I've gone." He had been coming here for eighteen years.

I commented on the large amount of debris on the beach—from where I stood I could see oranges and a coconut. He said there was not much here now, just seaweed. At times all kinds of interesting things, including hard hats, floated ashore. He motioned toward a large off-shore drilling platform in the distance.

I moved on less than a mile before stopping to set up camp. The dunes here formed a small amphitheater, and someone had left a bucket and a table made of plywood and driftwood.

I climbed a dune. I could see several miles north and south. The once-stranded red jeep was moving north slowly. Across to the west, the dunes undulated back and then the island leveled off.

Laguna Madre was about a mile and a half away. The land lay too low to see from this distance, but on the far side of the lagoon, somewhere to the northwest, was the mouth of Baffin Bay, where now-extinct Karankawa Indians had once lived. There were no trees here, just sand and grasses. On the dunes themselves rustled sea oats, the

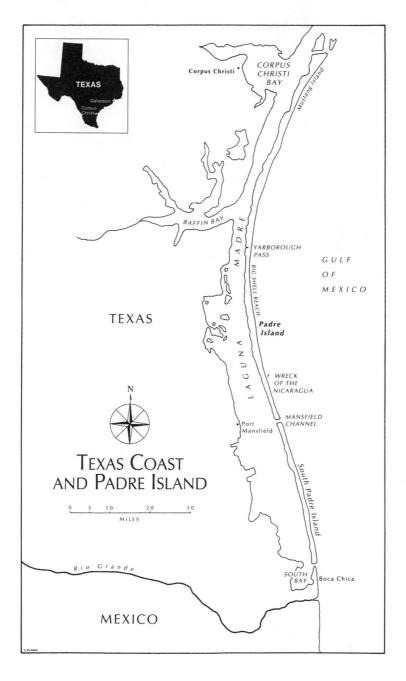

TEXAS

Corpus Christi

CORPUS
CHRISTI
BAY

Mustang Island

BAFFIN BAY

LAGUNA MADRE

YARBOROUGH
PASS

BIG SHELL BEACH

GULF

OF

MEXICO

TEXAS

Padre
Island

WRECK
OF THE
NICARAGUA

N

MANSFIELD
CHANNEL

Port
Mansfield

TEXAS COAST
AND PADRE ISLAND

South Padre Island

0   5   10   20   30
MILES

Rio Grande

SOUTH
BAY

Boca Chica

MEXICO

G.W.Ward

first plants to establish themselves on the salty sand. There were others—goatfoot morning glory, fiddleleaf morning glory, and sea purslane, which helped hold the sand.

I started to unload, pulling out the tent and poles, opening bags. But I was uncomfortable, still unused to the idea of traveling onto an alien beach. I stood there, hesitating, an uneasy tension in my solar plexus, a vague undistilled feeling. It was fear. But this was not rock fever, fear of being cut off from the mainland, of being stuck somewhere without escape. This was fear of being out here by myself, of being the person farthest out. Whatever was down the beach would meet me first. These were feelings I did not want to have.

I climbed the dune again and looked north. The red jeep was still in sight, maybe a mile away, but not moving. Maybe they needed help—meaning I would have an excuse not to remain so far out by myself. I quickly threw everything back into its box and headed upbeach.

The couple had gone a quarter-mile before the engine died again. The woman was there, the man again walking north for help. When I caught up with him three and a half miles later, he was angry at his ill luck, tired, and not talkative. This time I towed them the twenty-four miles to the first gas station at the northern end of Padre. They were delighted at my willingness to help; I was delighted at my excuse for not continuing down the beach. It was dark by the time I left them. I would start down the island again at first light.

The next morning a ranger told me conditions on the beach were moderate—there was a fair amount of debris to look out for. Stay high on the beach, he said. Stay off the wet sand in case you get mired and the tide comes in before you can get out.

The driving was difficult. The beach and the sand changed mile by mile, becoming wider or narrower; alternating between soft, clinging, loose sand and occasional hardpan; sometimes steeply eroded, sometimes flat; in places mined with ocean wrack. I crept along, mile after mile, avoiding the debris.

At fourteen miles I reached Yarborough Pass, a channel dug in 1941 from the intracoastal waterway in Laguna Madre across to the Gulf. It had filled in quickly; within five months the littoral drift overwhelmed it. A road passed from the beach through the dunes and to the lagoon a mile and a half back, the only chance I would have to get onto the back side of the island. Wellheads and tanks sprouted here behind the dunes; evidently a couple of others stained the sand elsewhere on the island, too. When the National Park Service had finally acquired Padre Island in the late 1960s, it had not gotten the mineral rights. This was, after all, Texas.

Once across the foredunes it was a completely different world—flat, with sea purslane, bitter panicum, seacoast bluestem, coastal dropseed, and of course the ubiquitous *Spartina*. Back to the east, there was no sense of the ocean, just the grassy backs of the dunes. To the west, Laguna Madre was flat, no winds riffling it for the moment.

The island had once been a ranch. In fact, it had supported cattle for more than two hundred years. The Spanish were running livestock on it and much of the Texas coast by 1760. (Reportedly a hurricane in 1791 killed fifty thousand head on Padre Island and the adjoining mainland, which belonged to just one rancher.) The Portuguese priest Padre Nicholas Ballí settled near the Rio Grande in 1800 and soon acquired the island—then called Isla de Santiago and later renamed in the padre's honor—via a grant from the Spanish crown. After Ballí's death his family continued to ranch, finally abandoning the island in 1844 in the face of the American annexation of Texas. After that, John Singer (whose brother Isaac made sewing machines) ranched the island till the Civil War. Then Richard King and Mifflin Kenedy, who established the million-acre King Ranch on the mainland, grazed cattle till a mammoth storm in 1880. Pat Dunn started leasing land on the north end for cattle, and by 1926 he owned almost all of Padre's hundred thirty thousand acres. In 1926 he sold the surface rights to Sam Robertson but kept grazing and mineral rights for himself. Robertson started to build a hotel, four houses, and a causeway; a hurricane soon destroyed them. The Dunn family continued to run livestock on the island till the last roundup in 1971. Somewhere out on the flats three of the old line camps survive, where ranchers used to hold cattle as they drove them north. Today Padre remains the longest stretch of undeveloped barrier island in the United States.

Back on the beach I began to notice flat asphaltum pancakes a foot and a half in diameter—big cow flops of congealed oil. They were everywhere on the beach, mostly in small pieces the size of coins; the bottoms of my shoes were soon black. Evidently this asphaltum occurs naturally, seeping out of the sea bottom in the southern Gulf of Mexico and washing up onto the beach. (In fact, the Karankawa Indians had decorated their pots with it.) But the seepage would not account for the volume here; much was coming from passing ships, oil spills, and the offshore oil wells. Throw it—or spill it—into the Gulf, and it will wash up on a Texas beach.

There was other debris, big stuff—a boiler from a ship and three mooring buoys, six feet across. And endless trash—plastic cans and bottles, rope six inches thick, barrels, a bird with a six-pack plastic wrapped around its legs.

Big Shell Beach stretched roughly from the twenty-two- to the twenty-six-mile mark, in the convergence zone for the coast. South of there, the littoral drift was northward, carrying sand and debris from the southern Gulf of Mexico; north of this zone the drift was southerly, bringing its load from the north and east. The beach here was primarily shells, evidently delivered by the converging littoral drifts and then exposed as the onshore winds carried the sand off the beach and onto the dunes. The dunes were large, thirty feet or more—as big as they got on Padre Island or almost anywhere else on the U.S. coast.

I stopped at thirty miles. Behind the island here, Laguna Madre was so shallow that it was hardly a lagoon. It was a wind-tidal flat, more sand and blue-green algae than water, only an inch or so deep at best, with sand hummocks rising from it. Since the lagoon formed about five thousand years ago, this section has been slowly accumulating sand. Some contend that ranching contributed to the process, the cattle destroying much of the island's plant cover and freeing sand to migrate. About a hundred fifty years ago a section of the lagoon finally filled. Nowadays it is under water only when the wind blows from the right direction, but otherwise it is almost continuous sand (except for the twelve-foot-deep intracoastal waterway scooped out of it). Here the sand sheet crosses to the mainland and forms the dunes that drift west across the Brownsville highway. The lagoon is a haven for birds; the oases of spoil pumped up in channel dredging offer ideal nesting sites for black skimmers, terns, white-faced ibis, snow and reddish egrets, great blue herons, laughing gulls, and the only breeding colonies of white pelicans on the U.S. Gulf Coast.

The lagoon is unusual for its salinity. With no significant river input, it is the largest hypersaline basin in the United States. The salt content in some areas can be close to that of the ocean, about 35 parts per thousand (ppt), or as low as 2 ppt in places after a hard rain. But generally it is a very salty 45 to 60 ppt. (The south end of Great Salt Lake, in northern Utah, by comparison, is about 50 ppt, which is considered hypersaline. At its north end the salinity rises to about 180 ppt.)

Even so, Laguna Madre is rich in sea life, a true Mother Lagoon. What it lacks in biologic diversity (many plants and animals cannot survive the salt), it makes up for in sheer numbers. It is a summer nursery for young brown shrimp and pink shrimp, which as adults are a large part of the commercial shrimp fishery in the Gulf. And there are fish: skipjack, pinfish, striped mullet, spotted sea trout, Atlantic croaker, and redfish. Its annual finfish catch is as high as a million and a quarter pounds. There was a time when the lagoon produced more fish than all the rest of the Texas coast; today it is second to Galveston Bay. As much as 90 percent of the fish and shellfish harvested in Texas depend on Laguna Madre and the other estuaries for their survival. In particularly hot, dry weather, though, the salinity in Laguna Madre and Baffin Bay can soar as high as 75 or 85 ppt; some locations have measured as high as 100 ppt. At these levels it kills the fish.

The sun was blinding, and the sharp-edged air smelled bitter when I inhaled. I took a long drink of water from a jug, then poured some into my hat and pulled it over my head. The cool liquid prickled my scalp and ran down my neck and forehead. I sat there a long time, enjoying the chill. I jammed the hat farther down. In spite of its brim, my face was already burning, my eyes sore from the sun's brightness.

At thirty-three miles I found a hard hat. Behind it a large overwash area had cut down the dunes and carried the sand all the way across the island to Laguna Madre. The island was narrow here, less than a mile. Two miles to the south lay another, more massive, overwash channel. No vegetation covered the dunes near the overwash—they were bare and unstable.

Three bars ran offshore here, maybe thirty yards apart. And there had been wrecks; some debris was visible on the receding tide. Now they were small iron skeletons with just a shark-fin metal triangle sticking out of the water, rusted and covered with seaweed. The rest was submerged and ghostly.

Ships have been running aground here since the first Western exploration of the Gulf. On April 29, 1554, three ships laden with silver and gold were driven ashore in a storm somewhere nearby, spread out along about five miles of beach. The *Santa María de Yciar*, the *San Esteban*, and the *Espíritu Santo* carried about three hundred men, women, and children in addition to sugar, medicine, silk, and more than one and a half million pesos' worth of precious metals. Though at first the Karankawas had appeared friendly to those who reached the beach, they were soon killing the Spaniards.

The survivors began to walk south, heading for Mexico, stalked by the Indians. As if the attacks were not enough, the Europeans did not know how to live off the land. As they marched, they died of thirst and hunger, eating the remains of their companions as they died. It is a familiar story; it goes on to say, probably apocryphally, that as the Karankawas saw them eating their dead, they decided the Spaniards must be tasty. From then on the Indians engaged in a running battle with the retreating Spanish, and the Karankawas' fame as cannibals was established.

The records are sketchy: perhaps thirty castaways managed to return to Mexico. Most of them probably salvaged a small boat out of the wrecks and sailed south. Of those who walked, only two are thought to have survived. Badly wounded by arrows, one of the two was taken for dead and buried in the sand. He revived and managed to pull himself out of his grave. He then walked to Tampico alone.*

By late July, about three months after the wrecks, a Spanish salvage fleet of six ships and a hundred men arrived and began to recover the

---

*There are plenty of these long-walk survival stories. In 1528 explorer Cabeza de Vaca, along with 241 other Spaniards, wrecked on the Texas coast. After seven years and some three thousand miles of wandering, de Vaca and three companions were rescued by Spanish slavers near the Pacific Ocean. Then in 1567, after a run-in with the Spanish in Mexico, the English ship *Minion* let off 114 sailors on a barrier island south of Padre Island. These men figured their chance of survival to be better afoot than aboard a ship where they were boiling their leather belts for stew. Three survived by walking the 2500 miles along the coast to Cape Breton, Nova Scotia. It took them a year. They must all have been great walkers in those days.

lost treasure. In later years some would call it the greatest salvage operation in history. They worked on the *San Esteban* first, for it was still partially out of the water. Dragging the bottom for the other wrecks, they found the *Espíritu Santo* and divided their crew to work both ships simultaneously. A few days later they located the *Santa María de Yciar*. Like the *Espíritu Santo*, which had split at the bow when she hit the sand, the *Santa María* had broken up and spilled her cargo onto the sandy bottom; some of the boxes of silver were already buried. The two ships lay in no more than eighteen feet of water.

The salvage operation ended on September 12, with the eleven divers taking an oath that they could see no more treasure. They had recovered about thirty-six thousand pounds of silver and a small amount of gold, less than half the riches. About fifty thousand pounds of precious metals remained on the bottom to haunt treasure hunters to this day. Occasionally someone finds a coin, and once again the local papers wonder about the Spanish treasure.

Ten miles beyond the modern wrecks, I found more treasures coughed up from the sea—another hard hat, then a fifteen-foot-tall green offshore navigation buoy, but no gold.

Birds were everywhere, more and more skittish as I moved south. I saw flocks of great blue herons, twenty at a time. With no sense of scale here, nothing to compare an object against, I could not tell how big they were. I took a heron in the distance to be a man standing still.

The beach was endless in both directions, curving slowly away toward the horizon till it tapered down to nothing. This had to be the middle of nowhere. Northward, forty-eight miles back to the road. Southward, twelve miles to the channel and another thirty-eight to the tip of South Padre—fifty miles in all.

Looking out over this endlessness and desolation, I realized that as I had traveled south, I had seen structures, every now and then a large pole set into the ground or a framework tacked together. Some of the framing could easily have been for stretching a canvas shelter. But the other posts, sometimes the thickness and length of utility poles, had been set erect. Had someone, I wondered, raised them in reaction to the isolation and flatness, the exposure, of the island? To hold something vertical in a horizontal landscape? Were they like the stacked cairns that some Arctic natives erect so they can see stone men on the horizon, so they will not be alone? There was a kind of indirect comfort in these assemblages; others had come here before me. And they were probably somewhere farther down the beach right now.

There was more tropical debris here—coconuts, fruit, and a *Pasta de Tomate* jar from Mexico. The longshore current was definitely from the south. A half-mile in that direction lay a yellow and black drum marked "Industrial Chemicals." (At the visitor center all those miles to the north, under a picture of men in yellow suits and respirators, a sign read: "Special suits are needed to handle this hazardous flotsam. Barrels with unknown contents wash up on the shore. Avoid these containers and report them to the ranger station.") If looking at the beach debris gives you a pretty good notion of the state of the ocean, from here it did not look good. One hundred forty tons wash up on the Texas coast each year.

Just past the fifty-mile marker lay the wreck of the *Nicaragua*. Less than a hundred yards offshore, it was mostly submerged, with its twenty-foot boiler sticking up. The rest remained a shadow lying parallel to the beach, almost a hundred feet long. Water broke against it. As each swell receded, a part of the wreck's far end would stand clear of the water; it might have been a foot across, little bigger than a sailboat winch, though it was hard to judge its size against the featureless water. The shadow in the surf was eerie and disturbing. It spoke of the foundering of this mysterious ship and of the survivors struggling ashore. More than that, the shape itself, half seen, a dark smear in the bright water, was menacing. Why menacing? Because it *was* just half seen, and thus unknown, undefined. Maybe, too, because to a sailor the shallows are always menacing—not deep enough to be safe ocean, too deep to be dry land. Rationale aside, it was menacing mainly because it was unseen, and one makes the half-seen shadow at the corner of one's vision into more than it is.

What happened here? Who were these men? Did any get off the island alive? No one knows much about the *Nicaragua*, but apparently it ran aground in October 1912. There are all kinds of stories about it, about its being used to run guns into Mexico to overthrow the government and instead running around after being sabotaged. More level-headed storytellers, though, say it was a banana boat that ran off course. The remains are always called the Wreck of the *Nicaragua*, though. Not the *Nicaragua*. The Wreck, as if it were an event, not a hulk.

At fifty-five miles I climbed the dunes. It was desert. The dunes ran back in graceful undulations of wind shapes. Behind them were hummocks with light vegetation, but mostly saltpans, deflations, and active, bare dunes that traveled across the island about thirty-five feet a year. (Some have been clocked at as much as eighty-five feet.) In the distance to the west I could see the massive back-island dunes—pure cream color, undisturbed by vegetation—poised at the edge of Laguna Madre. They shimmered in the heat, with mirage-water on this side.

Even in the shade of the jeep's canvas top the air stung my skin. The heat was purifying—from an all-encompassing, all-illuminating, all-revealing sun.

And again the emptiness. Endless sand dunes to a close horizon to the west. North and south, lines of dunes and surf stretching to the edge of sight. Eastward, the green and blue Gulf of Mexico to the horizon.

I stopped to consider. This was my limit. If I went the last five miles to the channel, I could not be sure of having enough gas for my return. I would not spend the night here—not because of the stories of drug runners, but because of the desolation. I would return to the head of the island. I wanted to be closer in, to have someone to the outside of me. I did not want to be the one farthest out. I was disappointed in myself, but that was the truth.

I lifted the jug over my head and opened its valve to let the water drizzle onto my head and down my back and chest. It flowed into my ears and, as I lifted my head to drink from the flow, into my nose. It brought me back to life. For a few moments it made the wind on my face cool.

I turned to go back. High thunderheads were forming to the north. The air was milder now, almost soft.

The return up Padre Island was easy. The tide, such as it was, had gone out. Despite the ranger's warning, I drove back on the wet, hard sand at the edge of the water. It was smoother than the mire I had worked my way through on the way down, and I was able to get the jeep into second gear at times—once even into third—so by the time I reached the populated beach I still had plenty of gas. I pitched my tent that night up island, a few other campers within a mile or two.

During the day the fine Padre sand had sifted into every crack of the jeep, and now, in spite of my precautions, it quickly began to penetrate the tent. As I crawled in, leaving my shoes outside and carefully dusting the sand layers from my feet and knees, I saw that sand had already covered the tent floor. And, I soon realized, it had embedded itself in my bedsheet and pillow. As I lay there, the grains began to grind the sunburn off my skin. *This does not happen on granite islands*, I thought at some point before I fell asleep.

In the morning I packed up, intending to do some more exploring. I wanted to go to Baffin Bay, where in recent years archaeologists had been digging for Karankawa traces.

A flat tire and a lock nut on the spare that would not break free kept me from going anywhere. After jacking up the jeep's front end, a piece of driftwood wedged precariously under the jack to keep it from burrowing into the sand, I pulled the flat tire off. Then I started to walk up the beach.

A man and woman driving by stopped to help—Tom and Eileen, in their late forties or early fifties. They drove the tire and me to a mainland service station, where a man of unusual patience fixed it and told me to bring the jeep around so that he could remove the lock nut. Tom and Eileen's jeep was old, dark blue with wide tires, no doors or seat belts, and the windshield folded down (evidently permanently). The body panels were rusted through and the right front disk brake was dragging; it smoked as we drove. A perfect car for the beach. Everything on it was frozen in place, Tom said, because they had stored it on the Coast for several months.

The two of them came down every year from Milwaukee, sometimes twice a year, to spend a month or six weeks in their camper. He was in the battery leasing business; that kept him busy winters, but it left plenty of time the rest of the year. From the look of their tans, they must have been newly arrived.

I was surprised, I said, that there weren't more people here.

"The park never has been used much," Tom said. Maybe this was the only place where America had not discovered the beach. "They've been trying forever to get people here. It's never worked. The reason is that for every hundred people who come to the beach, ninety-seven hate it and swear they'll never be back. 'Oh! There's so much sand!' " He mimicked a fastidious tone. "The other three love it and come back a month at a time."

How far down the beach had I gone?

Fifty-five miles, I said.

Had I seen the Wreck of the *Nicaragua*? He called it the *Managua* and then corrected himself.

"Yes, I saw the Wreck of the *Nicaragua*," I said. "It was something. I saw a couple of others in the surf on the way back."

"Shrimpers," he said.

"Right in the surf. Not much left of them."

"Right," he said. "One looks like a shark fin." The Wreck of the *Nicaragua* was as far as he had ever gotten down the island.

He had pulled about forty mired cars out of the sand over the years. One time on the beach, maybe thirty miles down, as he was driving south, a Val Girl—his words—jumped out of her convertible and asked him for gas. She had driven down to Mansfield Channel, figuring she would cross to South Padre and get gas there. She could not, so she had bummed gas from some of the fishermen and headed back. When she ran out, she waited for the next passerby.

Yeah, I said, I heard someone at the ranger station ask if he could get across at the cut. And when the ranger said no, he asked if they were going to build a bridge. You'd think that these people would at least look at a map before they headed down.

"Or," Eileen said, "they might figure, after a few miles down the beach, that they're headed nowhere."

"It's a strange feeling," Tom said, "going down the beach. You hit fifty miles and turn around to start back and you think to yourself there's fifty miles of nothing before I get back. What if something goes wrong? What if I can't get back?"

I was glad that I had not camped down there. I would have been fifty-five miles down the beach with no way to change the flat tire. I had thought of staying down there, I said, but it felt too exposed, too far away from anyone else. And I had heard about the drug runners.

Tom laughed. "Drug runners? Maybe, but not down on the cut. That place is jammed with fishermen. They're especially bad on weekends. The parade starts about three o'clock on Friday afternoon. There is a whole beach culture here. People who love the island and the beach come year after year, and they stay a month at a time."

Had they been to South Padre?

"South Padre? Gad. That's just like Coney Island, whatever Coney Island looks like. I guess it's all right if you like neon and plastic and high-rises. You might like it. Me, I like this. That's an awful place."

We went our ways. They would be down the beach, they said. They had a fire every night; I should join them.

I drove to the visitor center to tell the ranger about the chemical drum I had seen the day before on the beach. When I came out, I saw the man I had towed out two days before. He was looking for me; he had seen my jeep on the beach earlier and figured I needed help. He wanted to know if everything was all right—and he wanted to thank me again. We walked down to the vehicles. His wife was waiting in their jeep, parked next to mine. They offered me a beer.

He was in a much better mood than before, and his wife was talkative after a while, as seemed to be the way in this culture. His name was Darrell, he said. He had met his wife down here while he was in the navy—he was from Nebraska—and in the three years he was stationed here they had never gone to the beach. Now that they lived well inland in San Angelo, they came every chance they could. They had just gotten the jeep back this morning with a new alternator and so had gone back down the island. Not too far, she said, since she didn't trust the car yet. They saw a shark, at least she did, just where he had been fishing. She told him not to go back in. A couple of girls were attacked last year, she said, and one had her arm bitten off.

They wrote down their phone number in San Angelo. I should come by sometime if I was in West Texas.

And be careful of the snakes, Darrell added before I left. He had been bitten the year before—not here, at a snake roundup. The best way to avoid being bitten, he said, was to walk slowly and shuffle your feet: when your foot hits the ground, it scares the snake and it will strike to defend itself.

This was an island, I realized, where people watched out for each other.

A cold front was coming through. According to the radio, the temperature would rise to only eighty-five the next day. Rain was coming down in Corpus Christi. A massive squall line was moving through from the northwest, its thunderheads tens of thousands of feet high. Back at the campsite I pulled the jeep to the north side of the tent to shelter it from wind and then stretched a large fly over the tent. I propped the fly with aluminum poles, which I stuck at various angles into the sand wherever I could get a purchase, then guyed the structure in a snarl of rope to hold it against any gusts. It would, I figured, keep me dry, whatever came down. Now just after six in the evening, the air was cool, probably in the mideighties, as the clouds overtook the sun. The air was soothing and refreshing. Behind the forerunning thunderhead scudded some low, black, dense clouds—nothing threatening. The wind shifted to the north, then clocked around to the northeast. The sky continued to get darker as the front passed, but there was no rain.

I gave myself a bath in the dark, the five-gallon jug held over my head, water trickling down while I lathered up with a sand-embedded bar of soap. It did the job; I was clean. The night breeze dried me.

Tom and Eileen's fire down the beach was inviting, so I walked down. Friends of theirs, four other campers who also stayed by the month, had joined them. They offered me a beer and a spot by the fire.

These six loved the beach and spent as much time on it as they could. The last time here, Tom had trained some of the kangaroo rats to take food from his hand. One would even run up his leg and retrieve cookies from his pocket. He speculated about the next campers on this spot: he could just see someone settle in and put out a chair, then have a rat run up a leg.

"We trained a coyote, too," Eileen said. "We would give it food. It would come within about ten feet to take it." They had put out some beans but the coyote would not touch them. The next day, though, the beans were gone, with a series of tracks to a ghost crab hole. The crab must have taken them bean by bean. As we laughed, I wondered if a bean-fed crab would explode from the gas. They had made the coyote too tame, Eileen said. She heard the rangers had shot it later because it was coming so close to people for food. They were afraid it would bite someone. She was sorry she had fed it. If she'd known, she never would have done it.

"You saw the Wreck of the *Nicaragua*," Tom said. "Let me tell you another story." He told me about a big yacht that had once run aground very close to the *Nicaragua*. "Very big, very fancy, built for the owner about fifty years ago," he said. "So fancy that all the screws were countersunk with plugs driven in to cover the holes. They grounded on the third sandbar."

Tom had seen it on its side out there, about fifty miles down the beach. He had gone out several times and taken off all kinds of things. He still had the doors. The owner must have been diabetic, he said; there were lots of needles and syringes aboard.

One time when he had been down there stripping material from the boat, the skipper had come down. He had helped Tom and had told him more about the boat. They had been at sea for a while, headed south. The owner was very sick, and the skipper was afraid that this would be the old man's final voyage. The captain thought the old man might kill himself, just slip over the side some night. Earlier in the trip he had lost his dog overboard. The old man was pretty depressed. The captain wondered what he should do. And then they hit something and put a hole in the hull. With the boat leaking badly, the skipper turned toward Padre. They managed to get everyone off safely. The vessel's name was *Polly*, out of Dallas, Tom said. The skipper called her *Miss Polly*.

It was a story in which I felt things were not as they seemed. As Tom recounted the brief story, I had the sense of something eerie hidden in the details. A diabetic passenger? Maybe. Maybe other things were going on. But even if it was a story that was what it appeared to be, it was an uncomfortable narrative. A dog washes overboard. It had happened before. But it was a horrific image, the small animal meant for land, choking and struggling in the salty water, finally giving in and sinking into the darkness. And for a man to be contemplating the same for himself—it must have frightened the captain to think the old man would want such a fate.

I could imagine *Miss Polly* hitting an object that should not be there, an unnatural lurch in its motion and something terribly wrong. Then driving up onto the bar, its forward motion absorbed by the sand, a rumble penetrating the hull as millions of grains of sand ticked and scraped against it. The gleaming yacht now pounding against the bar, maybe next to the shark fin of the wrecked shrimp boat or alongside the dark shadow of the Wreck of the *Nicaragua*. The captain pulling crew and passengers into the surf, floundering about till they realize they can feel the sand island beneath them and they stumble ashore. The old man struggling to the beach, now all falling onto the sand, trying to figure out what to do next, waiting to be saved on this isolated beach.

I mentioned the wrecks of 1554, and how the people had not known how to find water or food.

There certainly was plenty of water, Tom said. "Did you know that if you dig down a foot or two you'll hit water? The cattle here would scuff it out and kneel down on their forelegs to drink. You could tell a Padre Island cow because its knees were callused." They used to butcher the cattle on the island, he said, at Packery Channel. Now closed up, at one time it divided Padre from Mustang Island, to the north. "They would dump the carcasses—they just wanted the hides—into the bay. The carcasses would get flushed out the channel to the Gulf and the waiting sharks." The sharks at Packery were very big.

My grandfather grew up east of here, on Galveston Island, and I remembered stories he had told me of diving off the pier for money. The water had been filled with large hammerhead sharks. They had not bothered him when he dove among them, but they had impressed the people throwing the money.

Later that night the front stalled over the Gulf. Then it backed up. The lightning became visible on the island some hours after midnight. It was far away to the east and south; twenty or twenty-five seconds passed after each flash before I would hear thunder. But even at five miles, the lightning was bright enough and the thunder loud enough to wake me. I thought of the aluminum poles that bristled like lightning rods around my tent and scrambled outside. I pulled them down and slacked the guys, letting the fly sink onto the small tent like a collapsed balloon.

I watched the storm approach for an hour before it reached me. It was immense. Sitting on the dark beach I had a sense of overpowering exposure.

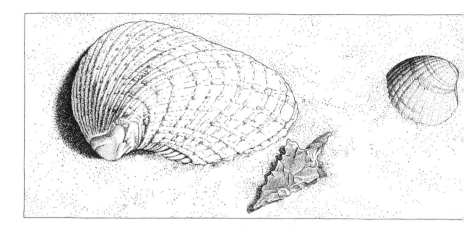

Treasure

Herman Smith had a couple of people he wanted me to meet. One was dead, but the other was alive and talkative. The dead man was Louis Rawalt. In 1927 doctors in Boston had told him that if he had any business to take care of back home in Texas, he had better do it. He had, they said, six months to live. So Rawalt had come back and headed out to Padre Island. And then he had died—fifty-three years later.

The other man was Gene French, known as Frenchy, a beachcomber and treasure hunter. Frenchy had started going out to Padre as a youngster in the early 1940s and probably knew the island better than any other living person. He and Rawalt had been intimate friends.

This idea came to Smith as we sat in his office talking about gold. A former Marine Corps pilot with 322 missions in Vietnam and what he called "a good number of snazzy decorations," Smith had given it all

up for archaeology. He was now museum archaeologist at the Corpus
Christi Museum of Science and History, and the world's leading authority on the Karankawas, which was, he admitted, better than not
being the leading authority on anything.

He remembered a collection of artifacts, including Karankawa
pieces, that Rawalt had gathered over his years at Padre. The museum
had once been interested in that collection. But evidently its curator at
the time had somehow offended Rawalt, who swore the collection
would never leave Padre. Let them build a museum on the island, he
had said. Smith was curious about the artifacts. He had never seen
them. What were they? Where were they? What state were they in?
Just to see them would be rewarding.

We could start out by talking to Rawalt's son, who had a bait shop
on Padre Island near the causeway. I could introduce myself as a writer
interested in his father. Maybe that would open a door, and we would
get to see what he had found.

We got nowhere. Charlie Rawalt looked at us as if we were from
Mars. He didn't know about his father, he said. Didn't know much
about the collection. I should talk to his mother. When I called Viola,
she seemed dismayed that her son had given me her name. But she
would talk to me about her husband. I should come late that afternoon. "It was more in the rough in those days," she said, apropos of
nothing. "Back then they weren't cleaning up the stuff that washed
ashore."

Smith and I headed to Frenchy's restaurant. A man in blue, Frenchy
joined us at our table looking out at Laguna Madre and the causeway.
He wore a pale blue jumpsuit, open in the front to reveal a gold chain
and anchor with a wheel about two and a half inches across. A blue
gimme hat with "Texas" and scrambled eggs embroidered in gold on
the bill stayed on his head. His pale blue eyes twinkled as he spoke
through the smoke of his cigarette-size cigars. He was slender, his age
indeterminate; he was vague about it, as he was about locations on
Padre. He was a man used to not revealing things.

I got to the point. Whatever had happened to Rawalt's collection?
Interesting question, Frenchy said.

Smith had heard it was a fabulous collection.

It was.

And that it was documented.

"It is. It is documented. He was a real smart man. Everything he would find, he would document it."

It would be of immense value to archaeologists and naturalists, Smith said.

He would talk to Charlie Rawalt about it.

Even if we just photographed and documented it, Smith said. Just to see it would be extremely valuable historically.

Frenchy said no more. That was as far as we were going to get. He would talk to Charlie.

He had known Louis Rawalt well, hadn't he, I asked.

Oh yes.

How had they met?

That was a long story, Frenchy said. He had first come here when he was three years old. "That's when I began to fall in love with the island. Then the causeway was gone, and I tried to figure out for years how the hell to get back." He was twelve years old when he started rowing across Laguna Madre. That was when he met Rawalt. "It was in the early forties, during the war. He caught me. 'Boy, what the hell are you doing on this island? You get your ass out of here.' He put me in the truck and took me back to my little boat. I came back and I came back. And the fourth time he caught me, that's when he said, 'You are the stubbornest son of a bitch I've ever met in my life. Get in the truck. I want to talk to you.' So anyway, he took an interest in me. He put me in his truck and set me down and told me a lot of stories. And at the time he was an old man. I thought he was." Rawalt had been in his early forties.

"That man taught me everything that he could teach a young boy. I wouldn't have known where to look. He could take me into these areas—Zachary Taylor, the Dunn Ranch, the Singer Ranch. I spent a lot of time with that man. He had a free hand. He was the overseer of this island. He was the only person that was allowed here."

During his Rawalt-inspired explorations, Frenchy had met others among the island's inhabitants. He pointed at his hand. "I even got rattlesnake bit right there. I reached down to pick it up and *bam!* got it. That's why you've got to be careful back in those dunes. I mean, going through that grass, you won't catch me walking through that stuff. I'd drive through that stuff. A lot of people don't believe the rattlesnakes. I say hell, it used to *rain* rattlesnakes."

Rawalt had been a very nice man, Frenchy said, a man who did not seem to care about wealth or material things. But he did care about history and the island. When he had told young Frenchy about the wreck of the Spanish fleet in 1554, he did not seem interested in finding the gold. He wanted to find the truth of the story and to prove that the wrecks existed.

Frenchy had been fascinated not only by the story of the flight of the three hundred, as it was known, but also by the prospect of treasure.

"It sounded unreal to me," he explained. "I just thought it was fiction, a story. But that was when I went to the libraries, and that's when I started studying. I found out, by God, he was telling the truth." Frenchy had spent fifteen years of his life, he said, and every penny he could muster, looking for those wrecks. He had walked the entire hundred-ten miles of Padre three times searching. He had gone through records and historical accounts searching for clues. But he had never found anything.

Then, in the late 1950s, he realized something about barrier island geology. One day his uncle had showed him a photograph of a shipwreck. "People had their hands on the hull and there were old Model-T Fords on the beach. And I said, 'Uncle Pauly, what is this?' And he said, 'Well, that's the Wreck of the *Nicaragua*.' I began to understand something. I had been looking in the wrong place all these years. I had found gold coins and silver coins all these years, always between the *Nicaragua* and the pass—the Port Mansfield Pass.

"At any rate, at the time, I could stand on the beach, and with the best surf rod it took everything I had to cast out to the boilers. So what did that tell me? It hit me like a ton of bricks. This beach has eroded! That *Nicaragua* used to be right on the beach and now it's sitting offshore. So I said, 'Wait a minute, where in the hell was this beach four hundred years ago?' I came back two days later, went down and measured all the way out to the boilers and back, right or wrong, to say I did it. And I went back to the calculator and I started figuring this was this and that was that, and my God, it's got to be four thousand yards off-shore." The island, he figured, had moved.

Frenchy started flying offshore, parallel to the beach. He did not know what he was looking for; he was just looking for something. Then the day came when he almost jumped out of the plane. He had spotted something and he wanted to look at it.

What had he seen?

"A long, dark spot. And I know what I saw." It was the *Espíritu Santo*.

With two friends he dove on the site and found bronze spikes and four gold coins. There had to be more buried under the sand. By now he was convinced he had one of the 1554 fleet. The salvage would take more divers and more equipment—a diving boat and prop blaster to clear the sand away from the buried treasure. Unfortunately no one would invest the money he needed. "They said, 'Frenchy, you're crazy.' I said, 'Where the hell do you think I got this stuff? Do you think I salted the mine?' Anyway, no one wanted to finance me, so I said, 'Well, to hell with it, I'll just do it myself. It's been there four hundred years and it'll be there another four hundred.'"

Then in 1967 the Platoro people arrived. A treasure hunting group from Gary, Indiana, they were determined to find the three wrecks. They approached French. They had heard that he knew where some of them might be. He could take them right to a wreck, he said, but what was in it for him? Ten percent of whatever they found, they said. What Frenchy said to them was roughly equivalent to "go fly a kite."

Forty-five days later one of the two divers who had examined the site with French told him that the Platoro group had a boat and six divers in the water on top of his wreck, less than three miles north of Mansfield Channel. Maybe the other diver had led them there. "There was not a God damn thing I could do. The irony of this story is that to this day I have not heard or seen from that second diver, ever."

Platoro started removing the goodies. Soon enough, though, the state of Texas called a stop. The *Espíritu Santo* and all Texas ship-wrecks, it said, belonged to the state. It would not bargain. The scavengers were to return everything they had recovered. Among the arti-facts they returned was a gold bar.

One gold bar. Frenchy laughed at that. "I know a lot of things about that wreck," he said. "I know for a fact that over two million dollars worth of gold was taken out by plane, including a cross with emeralds all over it."

Smith named a man—did Frenchy know him?

"Yeah. What do you want to know about him?"

They had met when Smith was down island in 1985 looking for the camp the Spanish had set up during their original salvage attempt. Smith had told me about him. "A real dirtball," he had said. The man had worked as a salvor, and Smith had paid him for information. He had said that while working for Platoro, he had loaded boxes from the salvage boat onto an airplane in the middle of the night. The boxes had been filled with gold bars, he said, and they were never seen again. Now Smith told this story to Frenchy.

"Well, what I told you did happen," he answered.

The mistake the Platoro people made, Frenchy said, had been to let on that they were finding anything. "When they took the cannon out—they were such damn fools—that's when they laid it on the dock, and that's when the whole world knew."

After the state stepped in, its researchers found a second wreck. The *San Esteban*, which they named 41KN10 (41 the official number for the state of Texas, KN the county, 10 the spot's registration number with the state), lay in 20 feet of water, 1,650 feet offshore, 2.5 miles north of the *Espíritu Santo*, 41WY3. In 1972 they began excavating 41KN10. The third ship, the *Santa María de Yciar*, had been obliterated when Mansfield Channel was dredged in 1957. They were convinced that, impossible as the odds seemed, the dredge had ripped right through the wreckage. Either that or it had been buried under the thousands of tons of stone laid for one of the half-mile-long jetties that protected the channel. Among the evidence for its presence were a two-*real* coin found in the sand dunes and an anchor of the type used by these ships found near the jetties.

The whole incident still haunted Frenchy. He had been so close to recovering a major treasure. And now it was not worth going after. He was disgusted with the state's pigheadedness on salvage. Two men from the state had come to him once, he said, to ask if he would help

find a certain wreck. He had offered them a deal. Put him on the research ship for a day and he would find the wreck. If he was wrong,
they had lost a day. If he was right, though, he wanted the state to guarantee that the artifacts would remain in Corpus Christi. He also
wanted full credit for finding the wreck. And he wanted a 10 percent
finder's fee. "Well, they said, 'We don't give a finder's fee.' And I said, 'I
don't give the information.'" Frenchy laughed bitterly.

Now he wanted a chance to find the third 1554 wreck. "I've got several readings," he said. "It's there. It's still there."

The state of Texas, Smith said, was satisfied that the third wreck
was under the stone jetties at Mansfield Channel.

Frenchy placed two mint candies and a pepper packet in a row on
the table. "Well, there's one, there's one, and there's one. Running
north to south, this would be the *San Esteban*, the *Espíritu Santo*, and
the *Santa María de Yciar*." He pointed to the mint candy in the middle.
"This is the first one right here that I went after. And then that one,"
pointing at the candy to the north. "But no one's ever gotten to that
one." He pointed to the pepper, the *Santa María de Yciar*. "That's the
one I want. Let me tell you what's supposedly unaccounted for. I think
there was fifty-three thousand pounds of precious metal and over two
hundred thousand coins unaccounted for."

That was correct, Smith said.

"I'd just like to have the freedom of going out there and just—I'd
love to spend a week, a month, whatever. I guarantee you, I blow out a
certain section, I'm going to come up with lots of stuff."

"Well, you may be absolutely right," Smith said. "We don't know
where it is. We've never found it." Maybe it really was sitting out there.

"Well, one thing's for sure: it's there. I'm convinced that you and I
could go right to the wreck."

"Do you think the third wreck is under the jetty?"

"No."

"You think it's somewhere else."

"I do not believe it's underneath the jetty. It's *possible* that it may
have broken up. That is possible. If they really dredged it, where is it?
Have you seen this material that they say they dredged up and got these
coins? I haven't. If that's true, then it's *possible* that that wreck could

have broken up. But I'm telling you, Herman, you find a way to go out there, we'll blow that thing out. I was just out there, just before summer. There are readings *every time* I go out there."

What would be in it for him? I asked. He couldn't take any of the treasure.

"Nothing," Frenchy said. He smiled. "Except one thing. If I hit it, I'll take what I can get and run with it. I'd be more than happy for the state to keep every artifact, every cannon, every anchor I can find—you give me the gold." He laughed again. I believed him.

Later that evening I met Herman Smith and a couple of his friends for a drink. He was excited when he arrived. A man had come in to his office at four thirty with some gold coins. A fisherman, the man had said, had found them on Padre Island. He thought they were from the 1554 wrecks. Were they authentic? Yes, Smith had said, they were *reales* and were worth up to five hundred dollars each. The man said the fisherman had three chests of them, with about eight thousand coins in each.

I multiplied the numbers for each chest in my head. There were six zeros each time I calculated.

Viola Rawalt was living in a suburb on the mainland near the road to Padre Island, a few doors from her son. Charlie and his wife had convinced her to move near them a few years before, a move she had resisted but was now grateful for. She was eighty-five years old, her hair pure white, her hands gnarled.

Her living room was filled with mementos of Louis and the island: an acrylic painting of some Padre dunes; a few arrowheads; scrapbooks of magazine and newspaper clippings about Louis and their life on the island; but mostly photographs of Louis. They showed a man with a long face, a long nose, pale eyes, and a high forehead. His hair was black in his younger years and still black later, though the hairline had receded a bit. His hands were long, his arms sinewed and muscular. He was tall and lean and well groomed, and in his old age his cheeks were creased, his skin dark from years in the sun.

Viola had met Louis in Boston during his two years in the Chelsea Naval Hospital. She explained that he had had malaria and then quinine poisoning. Her brother brought him to the house one day, this thin man in his late twenties—about ninety pounds, she said, and six feet tall. But, she said, he was a man who did not give up. When the doctors had told him in 1927 to go back to Kingsville, he had married Viola and brought her to south Texas for what was supposed to be their last six months together. Soon after they arrived, Louis took her camping on Padre Island for a two- or three-day introduction to the island and to fishing. They stayed two years.

On the way to the island they bought her a straw hat and a pair of boy's overalls. She could wear them with tennis shoes and one of Louis' shirts. "Tennis shoes are hard to wear down there," Viola explained. "If you're fishing, the sand works in them. So I went barefoot. Well, the wind was blowing and that hat worried me to bits, so the hat came off. By that first night—my skin was then very fair—by that night I was very, very sunburned. My eyes swelled up to where I just had slits to see through. My hands were swelled, my feet were swelled. And I'm very sure the good Lord had to be looking after me because I was in terrible shape. The sand was just like sandpaper against the sore. The first week was not a very good one. I never could get used to going to bed and having to shake the sand out before I got in, because it was always kind of rough."

Louis taught her to fish. At Corpus Christi Pass, on the northern end of Padre, they traded their catch for groceries. Somehow the weeks went by. Then they had a chance to move to the south end of the island. Sam Robinson had sold part of the island to the Jones brothers, and their representative, a Major Swan, offered the Rawalts a house and thirty dollars a month to look after things there.

I asked her what she had liked, herself, about being out on Padre Island. "Well, I enjoyed the water," she said. "I really did. And the fact that Louis was happy. He loved it. There were no conveniences. That was hard to take. If you wanted water you hauled it from a well. Louis dug wells everywhere we went. That was not hard to do over there. He'd take it down until he hit water and then he'd bail it out two or three times and that water would be just as clear.

"Going down the island, Louis loved to go in back of the island. He always loved to prowl. And, of course, he found one ship back there.

We were always going to dig down to see, because the top of the cabin looked like it was teakwood. But we never ever did. And eventually I think the sand covered it up through the years.

"The geese would fly, and the ducks. Louis would say, 'Well, you drop me off.' And he'd say, 'You cross over to the middle. And I'll drive up half a mile.' I would scare up any geese that were on the way. I guess, not knowing, there was no fear. Now you couldn't hire me to do it—there are snakes on that island. That was one of the things we had that was fresh meat. Of course, we caught fish. And sometimes the shrimp were out there."

Soon Louis had work looking after South Bird Island, a nesting sanctuary in Laguna Madre, and helping a geologist or engineer (Viola was not sure which) named Dr. Price, who was involved with dredging the intracoastal waterway. Viola described Price as "a truly wonderful man." Louis and Price drilled core samples on the island and dug up some sort of rock (Viola described it as being like coral) which Louis packed and shipped to universities around the country. Between times Louis fished. Eventually, with Charlie, he opened a small bait shop near the causeway. Louis and Viola spent most of the next fifty or so years on Padre.

Early on they saw very few people on the island, and then mostly fishermen. "Fish were everywhere," Viola said. "You caught so many big fish that a lot of them you had to throw back. I mean they would be enormous."

In the early 1930s they stayed almost a year and a half in a shack belonging to Major Swan on Big Shell Beach—little more, Viola said, than a room on stilts. Louis built a porch for it. There they fished.

One time a friend named Shorty came to do some fishing. "The two men were fishing that day with a net. The Gulf was glassy calm. It was beautiful. They were catching all the fish they could catch. In fact, they had to stop fishing 'cause they didn't have room to keep them. And about that time, I had started to fix something to eat. This little plane was circling, and they dropped a cork with a hole in it where they had a message with a streamer of orange cloth. So I picked it up and they said, 'Leave immediately.' And when that tide turned, believe me, that surf came in. We had to come back up the middle of the island."

Louis and Shorty headed back to the shack to save what they could. On the way they found a car left by some fishermen as they worked their way down the beach. The two men continued down island, hoping to find them. "Well, they got back as far as our camp and they were trying to grab a few things. And a wave came over, came clear up the sand dunes. And that is high down there. So they knew they could not get down to those men." The fishermen survived, though they lost their car. "They went way over in the big dunes and dug down in. And they weathered the storm. They didn't get drowned. They got hungry, but they didn't get drowned."

That was in 1933, when the wooden causeway washed away. Burton Dunn lost a lot of livestock in that storm, and Louis went to work for him, rounding up and rescuing what cattle he could.

"The next time we had an experience with a storm, we were way on down at what they call the telephone shack. It was just a makeshift shack, but when we'd go down there camping, lots of times we'd stay in that shack. It was a little protection. You know, you could cook there without quite so much sand in your food. Well, we hadn't been there a day. Louis sensed something wrong. He said he didn't like the sound of the surf. So we stayed that night, but in the morning we got out of there. That surf was clear up to that telephone shack. It was miserable. We got off there all right, but you weren't sure whether you were going to get through some of it or not."

Viola pulled out a scrapbook. "Here's something I want you to look at. You'll enjoy looking at it. I don't have very many ships." She had given Charlie the scrapbook with photographs of shipwrecks. They had seen, she said, probably eighteen shipwrecks while on the island, mostly shrimpers.

She returned from her digression. "Louis loved nature. And these are all pictures mostly of flowers. He could see the beauty in it, but not many people did—they'd see sand dunes. Louis would study those flowers. I mean, you don't think of much of beauty being over there, but he found it. There's a lot of very pretty flowers. And he knew the name of everything, flowers and birds. Now, there were a lot of birds over there. 'Course, Louis knew them all.

"We used to love to get up quickly after a norther and ride up and down the beach beachcombing. That was fun. One time Louis found a wooden bucket. I don't know what it would have held—probably twenty-five pounds or so. It was some kind of jam, and that jam was perfectly good. Another time he found a carton of lard. And perfectly good. Probably washed overboard or something. Then the time that the whiskey—I'm sure it was probably contraband or something, but it came in all along the island. Louis found some, and it was very, very good. I know that people in Port Aransas, when they got word of it, stayed happy for a good many days. Then one time when we were going down we found a fifty-five-gallon drum of excellent-grade gasoline. Now that was wonderful. We could ride up and down that island."

But useful things like fuel and jam were not the only treasures Louis and Viola found. "'Course, we were always picking up bottles and things. He loved—now, Indian artifacts—he prowled the sand hills all the time and he found all these different places where the Indians had their camps.

"Charlie has quite a bit of stuff that is packed away. If they ever have a museum on the island—Louis wanted it to go in the museum. He wouldn't put it in the museum downtown."

She pointed out a picture in a scrapbook. It showed some proud men with their catch, fifty-five trout. "That was nothing," she said. "They had their iceboxes full to boot. That was just one day. That's the way they used to catch fish down on the beach. There's no question about it." She looked at the men in the picture. "All these other—all four of them are gone." Louis had died on January 27, 1980, at age eighty-one. "We were married fifty-three years," she said. "It's a long time."

She paused for a moment, then returned to the picture and the fishing. "They had two trailers down there that they let us use, which were really very nice. One trailer had a little kitchen. It had a sink, no running water, but it had a sink. And it had shelves that you could put your stove and things on. Then a bar separated it and then a big long table in here with two benches, and one of those drum stoves was set in there. That was where we could eat. Then to sleep, and we always had company down there, there were three sections and the doors were screened. Twelve people, they could have slept there. So that was ideal that time. We just loved that.

"We came in one day. It was getting where it was almost dusk. Louis had built a well between the sand hills and this trailer. We are coming along there and Charlie, the little guy, you know, he's running out ahead. Well, Louise was not too far behind—our daughter—and all of a sudden she let out a war whoop and ran and grabbed him. Here laying right by the well where it is cool is a huge rattlesnake. Well, Louise goes way around and goes in the house. I don't know what she had, just a little gun, a twenty-two maybe; her daddy was teaching her how to use it. So Louise goes around. She gets the gun. She brings the bullets. She comes out. In the meantime that snake has crawled up on a little sand dune. It's got shrubbery on it. He stops in kind of a smooth place. She killed him, all right. But she shot him full of bullets."

Viola looked up from the picture. "What did you think of Charlie? He's not a little boy anymore."

I don't think he quite knew what to think of me, I said. That was why he told me to give you a call.

"He thinks I have a good memory. I don't really. Now Louis—the oil people coming in there, or the seismograph people, could always get ahold of Louis. He knew all the posts and geological markers down there. The different sand dunes had names—not all of them, but certain ones had names. Louis knew all of them. He never forgot anything. He had a wonderful memory. But I'm not that good."

We reached the clippings. She pulled out a *Saturday Evening Post* article published in the 1950s. "They love beachcombing more than parties," read one caption. The picture was a family portrait. "This was my daughter. And there was Charlie." She pointed at a toy in his hand. "He called him his duck, I think. He found that old duck on the beach and he just loved that thing. He carried it everywhere." Louis and Viola were in the picture, too. She was in her forties. Her face was wistful.

Her attention now was more on the scrapbook and its memories than on my questions. She pointed to a picture. "This is the well that the snake was lying down in." Another: "This was one of the trailers, and then there was another one over here." Then a picture of Louis walking alone in the sand, a hat on his head. It was an evocative image. "He could walk so fast," she said. "And I'd be over there with him when he'd go out hunting these arrowheads which he loved to hunt—he knew just the kind of places to go. And I'd stop to do something and he'd be two sand hills over, and I wasn't going to be left alone down there. I'd have to run and find him."

She pulled out a letter and handed it to me. It had come from a friend right after Louis died. I read aloud:

"It didn't seem real to me at first. I had just taken it for granted that Louis would go on forever. I remember I once told him, 'Louis, you would have to be a hundred years old to have done all the things you have told me about. But I believe it all, and I think you'll be here always. When the last man on earth is dead and only the coyotes remain on Padre Island, there will be Louis Rawalt walking along the beach.' "

I handed the letter back to Viola.

"I treasure it," she said.

Big Wind

The people of the Caribbean basin had a word for it: hurricane. To the Arawaks, it was *Hurakán*, the name of an evil spirit. The various Carib tribes called it *huiranvucán*, *aracán*, and *uricán*, which meant something like "big wind." From the Antilles to northern South America and up the isthmus to the Yucatán, its names sounded like echoes: *Hyoracán*, *Hurakán*, *Hurnraken*, the name of a god or a devil, or the name of the wind.

There are other names for this storm. In the northern Indian Ocean, it is a cyclone. It is a willy-nilly in Australia, a typhoon in the western Pacific, a *baguio* in the Philippines. But these are all the same: big wind.

When the winds of a tropical storm hit 74 miles per hour, we call it a hurricane. A hurricane is, in fact, the most powerful and destructive of all storms. There are stronger winds—tornadoes can reach 400 to 500 mph—but no other storm has more energy. The average Atlantic hurricane has about the same energy as a 10,000-megaton nuclear bomb. The bomb dropped on Hiroshima was about 20,000 tons, one half-millionth of a hurricane. Back when we tested atomic bombs in the atmosphere, one dropped on an atoll might lift 10 million (1×10^7) tons of water into the air. An average hurricane will squeeze out about 20 billion (2×10^{10}) tons of water in twenty-four hours—two thousand times the water of that bomb. One storm dumped 2.5 billion (2.5×10^9) tons of water on Puerto Rico in a few hours, only a fraction of the storm's total water. (I keep giving the scientific notation because of the amazing number of zeros.)

Comparing a hurricane to a bomb is a violent analogy, but it is appropriate, considering the violence to which hurricanes can subject human populations. There are other ways to look at their energy, although the numbers are so big that they hardly mean anything. An average hurricane releases 2.0 to 6.0×10^{26} ergs of heat per day. That is 16 trillion (1.6×10^{13}) kilowatt-hours, enough energy in a day to supply this country's electrical needs for more than six months. Other scientists calculate the output of a 500-mile-diameter hurricane at 10 trillion (1×10^{13}) horsepower. That is roughly equivalent to 24 billion Ford AC Cobras running flat-out. And a hurricane could easily maintain this output for nine or ten days.

The main source of all this energy is the latent heat released by condensation. A hurricane is a heat engine; its interior is warmer than its surroundings, and this temperature difference acts as a kind of pump. As warm, moist air flows into the hurricane, it rises. In the lower air pressure of high elevations, the air then expands and cools. The cooler the air, the less moisture it can hold. Thus, on certain evenings dew "falls" as the air cools to its saturation point. When the cooling hurricane air reaches its saturation point, some of the moisture condenses out, releasing heat into the atmosphere and feeding the pump. This air is pumped higher until somewhere above forty thousand feet it is ejected out the top of the storm and transported some distance horizontally. Now much cooler, it begins to sink.

This process explains why air pressure in a hurricane is low: the air is rising and reducing its pressure on the earth. The pressure inside a hurricane can be as much as 10 percent below that of the air outside it, and the lower the pressure the more violent the storm. Nominal air pressure at sea level is just below 30 inches of mercury, and it seldom goes below 29. Hurricane air pressure, though, has been measured as low as 25.69 inches; this was in a Pacific typhoon in October 1979, the lowest sea-level air-pressure measurement ever taken.

To form, these heat engines need a combination of warm ocean water (at least seventy-nine degrees Fahrenheit) and warm, humid air, along with some kind of force to kick the whole process into motion. This force can be an easterly wave (a trough of low pressure in the easterly winds south of the subtropical high-pressure areas), an intertropical convergence zone (an area where opposing trade winds meet), or the trailing end of a polar trough (the reverse of an easterly wave, a trough of low pressure in the westerly winds of the middle latitudes). Finally, the Coriolis force starts the air spinning counterclockwise (in the Northern Hemisphere, that is; to the south, it spins clockwise).

The eye, the hole in the middle of this spinning storm, is unique to hurricanes. The closer you are to the eye, the more violent the winds. As you pass through the cloud wall into the center, though, the rain stops and the winds are almost dead calm—sometimes as low as 15 mph, close enough to calm after bracing yourself against 100-mph winds. The eye is still enough that often you can hear the roar of the storm encircling you. In this oasis the sky above may actually show some blue through patchy clouds. Witnesses have often described the air in the eye as sultry or oppressive. This is no illusion. The air *is* warm; often the temperature rises rapidly as the eye passes overhead.

And the eye has something else: birds, often thousands of them, caught and carried along by this wind island. Tropical birds have been found in New England after a storm, and at times ships at sea will have their decks covered with exhausted birds as the eye passes over. (It is a strange sight, though not unusual. One time, about sixty miles offshore in a blustery northwest wind, a yellow finch landed on the deck of a sailboat I was crewing on. The bird was tired; it did not leave its perch on a lifeline as I approached with my guidebook to identify it. We set out some water, and soon it flew below deck and found a dark spot where it stayed for several hours. Apparently revived, it took flight and headed into the wind toward land.)

Hurricanes form pretty much the same way and in the same seasons all over the world—or at least where such storms form. North Atlantic hurricanes usually form off the western coast of Africa as tropical depressions and travel west, growing into tropical storms and finally into hurricanes. They last about nine days, though August storms tend to last about twelve. But these numbers are just averages; some have been tracked for three or four weeks, and one hurricane that formed on August 3, 1899, near the Cape Verde Islands, off the coast of Africa, hit the West Indies on August 8 and traveled north to Bermuda before turning west and crossing into North Carolina. It lasted five weeks.

Few hurricanes degenerate while they are over warm tropical waters. But they tend to move north as soon as they develop. And once they enter colder waters or cross over land they begin to die, or at least change into nontropical storms. Sometimes a hurricane will move north and hit moist low-pressure troughs that supply more energy and extend its life. The 1900 Galveston, Texas, hurricane passed through Oklahoma, eastern Kansas, and Iowa. It eventually reached the Great Lakes, where it was recharged and became an active storm again. Then it hit Montreal and tore through the Saint Lawrence region into New England. It went out to sea fourteen days and four thousand miles after destroying Galveston. Having crossed the Atlantic, it hit northern Europe and was last seen roaring into Siberia.

Hurricane season generally extends from June through October, with August, September, and October considered high season. Even so, there have been earlier and later storms. In the first six decades of the century, about 460 tropical cyclones are known to have formed in the North Atlantic, about 8 per year. More than half became hurricanes. Almost all of those hurricanes, about 222, hit land.

The incidence of storms seems to be increasing. Scientists noticed this change starting in about 1930, the same time, coincidentally, that sea level began to rise more rapidly. (The year 1933 set the record, with 21 tropical cyclones from May 4 to November 16; 9 became hurricanes.) The numbers might be larger partly because we are better at detecting hurricanes. Yet there are also more storms. Some scientists feel that a gradual warming of the atmosphere began at about that time and may account for this growth. During the last twenty years or so, the storm frequency has dropped. Both the Atlantic and Gulf coasts suffered relatively few storms. Now they are increasing again, and we may once more be seeing a rise in cyclic storm activity: the 1990 tropical storm season was the most severe in forty years.

We are still unsure of the details. We have been measuring things so briefly relative to the earth's time scale that it will be a while before we understand the nature of some of these climate cycles. Still, it seems clear that two factors are at work: the normal storm activity cycle due to complex natural conditions (such as cyclic rainfall fluctuations in western Africa), and the independent growth in storm frequency and strength tied to increases in ocean and atmosphere temperatures.

Global warming is caused by the greenhouse effect. As sunlight strikes the earth, its surface reflects infrared radiation back into space. Certain gases in the atmosphere, though, prevent some of this heat from escaping. Without these natural greenhouse gases, which include carbon dioxide, chlorofluorocarbons, methane, and nitrous oxide, the earth would be cooler by about sixty degrees Fahrenheit. But more greenhouse gases, particularly carbon dioxide, have increased the atmosphere's ability to hold heat. So everything gets warmer.

Why more CO_2? Our burning of fossil fuels (coal and oil) accounts for about 75 percent of the gain. On top of that, blame the loss of vast areas of forest for about 25 percent. That loss has decreased the environment's ability to reduce CO_2 back into oxygen and carbon compounds and thereby refresh the atmosphere. The concentration of atmospheric CO_2 has increased about 25 percent since the beginning of the Industrial Revolution. Global mean temperatures have already increased one degree Fahrenheit in the last century, and climatologists expect the earth to warm by as much as three to nine degrees in the next century. (To see the significance of this, realize that in the past two million years the earth's temperature has never been more than three to five degrees warmer than it is now.) Some politicians may want to discredit arguments for global warming, yet the real disagreement among scientists is not about whether it exists; it is about how much the temperature will rise and how quickly.

The effects of a warming climate are apparent in many small ways. For instance, European glaciers are retreating and the southern limit of codfish in the North Atlantic seems to have moved north. If the estimates are correct, in a hundred years San Francisco will be at least as warm as San Diego is today; New York could reach current Daytona Beach temperatures. More significant, higher temperatures mean more and bigger storms on the average, as well as increased vulnerability to them as the shore drowns, though there may be an upper limit on both the area and the intensity of hurricanes.

When we talk about just how big hurricanes get, we usually talk in these terms. Instead of horsepower, ergs, or megatons, we talk about area and intensity: how fast the wind, how heavy the rain, how high the seas.

Informally we often classify hurricane sizes by their frequency. People talk of ten-year storms and twenty-five-year storms and even hundred-year storms. Smaller storms develop more often than larger storms, so a twenty-five-year storm, one substantial enough to be likely to develop only every twenty-five years, is bigger than a ten-year storm. A hundred-year storm, then, is much larger than either, so huge that it is likely to develop only every hundred years or so. Of course, these time-defined sizes are all relative to the environment—a twenty-year storm in Maine might be a five-year storm in Texas. This way of looking at storm magnitudes can also be deceiving. People may think that if a so-called twenty-year storm hits their area, they are safe from such conditions for another twenty years. Not true, since the year number indicates only the likelihood of such a storm, not the certainty. This is especially so if global warming is indeed pumping more energy into storm systems and increasing the average storm size. Last decade's twenty-year storm may be next decade's ten-year storm.

There is a more formal classification system for hurricanes, the Saffir/Simpson Damage-Potential Scale, which describes the storm's conditions at any given time. Category One, which generates minimal damage, has winds of 74 to 95 mph, a surge of 4 to 5 feet, and barometric pressure at or above 28.94 inches. Category Two, moderate damage, has winds of 96 to 110 mph and a surge of 6 to 8 feet. Category Three, extensive damage, has winds of 111 to 130 mph and a surge of 9 to 12 feet. Category Four, extreme damage, has winds of 131 to 155 mph and a surge of 13 to 18 feet. Category Five, catastrophic, has winds of 156 mph or more, a surge of 18.1 feet or more, and baro-metric pressure at or below 27.16 inches.

In the average hurricane, the diameter of the area under hurricane-force winds (74 mph) is a bit more than 100 miles, with gales (40 mph) extending 350 to 400 miles. The Great Atlantic Hurricane of September 1944, though, had hurricane winds across 200 miles, and gales in a 600-mile diameter. And there have been even bigger storms. Hurricane Carla, one of the most intense storms of the century, entered the Gulf of Mexico on September 7, 1961. Its clouds spread 800 or 900 miles, covering the whole Gulf; its sustained winds reached 150 mph, double the minimum hurricane level. When Carla hit the Texas coast at Port O'Connor, winds near the eye had reached 175 mph. It was truly big wind—the area getting 150 mph extended 100 miles along the coast; the area of hurricane-level winds covered almost the entire Texas coast, from just north of Boca Chica well into Louisiana, more than 300 miles.

When a storm hits, the area of wind damage generally stretches 50 to 100 miles along the coast, though it can extend as much as 300 miles. The sustained winds (averaged over one minute) in a hurricane often reach 100 to 135 mph. With a sustained wind of 100 mph, you can expect gusts of 150 mph. And sustained winds of 150 mph might have gusts of 225 mph or more.

In fact, winds as high as 150 mph are probably not unusual in a hurricane, but they are seldom measured. Winds that high tend to destroy anemometers, so it is hard to measure the most powerful hurricanes. The biggest wind ever measured was at Mount Washington, New Hampshire, on April 12, 1934, though not during a hurricane. The sustained wind was 188 mph, with gusts up to 229 mph. (A wind speed of 197 mph was measured during Hurricane Inez in September 1966, but from an airplane flying through the storm at 8,000 feet; so somehow it does not count.) By comparison, in October 1944, a hurricane wind speed of 163 mph was measured in Havana, Cuba. In August 1969, winds in Hurricane Camille were measured at 172 mph in Main Pass Block, Louisiana—one of two Category Five storms to hit the United States in the past hundred years or so. Hurricane Gilbert, which in September 1988 devastated Jamaica and then continued on to the Yucatán Peninsula, had sustained surface winds at least as high as 170 mph. It is considered overall the most powerful storm in the Western Hemisphere during this century. In September 1955, Hurricane Janet measured 175 mph in Chetumal, Mexico, before the anemometer collapsed. The winds continued to increase and engineers later estimated that, based on wind damage, they must have reached 200 to 250 mph. Of course, these were all Category Five storms. In addition, hurricanes usually spawn tornadoes along their leading edge, and those winds can exceed 500 mph.

The force of these winds increases with the square of their velocity. So a 200-mph wind is four times as powerful as one of 100 mph. A wind blowing at 75 mph pushes against an object at about 17 pounds power square foot; thus a 150-mph wind will push at four times that, or roughly 68 pounds. A 6-foot-tall man might expose about 9 square feet to such a wind, which means it is trying to knock him down with about 600 pounds of force. The wind would win.

More destructive than the wind, though, is the storm's rain and the resulting flooding. As much as a quarter of the average annual rainfall in the southeastern United States may come from hurricanes. Generally a hurricane will drop 6 to 12 inches of water in an area, though the total depends on a number of factors, including the geography of the land and the speed at which the storm is moving. The slower the storm, the more water it drops in a particular place.

In 1955 Hurricane Ione left 16.63 inches in Maysville, North Carolina. An October 1947 hurricane dropped 1.32 inches in Miami in ten minutes, 3.60 inches in one hour. Hurricane Claudette, in July 1979, dumped 43.0 inches—more than three and a half feet—near Alvin, Texas, in twenty-four hours.

Even worse than rain is the storm surge, a rapid rise in water caused by onshore winds and the drop in barometric pressure. The surge reaches the coast at the same time as the hurricane's center and is the main cause of death and property damage. An Atlantic hurricane's surge (aside from the waves riding on it) can reach 15 feet. A one-inch drop in barometric pressure raises sea level about a foot (this is called the inverted-barometer effect); so the extremely low barometric pressure within the storm itself raises the sea under it in a kind of dome that moves with the storm. This dome, which can be 50 miles wide, is 3 or 4 feet high at most, though other factors affect it. If a hurricane moves into shallow water, for instance, the dome may rise because of resonance effects in the bay. The hurricane surge includes this dome and is highest to the right of the hurricane's center (facing the direction in which the storm is moving), since this is where the winds are strongest and where they have been blowing longest in the same direction. Possibly because of its shape, the Gulf of Mexico tends to have extremely high surges. Hurricane Camille had a surge of more than 20 feet when it came ashore in Mississippi.

On top of the surge, 35- to 40-foot waves may develop, with the greatest wave height again just to the right of the hurricane center. If two waves cross, their peaks may reach 50 or 55 feet. Seas in Pacific storms are even higher. In 1935 a typhoon with waves greater than 60 feet hit a Japanese fleet; in fact, one ship reported heights of almost 100 feet.

The first visible warning sign of an approaching storm is the swell, which can run several hundred, or even one or two thousand, miles ahead of the storm. These waves often move in a direction different from the local wind, since they are created by the distant hurricane, not the local conditions. They caused a Galveston weatherman to suspect a storm was coming in September 1900, even though he had received no official warning. The seas were moving against the wind and generated an abnormally high tide. The meteorologist was right in his prediction, and his early warning probably saved several thousand lives.

With these forerunning swells, the tides may rise to unusual heights before the storm arrives. These meteorological tides, as they are called to distinguish them from astronomical tides (astronomical not because they are big, but because they are caused by the moon), may start when the storm is as much as 500 miles away. Meteorological tides can be 3 or 4 feet above normal and may affect hundreds of miles of coastline. When Hurricane Carla hit Texas, the tides were 4 feet at Port Isabel, 175 miles southwest of the eye, and about 10 feet in Galveston Bay, 120 miles northeast, and to the right, of the storm's center.

Some hurricanes also bring tidal waves, though they have nothing to do with tide. These hurricane waves are extremely rare—at least authenticated cases are. Unlike the surge, which is rapidly rising water, the hurricane wave is more like a wall of water. Scientists do not agree on the causes, but they may be some kind of resonance waves. There have been a few documented cases. In 1737, a 40-foot storm wave hit the mouth of the Hooghly River, near Calcutta, India, killing an incredible 300,000 persons. In 1970, another killed 150,000 to 300,000 in Bangladesh. On August 27, 1893, almost a hundred years before Hurricane Hugo, a storm wave hit Charleston, South Carolina, and killed 1,000 to 2,000 persons. And the 1900 Galveston hurricane, the deadliest in U.S. history, had a hurricane wave of about 5 feet in addition to the surge. That Category Four storm killed 6,000 or more.

The forces involved with moving water are enormous: a cubic yard of water weighs more than three-quarters of a ton, and a breaking wave moves forward at 50 to 60 mph. A big wave breaking over you is like having a Volkswagen Beetle dropped on your head. It is no exaggeration to say that a storm wave hitting a house is going to strike with the force of a locomotive. If a 10-foot wave, not unusual in a hurricane, strikes a house 40 feet long, we are talking about half a million pounds of water hitting the wall at 50 mph.

Considering the forces involved, hurricanes are also major geologic factors on barrier islands. A large, slow-moving storm can move a barrier island's shoreline back as far as it would retreat in a hundred years of ordinary wave action. Hurricanes move sediment to the landward side of the island. And the storm surge is the main factor in this geologic effect.

Hurricane Carla's seas ripped mollusk shells, rock fragments, and coral blocks from sea bottom as deep as 80 feet and deposited them on the Texas barrier islands. The storm removed an area of foredunes 20 to 50 yards deep from the seaward side of Padre Island and left wave-cut cliffs in the dunes as much as 10 feet high. The foredunes were breached or completely leveled in many places, and Padre's wind-tidal flats, on its landward side, received large amounts of washover material, including a fresh layer of mud on its high mud flats. The storm also cut many channels through the island to Laguna Madre, but as with the ill-fated Yarborough Pass, longshore currents quickly filled them in.

Still, the main concern with hurricanes is not geologic change. It is their effect on people, the death and damage they inflict. We have seen that almost three-quarters of Americans live within 50 miles of a coast. And that percentage is increasing. About two hurricanes hit the East Coast each year, and their winds affect almost 2 million square miles of land, nearly a quarter of the country. About 30 million people live within an area likely to receive hurricane wind damage, and about 6 million are directly vulnerable to surge, the biggest killer.

As warning systems have improved, American storm deaths have decreased. But the trend is toward greater property damage as coastal development continues. Add the likelihood that hurricane activity is increasing, and clearly the numbers are going to get bigger. Average annual property losses from 1950 to 1970 were about $400 million. But when Camille hit in 1969, it caused $1.42 billion in damage. Losses from Hurricane Frederic, which came ashore at Mobile, Alabama, in 1979, were about $2.3 billion. Hugo, which hit Charleston on September 21, 1989, with sustained winds of 135 mph and a 13-foot surge, caused about $5 billion in damage. Then came Hurricane Andrew. It slammed into southern Florida on August 25, 1992, with 165-mph winds and an 8-foot surge, then crossed the Gulf of Mexico and hit Louisiana the next day. Andrew killed at least thirty people, destroyed eighty-five thousand homes, and left two hundred fifty thousand persons homeless. In Florida alone the initial damage estimate was $20 billion, the costliest natural disaster in U.S. history, and significantly more than all the hurricane damage in the previous forty years.

Hurricanes are hazards to us because we build and live in their path, and because we build in extremely risky places. That fact seems obvious, but to many people it is not. Most of us think that when a hurricane destroys a town, it is an attack, a challenge, from Nature. But Nature is indifferent to that town. Hurricanes are not the gods or devils the Mayans and Caribbean Indians thought; they are natural events that were sweeping the coasts millions of years before we started building on the dunes. A hurricane's size is only one aspect of the damage it does. That damage is also a function of the economic development and population of the area hit, and the nature of the area developed. Barrier islands are crummy places to build when it comes to hurricanes.

Galveston

At age five, my grandfather Milton Potter survived the 1900 Galveston hurricane with his family—his parents, Milton and Ada, and his elder sisters, Shelby and Helen. That storm killed more than six thousand persons, though no one would ever know exactly how many, and virtually destroyed the city. Half a century later he had told me of the cow that floated through a window and spent the storm inside the house, and of the family doctor who early on had come to tend someone. My grandfather watched the man walk up to the house and then saw a slate blown from their roof strike him in the head and kill him.

But these had been tales told before a fire in a living room safe on the mainland, no wind shaking the house, no sea eating at its foundations. I had been too young anyway to appreciate more than the gory thrill of the stories; I had had little sense of what these island people had gone through. Now my grandfather was a quarter-century dead, and I could not ask him what he had done and thought about during the storm, and whether he had been scared or excited. I could not know what it had *felt* like for a five-year-old boy. Of his generation of five brothers and sisters, only his baby sister, Tippy, survived.

My Aunt Tippy now lived a circumscribed life in a comfortable apartment in San Antonio, surrounded by mementos of a life of travel. She had moved from Galveston in 1923, and in a way she had left the island far behind. I realized, though, that in another sense it had always been with her in the way she had lived all those years since and in her vivid memory of her life back then. When I occasionally dropped by to have a chat with her, the island sometimes came up; some detail from her life that seemed to have been so long gone would somehow apply to what we were talking about in the present. Aunt Tippy was born in Galveston the year after the storm, but even so, she might be able to give me some sense of it. It was worth a journey to San Antonio to talk to her again.

It turned out that she had heard almost none of the stories of the storm and did not recall those that her big brother had told me. But she could tell me about the family.

Her father, my great-grandfather, was born in Galveston in 1855. During the Civil War, he and his newly widowed mother boarded a ship loaded with cotton that ran the Northern blockade and headed for France. He returned to Galveston at the age of seventeen. Later, as a cotton and insurance broker, he shared an office with his father-in-law, Colonel Denson. (The office later burned in the 1915 hurricane— Aunt Tippy remembered standing on the front porch with her father as he pointed out the glow from the fire.) The family went through the 1900 storm, she said, in a big white house on the northeast corner of 16th Street and Broadway, only a block from the island's highest point, an area that survived relatively intact. In fact, the house was still standing the last time she visited the island. The family had moved there only months before the storm; previously they had lived in the western part of the city, close to the Densons. Their old neighborhood suffered heavily, but the Potters returned to it soon after the storm.

"In those days you had a lot of servants," she said. "We had an upstairs and a downstairs maid and then a cook and then a nurse. That's the way you lived in those days. And the whole half of the house in the back would go to the servants, and all of their friends were there, praying and moaning during the storm." She began to talk about the 1915 storm, which she remembered well. It was Louis (nicknamed Shorty), their house servant, who had held the front doors closed while my great-grandfather and twenty-year-old grandfather braced them. Shorty was married to Stella, the cook, and in about 1904 replaced the two maids responsible for the inside of the house because his wife did not get along with them. He was tremendously strong, Aunt Tippy said; he had worked on the wharves as a cotton jammer, hauling bales, and had once fought Jack Johnson.

That storm lasted two nights, and during that time no one could go outside. "Oh," she said, "you don't know what those raging storms are. No one left the house. Not even Shorty. No one even stuck his head out." Galveston Bay filled, and the city flooded from behind, though not nearly so badly as in 1900. The family sat out the storm on the second floor. Sent to bed the first night, Tippy managed to get to sleep. But the second night, she said, she could not. The slate shingles had all blown off the roof, and the rain poured in all night.

Aunt Tippy did remember one of the effects of the 1900 storm. "Whole families, people we knew, were drowned," she said. "My father became one of the vigilantes who had to go out and collect the bodies, and oh, he never talked about it at all." After that storm the Densons moved inland. The colonel had already retired and had talked earlier about starting a farm. "They said they were going to raise mules," she added. "But you know you can't *raise* mules." She laughed when she said it.

That was all I got from her—enough to tantalize me, to give me some sense of what it had been like to go through a hurricane. It was also enough to draw me on to Galveston. Maybe I could find some traces of my family from its days there, and maybe I could learn more about the storm. It was an appropriate time to be in Galveston with such a purpose. A very big hurricane was ravaging the Windward Islands: that morning Hugo had ripped through Guadeloupe and was headed for the mainland.

At the time of the 1900 storm, Galveston was the state's most important port and its fourth-largest city, with a population of thirty-eight thousand. It was also the leading cotton port in the world, the fifth-busiest port in the United States and the country's second-richest city, based on per capita income.

Unfortunately it was built on barrier island sand. Only four and a half feet above sea level on average, and nine feet at its highest, Galveston Island was particularly vulnerable to storms. What few dunes protected it had long since been carted off to fill its creeks and marshes. Some had urged the city to protect the island with a seawall after a hurricane in 1875 severely damaged nearby Indianola, but most were indifferent to the dangers. The next hurricane, in 1886, had obliterated Indianola, after which some citizens proposed building a seawall and raising the grade of the city. But few cared. One weatherman even suggested that Galveston was well outside the "hurricane belt," though it had been hit by sixteen storms between 1810 and 1886.

Still, on a balmy September afternoon such as this, Galveston seemed a town no storm could hurt. The road atop the seawall that had been built after 1900 was jammed with traffic, some cars and trucks sporting bumper stickers that announced "BOI"—Born On the Island—a reminder that even here, where the economy depended on tourists, islanders knew who belonged and who did not. People strolled the seawall, the fat, the thin, the young, the old; large families hauling towels, sun visors, inflatable mats, soda cans, lotion, and embedded sand; sexy women and muscular men displaying themselves to each other. Lovers sat on the western end of the seawall, their feet dangling over the eroded shore. They looked out over the infinite and kindly sea. They embraced and kissed. Behind them a plaque commemorated the seawall's completion. Its first line read: "In God We Trust." *Good luck*, I thought to those lovers.

Wandering through the city, I knew no place to go to get a sense of the 1900 storm. There is no graveyard in Galveston to mark the storm's dead, for they had been burned or buried where the survivors found them. The city itself was the graveyard; the dead were everywhere underfoot.

I began my search at the Rosenberg Library, which held the archives of the city's history. There, I found letter after letter recounting the storm's horrors. Much in them was the same: the wind; the surprise at seeing houses break apart; the floundering in the water, pelted by debris; at times someone torn from the writer's arms and never seen again.

The library's photographs of the damage were overpowering. One, taken at 27th Street and Avenue N, showed "fourteen blocks of debris." The caption was correct. Two damaged houses stand in the far background. Otherwise the image is of a tangle of driftwood, something like a dry logjam. Another picture, a panorama looking toward the beach from 12th Street and Avenue I: houses in the foreground remain relatively intact, although every one is damaged and some sit at crazy angles with cocked roofs. To the west stand the walls of a church. But behind the houses, stretching south to the sea nine or ten blocks away, there is nothing, just rubble. Another picture looks like a huge field of torn-up timbers—as if a tornado had stirred up a lumberyard—with roofs in the distance, all at odd angles. The Bath Avenue School has one wall collapsed, torn away, the second floor dangling at a precarious angle, still connected to the building at its far corner, the bolted-down school desks still in place.

After a while, the photos of upside-down houses, ripped-out walls with destroyed lives and pick-up sticks of debris became meaningless. Yet two of the pictures remain in my mind. One shows the dead, their bodies bloated, limbs swollen and held away from the torso, stacked on a barge to be dumped in the Gulf. The other, easier on the eye, shows weary men clearing the wreckage.

Poring over these photographs and the accounts, some written in a now-shaky hand as the writer looked back across many years, I pieced together a story, at least a fragment, of what some of those in the storm had endured.

The first hints arrived on Wednesday, September 5, when Isaac Cline, head observer for the Weather Bureau in Galveston, received a message from the bureau's central office in Washington, D.C., warning of a "disturbance" near Key West that was moving to the northwest. Vessels bound for Florida and Cuba were warned that the storm was likely to become dangerous.

During Thursday the storm moved north along the west Florida coast. That night it turned sharp left and headed toward Galveston, closing on the island at about 12 miles an hour.

By Friday the winds had picked up and long swells were breaking on the beach from the southeast, against the wind. That afternoon and evening the seas became rough, driving high up on the beach. The swells continued throughout the night, and the tide rose to an unusual height—normally the opposing winds would have kept it from rising.

By five o'clock on the morning of the eighth, Joseph Cline, Isaac's brother and chief clerk, reported that the tide was well up in the low parts of the city. Isaac hitched his horse to a two-wheeled cart and drove to the beach, where he timed the swells. They were coming faster and still growing. He was convinced they were building into a storm tide—they were already damaging houses along the beachfront.

Isaac drove the entire beach to warn people to move to higher ground. He told about six thousand visitors summering on the beach to get off the island immediately. He warned those living within three blocks of the shore to move back and prepare for the worst.

Back at his office, he wired Washington: "Unusually heavy swells from southeast, intervals one to five minutes overflowing low places south portion city three to four blocks from beach. Such high water with opposing winds never observed previously." No local weathermen were allowed to issue storm warnings, but when Washington failed to post any, Cline did anyway. The surge, he later wrote, "told me as plainly as though it was a written message that great danger was approaching."

The first house washed into the sea at 7:30 A.M. The rain began three-quarters of an hour later. Even so, hundreds of unconcerned islanders went to the beach to watch the spectacular surf. After all, they had ridden out the 1875 and 1886 hurricanes safely; why should this be different? As the Gulf waters began to run through the streets, many still did not take the storm seriously.

By ten o'clock the surf was damaging houses as far as three blocks from the beach. By noon rising water had destroyed the one wagon bridge and three railroad bridges to the mainland. Soon the islanders started getting worried, and those who lived near the beach or in small houses began moving their families to the center of the island for protection. Those living in strong buildings a few blocks from the beach thought they could weather the wind and tide. They were wrong.

At 1:00 P.M. the winds reached storm velocity. At 1:15 rising water forced back the last train trying to take people off the island. After driving to the bay and then to the Gulf, at 3:30 Cline wired Washington: "Gulf rising, water covers streets of about half city." Storm waters were already eight feet high and in places stretched from the Gulf to the bay. Soon there would be no island at all, only houses standing in open ocean, with waves rolling between them.

Cline headed to his house at 25th Street and Avenue Q to check on his pregnant wife and three daughters. He had to wade the two miles in waist-deep water, dodging flying timbers and roof slates. When he arrived, he gathered about fifty neighbors into his house. It had only recently been built with such storms in mind, and the islanders mistakenly believed it was secure.

At 4:00 the storm reached hurricane strength. Fifteen-year-old Harry Maxson, working at the Santa Fe Railroad's freight depot, was sent home. Wading west on Avenue H, he saw the roof lift off a house. He began to run to avoid the shower of slate shingles. As they hit him, he stumbled and fell into the water. To his surprise, it was salty.

At 5:15 the wind was blowing a steady 84 miles an hour. It reached 100 mph for two minutes, and then the Weather Bureau's anemometer blew away.

At 6:30 Joseph Cline left weather observer John Blagden to man the station while he returned to the Cline home. In places the water was up to his neck. He reported to his brother that all wires were down; they could get no more messages out. Galveston was completely closed off and fast disappearing under water.

The water rose steadily till about 7:30, when at Cline's house it suddenly rose four feet in as many seconds. As he stood at his partly open door watching the water, it rose from around his calves to above his waist before he could move. It was now ten feet above the ground, which at his house was five feet above sea level, making the tidal surge there fifteen feet. Over the next hour, it rose nearly five more feet.

Cline estimated that the winds reached at least 120 mph from the northeast by 8:00 P.M., when the eye apparently passed to the west of the island. There was a lull, and then by 8:30 the wind began to blow out of the east harder than before.

At the height of the storm, someone at John Sealy Hospital, most likely a nurse, though her identity is unknown, was writing a letter. "Everything washed away," she wrote. "Now flames in the distance. It is all a grand, fine sight, our beautiful Bay, a raging torrent . . . Am beginning to feel a weakening desire for something 'to cling to' should feel more comfortable in the embrace of your arms . . . Darkness is overwhelming us, to add to the horror. Dearest—I—reach out my hand to you. My heart—my soul." No one knows whether the writer survived.

Those at Cline's house soon retreated to the second floor, where they watched wind-and-water-borne wreckage destroying buildings. Timbers and roofs flew through the streets, splintering houses and killing those caught outside. Debris piled up as much as fifteen feet. Several swept-up houses lodged against the Cline house; driven by the force of the waves, they pounded against it. Still, it held.

Then at about 8:30 the seas drove a quarter-mile length of streetcar trestle against the house. The structure tore the house to pieces, carrying its refugees with it. As it went down, Isaac saw his brother near a window with Isaac's two oldest children. Joseph knocked out the glass and took the children onto the floating wreckage grinding against the house. Isaac, his wife, and their four-year-old were in the center of the room. The collision threw them into a chimney that carried them under water as it collapsed. Timbers pinned Isaac. He was drowning. As he lost consciousness, he felt he had done all he could do; it was useless to fight for his life.

He awoke in the darkness sometime later, hanging between heavy timbers. A flash of lightning revealed his daughter, still alive, floating on wreckage a few feet away. He retrieved her but could not find his wife. Then with another flash he saw Joseph clinging to nearby debris with his two other children.

During the night the two men spotted another four-year-old on some wreckage and managed to save her. They protected themselves from flying timbers by huddling behind planks. Often the force of the debris would knock them several feet into the swirling waters, and they would fight their way back to their raft. The small group drifted on the wreckage till almost midnight, while it continued to ram into other houses and destroy them. Though they could see nothing, they could hear the houses crashing under the assault, as well as the screams of the injured and dying.

Finally they were able to climb to a house at 28th and P, only three hundred yards from where they had started. There they left the foundling with others for safekeeping. They had learned from her that she and her mother had been visiting her grandparents, but the child did not know what had happened to them. (About two weeks later Joseph Cline met a man who was searching for his wife and daughter, who had been visiting his mother-in-law; he feared he would never see them again. Recognizing his name, Joseph told the man where he could find his daughter.)

Sometime before midnight young Harry Maxson opened his kitchen window during a lull in the wind. He heard a woman cry, "For God's sake, come and save us!" He closed the window and tried to forget the woman's voice. He hoped it had been only the wind. Between gusts he opened the window again, and again he heard the cries. Maxson was a poor swimmer, but he knew he had to help her. After two other men refused to attempt a rescue with him, a young neighbor agreed. While the man said goodbye to his wife, Maxson told his father what he was going to do. But he could not bring himself to tell his mother goodbye.

Easing themselves out the door, the two men began to ride the waves, half wading, half swimming toward the house where they heard the woman calling. Now afloat, it was already breaking up— each gust of wind tore off a piece. An hour more and it would be gone.

They found twenty-three adults and thirteen babies inside. They decided to take the children first and asked the ten men inside to help carry them to Maxson's house. But the men were too frightened; none would come out. Maxson threatened to leave them all except for the two children in his arms. Finally a man came forward with a child, and soon others joined in. The group worked its way back single file, each holding onto the person in front. They struggled three blocks and reached the Maxson house safely. The two rescuers immediately turned around to save the rest. About one hundred fifty persons spent the night at the Maxson house. All of them survived.

Blagden had stayed all night at the Weather Bureau office and escaped injury. At dawn he headed out in search of his boardinghouse. It was Sunday, September 9, a beautiful day. The sky was clear and the sea almost calm. Yet it was a scene of unimaginable horror. A line of debris, head high and four to ten feet deep, stretched for thirty blocks. It was filled with sand, trees, pieces of houses and their contents. Thousands of dead lay scattered through the wreckage, drowned or crushed by the debris. "I could not help seeing many bodies, though I was not desirous of seeing them," he wrote to his family the next day.

Out on the street, Harry Maxson found the bodies of a woman and twin boys about five years old. The boys were holding onto each other. He began to dig a shallow grave for them. A man sat at the curb near the body of the woman, his wife. He had been looking for her all day, he said. He had not been able to get back to their house during the storm, and it had washed away. The two men laid the woman and two children into the grave, the man all the time mumbling her name. When they were finished, the man thanked Maxson for his help and walked south toward the Gulf. Maxson never saw him again.

Of the fifty in the Cline house, "all but 18 were hurled into eternity," Isaac wrote later. (Two weeks later Mrs. Cline's body was found under the wreckage on which her family had survived. She had traveled with them throughout the storm.) No one really knows how many died; maybe six thousand, although some estimate twelve thousand. For the next several weeks the *Galveston Daily News* published page after page listing the known dead.

About thirty-six hundred houses—half of Galveston, and home to twenty thousand persons—had been completely swept away. No building escaped damage. The entire west end of the city was gone. In addition, about three blocks, more than a thousand feet, of Galveston's shorefront had vanished, the island itself washed away by the storm. The total loss was estimated at $30 million.

The full scale of the disaster would not be clear for days. Reports coming out of the city were almost uniform in their tone and assessment. "Words are too weak to express the horror," they would say. "The suffering and damage are incalculable." Rescuers reported seeing the naked bodies of men, women, and children floating in Galveston Bay. They found survivors standing in small groups among the wreckage, still stunned by their ordeal. "The stores were ruined and deserted and the blight of destruction was visible as far as the eye could reach," wrote George Baily of Dallas, who came to help. "As horrible as all this was, it was as nothing to the hopeless faces of the miserable men, women and children in the streets. . . As long as I live I shall never forget them. Many I knew personally, and these gave greeting, but God, it was nothing but a handshake and tears . . . The tears in their eyes, the quiver in their voices, the trembling of lips! The brand of agony was written across their hearts."

To keep order during the first days, martial law was declared. The military patrolling the streets were quick to shoot looters and "idlers," those who appeared healthy but were not helping clear debris or bury the dead. "I understand four men have been shot today for robbing the dead," Blagden wrote on the tenth. "I do not know how true it is, for all kinds of rumors are afloat and many of them are false . . . A famine is feared, as nearly all the provisions were ruined by the water which stood six to fifteen feet in the streets and all communication to the outside is cut off."

The cleanup began immediately. The greatest problem was what to do with the dead. Three morgues were established to collect them. Those moving the bodies covered their noses with handkerchiefs soaked in camphor to hide the smell and drank large amounts of whiskey to ease their horror. "Hundreds are busy day and night clearing away the debris and recovering the dead," Blagden wrote. "It is awful. Every few minutes a wagon load of corpses passes by on the street."

The dead were too many. For the health of the survivors, they would have to be quickly burned or buried at sea without being identified. Men were impressed to search for bodies, which they carted to the wharves to be loaded onto barges. Fifty black men were forced aboard at gunpoint to handle the bodies. The barges were towed eighteen miles into the Gulf, where the men tied weights to each of the seven hundred corpses and dumped them overboard. The next day the men returned, reportedly ashen in color.

Two days later a body that had been tied to a two-hundred-pound rock and buried at sea washed up on the beach. Soon others were cast up on the west end of the island. "'The sea as though it could never be satisfied with its gruesome work washed these bodies back upon the shore, the waves being the hearses that carried them in to be buried under the sand," one survivor wrote. "The terrible odor from thousands of putrefying bodies was almost unbearable."

Finally, in an effort to stave off sickness, the islanders burned the dead where they found them, afterward burying them in mass graves. For more than a month islanders uncovered bodies at the rate of about seventy a day. They found the last body, a fourteen-year-old girl, on February 10, 1901, ten miles down the island from the city. Well into November the glow from the immolations was visible at night from the mainland.

The story I had pieced together was horrifying. Strangely, though about six thousand persons moved inland after the storm, there was little talk of abandoning Galveston. Too much money had been invested in the city. Too many people lived there. Instead, islanders decided the storm had been a challenge; the only courageous response would be to take up the gauntlet and rebuild.

To assure themselves this effort was worth it, they tried to convince themselves that no such storm would hit again. Community leader George Sealy was quoted in the *Galveston Tribune* on September 20, less than two weeks after the disaster, as saying, "The storm that swept over the city was exceptional and . . . such a storm will never be seen again."

Yet people realized that if they were going to stay, they would need to protect themselves. On September 23 Isaac Cline delivered a special report on the hurricane in which he said, "It appears that a sea wall which would have broken the swells would have saved much of the loss of both life and property." One Chicago engineer told islanders that a seawall would make Galveston "a city that can not be destroyed by such storms . . . You will have the confidence of the world."

Within a year and a half Galveston had a plan to build a seawall and to raise the city. The wall would be constructed of granite and steel-reinforced concrete, anchored with pilings driven fifty feet into the sand. It would be seventeen feet high, with twenty-seven feet of riprap stone seaward of it. The top would have a thirty-foot-wide pavement. The raised grade itself would be highest at the seawall and slope back to about eight feet at the bay.

The initial three miles of seawall were completed in 1904. Other sections were added over the years. When the last 1.2 miles were completed in 1962, the seawall stretched 10.4 miles, a third of Galveston Island's oceanfront, and islanders boasted that it was the longest seawall in the world.

The grade raising was completed in 1910; it was an immense engineering feat. Before the filling could begin, islanders had manually jacked up 2,156 buildings (including the six-million-pound Saint Patrick's Church, which they raised five feet with seven hundred jackscrews without interrupting services) along with sewer, gas, and electrical lines. During the raising, people walked on elevated catwalks. To deliver the necessary eleven million cubic yards of fill, they dug a two-and-a-half-mile canal the length of the city to accommodate hopper dredges that worked six years pumping wet sand from Galveston Bay onto the island. The filled areas took months to dry out.

Now, almost a century later, I sat there in the library, wondering whether the island wasn't still in danger. Common wisdom among geologists holds that when you build a seawall, you sacrifice the beach. Unfortunately, for reasons that scientists are still discussing, seawalls increase the erosion rate of the beaches in front of them. Evidently the seawalls not only interrupt some sand transport processes but also may amplify the energy of the waves in the surf zone and thereby help them scour the beach. The sand in front of Galveston's seawall has long since gone as the shoreface has steepened, and stone groins stick out every two or three hundred yards in a futile attempt to trap any passing sand. That sand loss removed more of the island's seaward storm buffer, and today storm seas beat hard against the seawall, increasing the chances of its failure. Ironically, as the structure has been undermined, the original row of riprap placed at the seawall's foot to protect it has in places been supplemented with a second row to protect the first row; indeed, a third row, in turn, protects parts of the second.

The beach to the west of the seawall is also eroding rapidly. The seawall itself may have contributed to the erosion by cutting off part of the sand supply. When the western end of the seawall was completed some thirty years ago, the road on top ran off the end and down onto the beach. Now the old roadbed leads into the Gulf of Mexico; the beach lies more than two hundred feet inshore of it. In addition, since the 1950s Galveston's suburbs have expanded west of the seawall, out of its protection and onto land that has not been raised. There have been few storms lately, and people forget about the danger.

But that does not matter, really. Nor does it matter that barrier islands are the worst possible places to build. It is too late for that; sixty-five thousand people live on the island, and they are not going to leave. The population in summer, the most vulnerable time, swells to about one hundred twenty thousand.

The real question is whether these people can escape before a storm. Officials estimate that evacuating the island would take twenty-six hours. Unfortunately, the National Hurricane Center can predict landfall only about twelve hours in advance. And with the escape routes lying so low—the road from western Galveston to Follet Island floods with only a two-foot rise in sea level, and the main highway to Houston is about four feet above water in places—rising water would cut off the island long before those twelve hours elapsed. By the time forecasters knew that 1988's massive Hurricane Gilbert would miss Galveston, it was already too late to evacuate.

Even if there is time to evacuate, a large number of people simply will refuse to go. Most of them, according to one islander, are BOIs. "They say their grandfather and great-grandfather went through the hurricanes and they will, too," he explained to me. "'No damn hurricane is going to drive me off.'" Most of these people have never been through a hurricane; they are likely to get religion sometime during their first one.

Hurricanes have continued to hit Galveston in the years since the storm Isaac Cline called "one of the most important meteorological events in the world's history." Even though bigger storms than the 1900 and 1915 storms have entered the Gulf of Mexico since, none has reached the island. There are much bigger storms out there, Category Five storms with winds exceeding 155 mph and a tidal surge greater than 18 feet. Hurricane Allen, in August 1980, was one of those, a storm so big it filled the entire Gulf of Mexico. Its winds reached 185 mph. But Allen hit the thinly populated lower coast and faded fast. Galveston was lucky that time.

Before leaving Galveston, I wanted to find some last traces of my family's time there. At the Rosenberg Library, the 1896 city register listed the Densons as living at 3110 Avenue O and the Potters at 1601 31st Street. Both these addresses were on the northwest corner of 31st and O, the present Artillery Club. Aunt Tippy said her grandparents had owned that land, but I saw no trace of any old buildings. The storm had destroyed the area, a block and a half from relative safety.

By 1899 both the Densons and the Potters were living at 3318 Avenue N, on the northwest corner of 33rd Street. Across the street the block had been obliterated, but this was an area of only partial damage. Still, I found an empty lot surrounded by chainlink fence, what we as kids had called hurricane fence. It was a beautiful spot, at least five lots wide, with large palms and live oaks, some as high as thirty feet. It was for sale. I called the bank holding the property. For forty thousand dollars I could come back to the island—thirty-five thousand if I paid cash.

The register did not list the Densons in 1901. Presumably they had already left the island. I did, however, find "Potter, Milton H, broker, notary public, also agt. Mutual Life Ins. Co. office 2205 Strand, r. 1703 31st phone 924." The Potters were back in their old neighborhood, across Avenue O from their 1896 address, an area totally destroyed earlier. Aunt Tippy was born there in 1901, and her baby brother, Bill, in 1903. It had been "a great big house," she said, with a big yard. When I went there, I found a newer house, with a red brick and white fake-timber facade. It faced Avenue O and therefore carried no 31st Street number. The original, my aunt said, had been broken into three houses. No matter how I figured it, this Potter house, too, was gone.

There remained only the two-story house on the northeast corner of 16th and Broadway, where the family had ridden out the storm. Aunt Tippy had seen it the last time she visited the city. But when I got there,

there was no house, just grass ringed by live oaks and palm trees, as if a house had stood there recently.

My family's relationship to Galveston had proved tenuous. Its homes had all been washed away or torn down.

I crossed the street to the northwest corner. Surrounded by live oaks and tall palms and shut off from the street by a seven-foot brick wall, that house was hard to see—tan brick, two stories, a second-floor gallery. The shutters were a faded, chalky blue, with a red Mediterranean tile roof and overhanging eaves, a perfect tropical house. Maybe these people would know when the house had been torn down. A yellow Mercedes station wagon pulled up to the wall, and a metal gate rolled up to let it in. The gate closed before I could reach it. The nine-foot-high door beside it sported two security alarm stickers and a bell. I rang. No response. I pushed the button again. A door slammed. But no one came to answer my questions.

I went back to the Rosenberg Library and began to search through the lists of the dead. In the September 23, 1900, *Houston Daily Post* I found 4,967 names. But after that were two more pages of names, "Some People Who Survive," listing those who had previously been thought dead. There I found "POTTER, Milton, and Wife." My great-grandparents.

Delta

Orrin Pilkey had suggested I see the geologist Shea Penland, at the Louisiana Coastal Geological Survey. That state was in big trouble, he
said. If I wanted to know the future of America's barrier islands, I need
only look at Louisiana. And Penland was in the middle of it.

Studying a map, I could see that the state has problems. Its coast is
a corrupt leaf. I could see the rot, the crumbling seaward edge of the
land reduced to an open filigree of salt marshes as the sea overwhelms
the coast. The shoreline is eroding at a horrifying rate; a map of the
coast ten years from now will not look like today's—there will be far
less land.

The average coastal erosion rate nationally is about 2.6 feet per
year. In the Gulf of Mexico it is 5.9 feet. Louisiana, by comparison,
loses an average 13.9 feet of land annually, the highest rate in the country, more than five times the national rate. The state loses almost 60

square miles per year to the sea, more than 100 acres per day. West of the Mississippi River, Terrebonne Parish alone loses 6,000 acres—9.4 square miles—every year. Its coast is eroding as much as 50.5 feet per year in places. In a hundred years it may be half its present size, its coastal plain and wetlands entirely gone, reduced to open sea. Houma, now on relatively high ground some twenty-five miles inland, will be a port on the Gulf of Mexico.

The cause of all this erosion? Louisiana's landscape is submerging. Sea level here is rising about half an inch per year, a ruinous rate for a place such as Louisiana: with its flat coastal profile, a small sea level rise means a big shoreline retreat.

The rise plays hob with Louisiana's barrier islands. In the past hundred years they have been reduced to two-thirds their former area. Between 1955 and 1978 the islands in Terrebonne Parish lost 42 percent of their area. Their geology makes other barrier islands look slow. Louisiana's islands are young—Grand Isle, the state's only inhabited barrier island, is three hundred years old, and the Isles Dernieres are maybe six hundred—both are disappearing fast. They move landward as sea level rises, but the sea eventually overwhelms them. One hundred fifty years ago the four Isles Dernieres were a single island, separated from the mainland by less than a third of a mile of open water; today they are more than four miles offshore. They are a third their former size. In one storm alone, Hurricane Juan in 1985, the islands lost 10 to 20 percent of their land area. In forty-five years they will be reduced to submerged shoals; ten years after that so will the rest of Terrebonne Parish's barrier islands.

The effects of the barrier island loss and the associated wetland damage are potentially devastating. Hurricane dangers for coastal communities and wetlands will increase—they will be more vulnerable without these barriers between them and the open Gulf. When the islands go, so do the estuaries behind them. And then the wetlands will erode even faster with direct wave action from the Gulf.

Louisiana contains 41 percent of the nation's coastal wetlands. And marshland is the richest land on earth, one acre yielding four times more organic material than a cornfield. Some estimate that if you include their income-generating ability, the salt marshes of the Gulf and southern U.S. Atlantic coasts are worth about eighty-two thousand dollars an acre. Louisiana's wetlands support two-thirds of the fish caught in the state's waters. The Barataria estuary, east of Terrebonne Parish, for instance, produces more than six hundred fifty pounds of fish per acre. The Gulf Coast from Galveston, Texas, to Apalachicola, Florida, has been called the most productive fishery in the world. Louisiana alone accounts for 25 percent of the nation's fish and half of its shellfish catch. More than two billion pounds of fish and shellfish come from nearby waters each year.

Yet biologists estimate that the state's wetland losses in the last twenty years have caused an annual shrimp loss of more than sixty-three million pounds. The Army Corps of Engineers says that within thirty to fifty years the state will lose 30 percent of its fishery. Lose the islands and you lose the fishing.

The reason for the rapid sea level rise is that the sea is rising while the coast is sinking.* Eustatic sea level is rising worldwide about 0.05 inch per year; as the icecaps have melted since the last glaciation, the additional water has raised sea levels.

The situation is worse in Louisiana, though. Aside from whatever the sea is doing, the state's coast itself is sinking as much as 0.46 inch per year. Add eustatic rise and subsidence together, and relative sea level rise in Louisiana is ten times the global eustatic rate. And it has accelerated since 1932; in 1980 it was triple the 1940-to-1960 rate. If it keeps this up, by 2075 sea level in Terrebonne Parish may have risen as much as 43.70 inches—that's barely more than eighty years away.

Global warming only exacerbates the problem. A warmer climate melts more polar ice and thus increases the amount of ocean water; it also warms the seas, increasing their volume. The Environmental Protection Agency (EPA) claims that if we add the expected effects of global warming, sea level in Louisiana could rise by as much as 1.10 inches per year, raising sea level at Terrebonne Parish by the year 2075 more than 7.5 feet, instead of that mere 43.70 inches.

*We need to distinguish eustatic—true—sea level rise from relative rise. In some places sea level appears to be falling. But in fact such coastlines are themselves rising faster than the sea. In these places, relative sea level is falling while eustatic sea level is rising.

The causes of subsidence, the main contributor to relative sea level rise, are complex. Essentially the land is so heavy that it is slowly consolidating, collapsing in on itself. The weight also warps the earth's crust downward, though this amount is small compared to subsidence from consolidation. The shallow-water sediments (formed in less than 65 feet) along the Louisiana coast are about 40,000 feet thick. For the last sixty million years they have been warping the crust about 0.008 inch per year.

The primary reason why this depressing weight problem is, in fact, such a problem is tied to the nature of the Mississippi River and to how we have used it. After the last glaciation, the river began to build a delta plain out into the Gulf of Mexico. By flooding and by breaking through its levees—which, under natural conditions, happens about every three years—and bifurcating, the river also built its delta upward. When a river floods, the slowing water drops its sediments. As the delta builds farther out onto the continental shelf and rises, it becomes hydrologically inefficient and diverts: the channel switches to a shorter, steeper course. Here it builds another delta lobe until this lobe, too, is high enough and extended enough for the river to change course. The abandoned delta's headland, in the meantime, becomes the sand supply for a barrier island arc flanking it.

In this way the river maintains a series of deltas and their associated barrier islands, replenishing one and then moving to another. Because these deltas are sinking, when the river diverts, it tends to move to the one that has subsided the most (usually the oldest) and is therefore the most efficient for the river to flow across. This back-and-forth refreshment cycle keeps the deltas at a relatively stable level overall. In the past seven thousand years, it has produced a delta plain covering 9,400 square miles, consisting of six deltas, each built of several subdeltas. These radiate southeastward from the Mississippi valley between Baton Rouge, on the river, and Lafayette, 50 miles west, and form 300 miles of coast. About 20 percent of the delta plain is receiving sediment. The rest is abandoned.

Looking at the map, you can see the different deltas. (Well, most of them; some you have to imagine.) Clockwise from east to west are the Saint Bernard delta, from Lake Pontchartrain to east of the current riv-

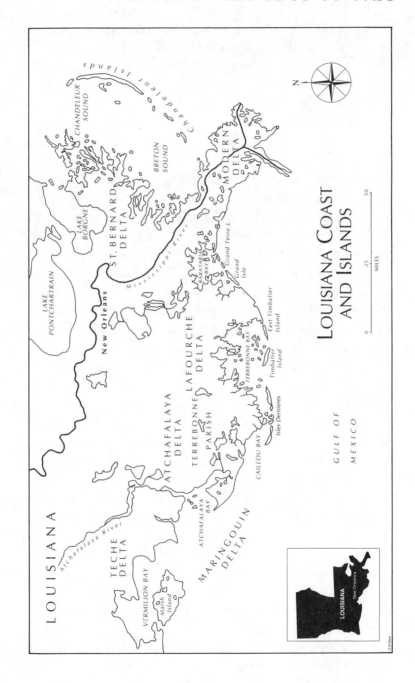

LOUISIANA COAST AND ISLANDS

erbed and including the Chandeleur Islands; the Modern delta, extending well into the Gulf to the continental shelf edge; the Lafourche delta, including Grand Isle, the Timbalier Islands, and the Isles Dernieres; the Atchafalaya delta, extending into Atchafalaya Bay; the Teche delta, under parts of the Lafourche and Atchafalaya deltas, westward to include Marsh Island and Vermilion Bay; and the Maringouin delta, now completely submerged, and extending offshore from under the Teche, Atchafalaya, and Lafourche deltas.

In his model of the evolution of abandoned deltas, Shea Penland has defined three stages. In the first, the eroding shoreface reworks the deposits in the abandoned delta headland into flanking barrier islands. Longshore transport moves its sand laterally, and the islands are still connected to the headland. In the second stage, rising sea level separates the barrier islands from the retreating mainland and creates a transgressive barrier island arc with large lagoons behind it. In the third stage, the migrating barrier islands cannot keep up with sea level rise and drown, reduced to inner-shelf shoals, their associated lagoons destroyed. Eventually a new delta reoccupies this remnant and the cycle begins again.* Today's active deltas are the Atchafalaya and the Modern, which is the current Mississippi River outflow, active only near the mouth. The Atchafalaya delta began to form after an upstream diversion in the Mississippi River in the late 1800s, and the Atchafalaya River now receives 30 percent of the Mississippi's flow. It would receive more (in fact, it would be the main outlet of the Mississippi) if the Army Corps of Engineers had not intervened to control it.

The youngest abandoned delta is the Lafourche complex, west of the Mississippi River and active from about thirty-five hundred to

*Penland's Stage One corresponds to Gilbert's theory of barrier island formation by mainland spit growth. Likewise, his Stage Two fits McGee's model of formation through separating beach ridges from the mainland during sea level rise. None of the cycle corresponds to De Beaumont's theory of formation from the upbuilding of submerged shoals, except that in a way Stage Three looks like De Beaumont in reverse. Just east of these deltas, in Mississippi, the geologist Ervin Otvos is the main proponent of this upbuilding theory, saying that some of the barrier islands of the Gulf of Mexico coast formed that way. Penland, however, scorns this notion, calling it ludicrous. There is, he says, no evidence for this kind of barrier island building in the Gulf, no matter what Otvos says.

three hundred years ago. It incorporates several smaller deltas, two of which are apparent on the map. To the east, the headland containing Bayou Lafourche is younger, abandoned some three hundred years ago. It is still intact, its flanking barrier island arc (the Timbalier Islands to the west and Grand Isle to the east) still coherent, a Stage One delta. Even so, the headland and its islands have retreated about two miles in the past hundred years. To the west, the delta containing Bayou Petit Caillou, for which Isles Dernieres are the flanking barriers, is older, abandoned maybe six hundred years ago. It has made the transition from a Stage One to a Stage Two delta in the past hundred fifty or so years. The islands are now detached from the submerged headland and are crumbling as the mainland retreats.

The easternmost delta, the Saint Bernard, was active from about forty-six hundred to eighteen hundred years ago. Its Chandeleur Isles and associated shoals are the oldest barrier island arc in the delta plain. The Chandeleurs are now more than 19 miles offshore, and the mainland delta is reduced to a series of open salt-water marshes, the map's leaf well rotted. The Chandeleur Islands are shrinking. Still, the northern end of the 46-mile arc remains relatively intact because of plentiful sand and because of its angle to the prevailing waves; though hurricanes will disjoin the islands, they are able to reconsolidate during quiet periods. The north end is moving inland at about 16 feet per year while the ephemeral island fragments of the south move as much as 50 feet per year. The arc is expected to survive another three hundred fifty years.

The next two abandoned deltas, both Stage Three, have no surviving barrier islands. The Teche delta, abandoned about twenty-five hundred years ago, has a transgressive shoreline, and few of its coastal features survive. Trinity Shoal, about 10 miles offshore from Marsh Island and approximately 30 miles long, is a remnant of that delta's barrier arc. The Maringouin delta remnant, maybe six thousand years old, is so far gone that none of it remains above water. Nautical charts from the 1700s and 1800s show a small island at the western end of Ship Shoal, which lies about 10 miles offshore of Isles Dernieres. But that island has not been seen since 1816. The 30-mile shoal is the delta's last feature, footprint of a barrier island arc moving landward before the rising sea overwhelmed it. The shoal is still moving inshore as much as 50 feet per year in places.

Thus the Louisiana coastal delta dynamic is a kind of balancing act, like some vaudevillian trying to keep six plates spinning on six sticks. As one slows and starts to wobble, he sets it to spinning faster and turns his attention to the next one that has started to wobble. It all stays in balance as long as the vaudevillian pays close attention to all six disks.

But human use has changed the dynamic balance. First, we have reduced the Mississippi's sediment load, mainly by constructing upstream dams and reservoirs, so less material is available for upbuilding. The river has lost 41 percent of its sediment load since 1963. Even so, it is still carrying a lot of stuff—after all, it drains 41 percent of the area of the lower forty-eight states. About two hundred fifty million tons pass down the Atchafalaya and Mississippi each year. Most of this available sediment does not reach the delta; instead, it is deposited deep in the Gulf. Why? Because of our second disruption of the balance: we have leveed the river.

Historically we have occupied the natural levee ridges of the Mississippi River and its bayous—the dry areas. To keep the river from flooding, we have raised and strengthened the natural levees—something we have been doing, more or less, since the 1700s. Two-thirds of the river's flow is now confined within levees and channels, and delta building has stopped. The river cannot change its course or overflow its banks; it can no longer refresh the soils of most of its current delta, much less move on to rebuild abandoned deltas.

As long as the river cannot rebuild the deltas, they are going to sink and Louisiana is going to have an enormous land-loss problem. The barrier islands are collapsing for lack of sand. And, as Penland has put it, "The wetlands are falling apart like crazy behind them." By cutting off the sediment, we have kept our busy vaudevillian from four of the plates. They are wobbling so badly that they are about to fall, while he spins only two. And he spins those faster and faster and faster.

Other factors are at work, too, though some geologists, including Penland, do not feel they are particularly significant compared to the disruption of the delta cycle. Extracting water, oil, and gas from the delta has helped make the sediments collapse. (The world's first producing offshore oil well was drilled half a mile from Louisiana's coast in 1937, and since then another twenty thousand wells have been drilled in the Gulf.) About ten thousand miles of canals penetrate Louisiana's wetlands, mainly for navigation and access to oil and gas facilities. These canals have increased saltwater intrusion and erosion; between 1955 and 1978, some geologists estimate, they accounted indirectly for 14 to 43 percent of Louisiana's wetland losses. Moreover, those canals cut into barrier islands make the islands vulnerable to overwash and breaching, as do pipelines cut through them.

In responding to these problems, we have at times only made things worse for the barrier islands. Attempts to stabilize the shore are directly to blame for more than 10 percent of all the barrier island area loss between 1880 and 1980. The Timbalier Islands, part of the Lafourche delta complex, actually grew some between 1935 and 1956, owing to a low tropical storm frequency. (Even with rapid sea level rise, barrier islands flanking a large, active sediment source tend to build.) After 1956, though, both islands started to shrink; the construction of jetties at Belle Pass and a seawall along East Timbalier Island to protect oil and gas operations there interrupted sediment transport from the Bayou Lafourche headland. The 1969 extension of the Belle Pass jetties increased the erosion. Today the two islands are half the size they were in 1955.

Look at that map again. Notice where the Mississippi River flushes its sediments into the Gulf of Mexico. The land protrudes far out to sea, well beyond the surrounding coast and barrier island arcs. This is the Modern delta, the only place where the river can build, beyond the last levee at Venice and out to the edge of the continental shelf. My first stop in Louisiana was to see Shea Penland in his office at Louisiana State University (LSU), in Baton Rouge. As soon as I settled into a chair he jumped up and strode to a large map on the wall. That protruding delta—or birdfoot, as geologists call it—was the first feature he pointed out. "This thing," he said, tapping the protrusion and calling it a chickenfoot, "is an abomination of nature. It would never have gotten that far without the levee system."

As coastal geology supervisor for the Geological Survey, Penland had the job, among other things, of monitoring the coast and its barrier islands. And that meant watching them disappear. He talked fast, a man with much to say, illustrating a point by reaching for a book, a sheet of paper, or a photograph among the many scattered across his office. He had names, people I should talk to, places to go—talk to Bobby Jones, parish engineer for Terrebonne Parish; talk to Jim Sothern in Houma, who knew about the history; get down to Cocodrie, at the edge of the collapsing marshes—I could stay at a research lab there. I took notes fast.

Penland was outspoken and profane and honest about his opinions, a good person to talk to for a notion of what was happening, especially considering how readily Louisiana's coastal issues could become political. Given the high price of doing something, or for that matter of doing nothing, and given the number of people risking dislocation and loss of their way of life, any discussions of Louisiana's coastal problems were likely to be contentious.

In some ways Penland did not like Louisiana much. He certainly disliked the politics. He was also an unregenerate surfer, and if he had had his way, he probably would have been waxing his board back on a beach in western Florida. One thing kept him from leaving, though— the geology. It was too interesting for him to live anywhere else. "It's really neat," he explained with surprising enthusiasm, given the gravity of the problem, "because you can really see the coastline evolve. I swore to God I'd never live here after I did my graduate work here. My second wife is from California, and I took her to the beach one time and she just said, 'God damn.' And I said, 'Well, sweetheart, it may not look like much'—and you'll learn that—'it may not look like much, but the geology's great.'"

Great geology or no, the people of Louisiana are facing disaster. "It's very controversial right now, what's happening in coastal Louisiana," he said. "There's a lot of infighting among state agencies about what needs to be done. The state of Louisiana is asking, 'What can we do?' I used to be on the governor's technical committee. After dealing with a bunch of politicians, people who make decisions based on politics . . ." Penland's voice trailed off and he shook his head. He did not want to talk about politicians.

What are the options? He began a litany. "One of the big questions facing coastal Louisiana is, should we even do anything? Well, the EPA says it's cheaper to do something than nothing. You're looking at strategic retreat; that is, some parts of this coastline you can't save. The people who are living there will have to move. Orrin Pilkey says retreat, don't spend the money on the coastline, and all that kind of bullshit. Orrin plays both sides of the fence."

(Both sides, evidently, because Pilkey writes about how we should abandon the barrier islands, while he also has published a series of books on where we can build on them. I asked Penland about Pilkey. He started to laugh about how the man confronts developers at public meetings. "Good old Orrin, nothing's going to keep him down. That guy—I love it. Pilkey's saying, 'You shouldn't be allowed to build seawalls. Retreat. You shouldn't be developing the coastline.' The developer turns around and says, 'It's my God-given right to buy property and protect it.' So I tell Pilkey, I say, 'Well, Pilkey, you're such a great son of a bitch'—Orrin and I, we're great friends—'you can't lose in your business.'")

The next option, according to Penland, was to divert the Mississippi during flood to get some of its sediments back onto the delta instead of losing them off the edge of the continental shelf. "The cheapest one, five hundred million bucks," he said. "The first one that's coming on line, which is not sediment diversion but freshwater diversion, is 10,500 cfs [cubic feet per second] for sixty million dollars. So they're not cheap. If you want to do a 100,000-cfs sediment diversion, you're talking about big projects requiring ten to fifteen years of planning, if you've got enough money in the pipeline for engineering and environmental considerations to merge."

Two diversion projects have been considered in recent years near New Orleans, to increase the freshwater levels in marshes and to build up the delta. Some geologists feel that diverting 5 percent of the Mississippi River's flow would allow a delta growth rate of as much as three-quarters of a square mile per year.

Then there is marsh management. "Marsh management can be a sixty-thousand-dollar freshwater diversion, trying to keep the marshes from becoming intruded by salt water, to a two-hundred-thousand-dollar marsh management of a thousand acres of marsh and building a levee, just trying to control the water level and trying to maintain the marsh. But the problem with marsh management is that it's very controversial, because people manage marsh for different reasons. The Department of Wildlife and Fisheries manages the marsh for ducks; so they don't want marsh, they want shallow ponds. So there's a moratorium now on marsh management plans; we have a three-year study we're doing to identify which marsh management strategies are most effective.

"Terrebonne Parish engineer Bobby Jones does barrier island projects, marsh management projects for one parish. How would you like to be the drainage engineer for a parish that's sinking at rate of 1.25 centimeters per year, in charge of hurricane protection? As he explained to the parish council, 'Well, when the pumphouse was three meters under water during the last hurricane, I guess we just couldn't keep the pumps running.' This is the guy at the parish level trying to hope that the big-brother state will help him out. Well, the big-brother state and the feds aren't . . ." He did not finish his thought.

"The cheapest thing to do is restoring the barrier islands. You're looking at about three hundred and fifty dollars a linear foot, a million a mile. You're talking about your five-million- to twenty-five-million-dollar projects.

"And then the *cheapest* thing you can do is research. What you hear a lot is 'We've studied the problem enough! We're ready to start doing stuff.' But they don't understand natural systems at all. So that's why the LSU research community is pissed off at the state, because the state doesn't listen. The state makes all its decisions based on politics, not on good research."

He stopped. Five years ago, he explained, the state had asked him to put together a map of what the Louisiana coast would soon look like. The map so appalled the politicians that they refused to release it to the public.

How bad was it going to be? Penland sighed. "If this greenhouse effect is true, with additional subsidence on top of that, man, you're looking at some radical changes. You're looking at New Orleans being Gulf-front in a hundred years. Terrebonne Parish, if the land loss rate that occurred during the last twenty-five years occurs for the next hundred and two years, then the entire parish will be open water. Plaque-mines Parish, fifty-six years. What do you do when you're a coastal planner for a parish and you come up and tell the mayor, 'We're going to be gone in a hundred and two years'? And he says, 'Do something about it.' These guys throw rocks on it—they have all kinds of ideas—throwing old cars out in the bays and putting dirt on top of them and planting marsh—we've done some bizarre things in this state.

"Cybernetic architecture! The newest thing I've got to review is turning the beach into a driveway with marine cement. Some state senator says, 'I've got boudin bags [so named because they look like giant Cajun boudin sausages], concrete bags,' so one project, they stacked nine-foot-long concrete-filled bags vertically, *just stacked them up*! And they had a choice of doing that, which cost four times more per linear foot than beach nourishment, and they had a source of sand from a dredging project. Well, of course with the senator tagged to it, they went with the boudin bag project. But now they're having to fund the beach nourishment project to protect the boudin bags." Penland gave me a bemused look. "This is where research plays into the decision making. We recommended to them no, don't build these boudin bags. What you should do is set up a permanent spoil disposal pipe along the beach so that every year when you do maintenance dredging, hook up to the pipe, turn on a little gate, cell number one spews out." But no luck.

"Do you know cybernetic architecture? We did a project—some state senator got turned on, somehow—you get four fence posts, some chicken wire, and string it around them. You get a solar panel and a twelve-volt battery, two alligator clips, hook them together, and run current through the chicken wire. The current makes calcium carbonate precipitate out and form like an oyster shell. The materials for the project probably cost two hundred and fifty dollars, but I think the final bill was for something like a couple of hundred thousand. And what they didn't realize was that the chicken wire rusted faster than the calcium carbonate could be secreted out. They made a nice hit and ran."

Penland tapped a piece of paper on his desk. "You see this? Pouring marine cement on the beach with a rototiller and turning the beach into a driveway." I got the idea.

"Some people feel that the barrier islands serve no functional role in the ecosystem of south Louisiana, if you believe that. Some people feel that you should only throw rocks on the beach. Some people think that we should go with cybernetic architecture. You will find that East Timbalier Island is the most abused barrier island in the country, ringed by a complete rock wall. We poured sand on top of the island. This cost twenty-five million dollars—two million dollars a year to maintain it."

Penland does not think hard structures will solve Louisiana's problems, a controversial position in a state that often drops rocks on erosion. He has written that hard engineering has proved expensive and ineffective in stabilizing Louisiana's barrier islands. In fact, hard structures do more harm than good, because they disrupt sand dispersal. He does, however, like soft engineering, adding sand to the system through beach nourishment and island restoration, and stabilizing the islands with vegetation.

"You've got to work with the system. If the barrier island is losing sediment and is needing sediment and new vegetation to maintain its integrity, you don't throw rocks on it. You throw sand back into the system. And you study the barrier islands to learn how they operate. Because some of the barrier islands can't keep pace with sea level, you look at those barrier islands and say, 'Well, we're going to have to design a barrier island that's like the northern Chandeleur Islands.' All of a sudden you're coming to landscaping at a new scale. A big scale.

"You have to protect the estuary. You have to maintain the seaward framework and then rebuild the marshes from behind. At the Isles Dernieres, if you lose that barrier system, you lose the bay behind it, that estuarine water-column habitat.

"The state's position is that the barrier islands are not important to the coastal ecosystem. Well, that's politics right there, that's a hundred percent politics. With Bobby Jones it's open warfare, as far as he's concerned. He's gunning for the state officials. We're the laughingstock of the nation. A month ago a fellow got up at a conference about maintaining barrier islands and told the entire conference that the state sees beach nourishment does not work—it's now the nationally accepted way to protect beaches—and the state's policy is to build more seawalls, and the state's policy is they don't care about barrier islands, because they don't have any functional—This guy was laughed out of the conference.

"The Department of Wildlife and Fisheries, who regulate the fisheries within the bays, are going crazy. They're going, '*What!*' The shrimp's life cycle goes from ocean to bay to marsh and back, and if you remove the bay habitat on which the fisheries are dependent, you lose the salinity gradients; the environmental stress on the shrimp population and the fish population that uses that marsh-bay-barrier ecosystem is severely damaged. And that billion-dollar-a-year productivity will just fall apart."

Penland shrugged. "This is Louisiana," he added, his voice heavy with meaning.

Fingers in the Dike

I went out to the marshes—south past Thibodaux into Terrebonne Parish, past Houma with its sale on generators ("Hurricane season is here!"), past Dulac, and down along the bayous, with their low-lying houses and large shrimp boats parked behind them, often longer and always taller than the houses themselves. Here the graveyards perched above ground, rows of tombs keeping the dead dry. Cypresses and moss-bearded live oaks populated the bayou ridges, and dense fields of sugar cane stretched from the road's edge. The ground was only a foot or so above water. Soon it was not even that, dry land giving way to marsh, the road raised on a bed of shells.

South past Cocodrie there were no roads, just the sinking marshes.

Here was the deep irony of this place: when the French had called it *terre bonne*, they had been speaking of the "good land." Now, eight miles across the marshes stood open water; thirteen miles away lay the degenerating Isles Dernieres. This was as close to the Gulf as one could get and still remain on fairly solid ground. A few informal houses stretched along Bayou Petit Caillou. An oil-company facility and a dock full of shrimp boats exploited the nearby Houma navigation canal for access to the Gulf. And here too stood LUMCON, a research laboratory run by a consortium of Louisiana universities to study the state's wetlands, bays, and barrier islands. Those who used the lab, Shea Penland had said, called it Marine Lab Galactica.

The characterization fit. The building was modern, all sand-colored concrete and dark mirrored glass spreading in several wings from a tapered glass conning tower rising three stories above them. The entire structure hulked over the flat surroundings, pilings holding it clear of rising water. It looked like something freshly landed, something alien, a UFO of the marshes. Inside, the building rumbled faintly with air conditioning and unidentified machinery—noise almost too deep to hear, but which the body feels, the way it feels the thrumming of a ship at sea.

This would be my base for a few days. Except for the hum, the lab was strangely quiet. I saw a few people: the receptionist at her station in the central hall, the librarian by the books, the director coming and going, a woman behind a glass wall working at a computer. But by late afternoon everyone was gone.

I climbed the tower to see the marshes. The prospect was dark and moody, the sky gray, with patches of black clouds scudding by. For two days there had been a low overcast. The air was humid, the temperatures in the low seventies. Now the wind darkened the marsh waters and whistled along the tower's edges. I could make out three large, low-flying egrets headed for the grasses at a pond's shore. A shrimper headed southwest down the bayou for open water. The marshes seemed separate, another world from this sterile, technical structure.

Outside, though, where I could feel the damp breeze, the open expanse of marsh was very much there. The *Spartina* ruffled in the wind. Faint sounds drifted up—crickets and a distant mix of birds squawking and chirping and falling silent. I could not tell one from another. Somewhere out there in the brackish nursery, oyster spat were making a home, recently hatched shrimp were busy grazing on debris, and countless varieties of crabs, fish, worms, snails, and other little animals were making babies and eating and filling the marshes with life.

Overhead a flight of white pelicans circled high in a rising thermal, their black primary and secondary feathers clearly visible. I counted more than eighty. They held to the gyre for several minutes, their wings barely flapping. Then, forming up into a long, ragged vee, the ponderous birds headed east. After three or four minutes I could scarcely see them without field glasses. The formation broke, and again they began to circle. The dark shapes suddenly flashed white against the darker overcast as they wheeled, their white backs and wing tops catching the light. It happened in unison—the mass of birds turning white, then darkening as they angled away. The circle drifted east toward Terrebonne Bay and the edge of the Lafourche delta till I could not pick them out from the dark sky.

That night I wandered through the building. Doors stood open, the library lights still on, but except for the guard sitting in the central hall, I saw no one. Even out on one of the decks, there was nothing to see in the encircling darkness. With only the hum of the ventilation system for company, I did briefly feel as if I was floating alone through space—or at the edge of the sea.

Later in the kitchen of the dormitory wing I met a man sipping beer, watching the Browns-Bengals game on television. I joined him, opening a can myself and settling into the institutional approximation of an easy chair. His name was Sean, he said, and he was working on his Ph.D. at LSU, studying genetic evolution. He was from California, and he and his wife had been in shock for a year when they moved to Baton Rouge. He did not come to LUMCON for the wetlands but for the lab itself, where he was studying oysters. He did not work outside at all, he said.

Still, he liked the marshes; the fishing was great. He would set up a floodlight in the marsh at night. After dinner he would go back out to fish. He caught big, big speckled trout, he said, and red drum. The trout were wonderful. These waters were incredibly rich with nutrients—so murky that you couldn't see two feet down. Not like California, where the water was a beautiful turquoise blue but couldn't sustain much. Here it was a real broth, full of life.

He also bought shrimp from the local fishermen. They were funny people, the Cajuns, he said, very suspicious. But after they talked to you, they warmed right up. He'd go down on a bicycle and they'd laugh at him. "What is that language they're talking?" he asked, mocking. "It certainly isn't French."

At about 10:00 P.M. he abandoned the game for fish. He would leave me a trout in the refrigerator for breakfast, he said. After he left I watched cockroaches scuttle across the floor. Yes, he was right; there was lots of life here.

In the morning a heavy speckled trout waited for me in the freezer. That night I hacked rough fillets out of the deeply frozen fish and simmered them with scallions in olive oil, deglazing the pan with beer. I ate it with a ripe tomato on the side. The fish was delicate and sweet.

Robert Jones was a busy man when I arrived in his Houma office. The phone kept ringing, interrupting my attempt to talk to him. Finally, he told the next caller he would phone back. A deep Cajun accent colored his speech. He talked fast, jumping from subject to subject, moving around the room from drawing table to desk to wall to illustrate a point. Underneath he was a bit frantic, a man who, having stuck his fingers in a dike—or maybe a levee—was now running out of hands.

He had a harrowing job, keeping his parish from drowning as it sank. And it would not take much to drown. Though Houma was forty-five miles from the present coast, it was only five feet above sea level. Jones fought his battle while trapped between the Army Corps of Engineers, several federal agencies, and the state of Louisiana. Each seemed to have its own restrictions, priorities, and notions of what could, should, and might be done. And each, it seemed, needed to give its approval before Jones could do anything.

He tapped a series of points on a topographic map. "This is a forced drainage system," he said. Tap. "A forced drainage." Tap. "This is a proposed forced drainage system down here." Tap. "This is existing

forced drainage." Tap. "Existing forced drainage." Tap. "This is existing forced drainage." Tap. "Everything north of here is existing forced
drainage." Tap. "Everything north of right here is existing forced
drainage. Existing forced drainage. Existing forced drainage." Tap tap
tap. "Terrebonne Parish has fifty-two or fifty-three pump stations, a lot
more than the city of New Orleans does. They're not as big. Basically,
a lot of our lower areas that are habitated will have forced drainage
protection, and that's how we deal with subsidence."

He had a problem with the drainage system: most of it had been in-
stalled before 1975, and now the federal government said it was illegal. Environmental restrictions had changed, and the feds wanted the
parish to meet new regulations. "I'm sorry," Jones sighed. "You can't
go back and physically undo things that were done. For instance, say
we bulldoze the levee. Some of those areas are at minus-two-foot elevation now. They'll never return to wetlands; they'll return to open
water."

The parish had finally persuaded the Corps of Engineers to accept
its mitigation project to maintain and improve marsh areas as part of
its program of pumping out leveed areas. Then suddenly, two months
ago, the EPA had stepped in. "EPA said, 'Hold it! That's against our
no-wetland-loss policy.' Well, the no-wetland-loss policy just was in-
stituted in the last year." The program would have helped keep salt-
water intrusion from the Houma navigation canal from killing off
much of these wetlands. That was not good enough for the EPA. "EPA
focuses in and says, 'Well, it already exists as wetland,' and we say,
'Yeah, but you can't think of today, boys; you've got to think of the
fifty-year life of this project.' "

He pointed at the map again. "This area that's green is a lot of open
water, and this area, which is supposed to be marsh, is almost all open
water. I mean, you look at a map." He stroked his hand across a marsh.
"It's not there; it's not like this any more. What's there ain't there." The
map was based on aerial surveys done in 1955. The EPA, he seemed to
fear, didn't get it. Without human meddling the wetland situation
would get worse, not better.

It was a frustrating position for Jones. It had been difficult enough, he said, to get the Corps to approve the project. The parish had had to come back again and again with revisions after having the plan rejected.

Why had the Corps turned it down in the first place? No one would say. "They let you keep proposing stuff and they keep saying, 'No, no, no,' or 'That's not good enough.' The Corps of Engineers, if you do a project in the wetlands, they're not going to tell you how to mitigate for the damages it may cause. They'll just approve or disapprove of what you propose to them. They're never going to tell you how to do it."

Back to the map, to a dotted line crossing east to west through its heart. It marked a levee the parish was starting to build, a kind of barricade. "They're saying we're going to save everything above this, we're going to protect it from hurricanes. Obviously, if the dotted line is completed, that will be our final line of defense unless we just abandon the parish entirely. If we abandon the parish entirely, there will still be some of Terrebonne Parish left, but there won't be a lot of its wetlands left."

By that time, less than fifty years from now, the new parish behind the levee would be half its present size. The line was at least thirty miles inland from Cocodrie. A lot of people would be displaced. "You're talking about an entire culture. You're talking about the latest rage of Cajun culture and wiping it out. You're talking about the city of New Orleans being a leveed island out in the middle of the Gulf of Mexico, if you're talking 'Let's just give up and move.'"

I wondered whether there was anything to be done. "That gets down to whether you think you can save what's out there or not," he said. "Do you think you can save a barrier island? Well, Terrebonne Parish does." He picked up a packet of photographs from the drafting table. They showed a part of the eastern end of Isles Dernieres being rebuilt—men surveying, dredges dumping sand, bulldozers moving it. They had rebuilt overwashed dunes on its front, back, and sides and then filled in with sand dredged from the bay behind it.

He pointed to a photograph of bulldozers shaping a dune. "We made a real effort to approximate the existing beach slopes. So we ended up with a dune which, if you looked at it in comparison to what was already out there, it looked like just an extension. We elevated what was in essence a three-foot-elevation island. We took what would probably now be open water (there were areas of the island which were in better shape than this that are open water now) and elevated it to a six- to eight-foot elevation and then planted it. Obviously, we have found out that planting grass seed on the islands works great. We bought the entire supply of grass seed in the continental United States one summer and gave it to summer students to go out there and plant grass."

The project cost the parish about eight hundred fifty thousand dollars and used three hundred fifty thousand cubic yards of sand. In the end a thirty-two-hundred-foot stretch of island—thirty-eight acres—was repaired and filled in a twenty-nine-day period in March of 1985. A storm overwashed the island with minimal damage once during reconstruction. Since then, three hurricanes had hit it. Two knocked down a sand fence. The third, Hurricane Juan, did more, removing part of the foredune. Even so, the repairs prevented heavy breaching. And, as Jones said, "It's still there."

Unlike the parish, both the state of Louisiana and the Corps of Engineers felt that a barrier island was not worth saving. Such rebuilding, the Corps had said, was not economically efficient. This from an organization famous for dredging sand and rebuilding islands, an organization that has seemed to some at times to be more interested in moving the earth than in attending to environmental reality.

"You know," Jones said, "the colonel was quoted down here in one of the recent hearings as saying it would be presumptuous to think we could alter the course of nature and save coastal Louisiana—it *might* be presumptuous. Made all the headlines. My question to him would be, if it's presumptuous of us to think we can save coastal Louisiana, then how presumptuous is it of us to think we're going to control the course of the Mississippi River for the last hundred and fifty years? The Corps spent hundreds of millions and hundreds of millions at the old river control structure on the Atchafalaya River. Is that presumptuous?"

Or, I added, was it presumptuous to replenish every stretch of sand on the Atlantic coast?

He laughed. "That's right. At no matching cost, by the way, along

New Jersey. Some people—back when the Corps said they needed to spend another three hundred million on the old river control structure—said that maybe we ought not to build that, maybe we ought to let the river change its course. The Corps certainly wouldn't have to keep dredging the mouth of the Mississippi if the sediments weren't coming down there all the time. New Orleans might have become one of the best nondredged deep-water ports in the world."

The problem, as Jones saw it, was that the Corps did not want to become involved with wetland issues. The reason was that in dealing with the Mississippi River it was already overwhelmed. "I mean, if you've got this big sinkhole that you keep putting your money into, then do you have any left over? You're fighting a rear-guard action not to have to spend the hundreds of millions of dollars a year it takes to save coastal Louisiana. Whereas on the East Coast or the West Coast, it's a question for them of do they build a beach, or do they build a jetty for three hundred pleasure boats all owned by millionaires. And there is not the competitive demand for their services. There's no telling with the Army Corps. It's interesting how reluctant they are about some of these things, given their tendency to go after any dredging project they can."

What about the state? Would it help rebuild the islands?

The state, he said, had agreed to help pay for some marsh management projects. But it would not talk about barrier islands. In fact, as long ago as 1982 the parish had determined that if it was going to protect its coastline, it would have to do so entirely at its own expense; it could not depend on any state or federal money.

Jones handed me a study. "Read that paragraph," he said. I glanced over it. The state had concluded, in effect, that based on extrapolation of U.S. Fish and Wildlife Service land-loss rate figures, restoring the barrier islands of the Grand Isle chain would reduce marsh loss by only 10 percent between 1990 and 2040 and would not be worth the cost.

Jones looked me in the eye. "Okay, what's wrong with that statement?" It was, he said, based on irrelevant land-loss figures that had nothing to do with the realities of barrier island rebuilding, so its conclusion was illogical. If, instead of 10 percent, they had picked 20 percent as the amount of land saved from a restoration program—reasonable, Jones felt, since either number was essentially picked out of the air—suddenly everything would be cost effective.

Asked for help with the islands, the Corps had responded that maintaining the barrier islands and barrier beaches would be "extremely expensive."

"I don't disagree with that," Jones said. "Of course they're spending sixty million dollars to do seven miles of the New Jersey beach line. How about spending twenty-five million to redo fourteen miles of one of our islands?"

Furthermore, it seemed to Jones that, aside from the question of how much marsh would actually be saved, the Corps had skewed the study by including the cost of protecting Fort Livingston, on the western end of Grand Terre Island, just east of Grand Isle. (The fort had been built in the midnineteenth century on the worst possible spot on a barrier island—on the beach, the least stable part of the island front to back; and at an inlet, the least stable side to side—and very quickly the sand in front of it had eroded. Today surf breaks against its walls.) Protecting the fort, he felt, was a historic preservation issue and did not belong in a coastal restoration program. What would happen to the cost-to-benefit ratio, he wondered, if the Corps did not include that project? "See, to me, if you control the assumptions, you can obviously control the conclusions. It's full of these little illogical-type connections, and things like 'Let's protect Fort Livingston.' Well, that increases the cost of whatever protection program you propose greatly. 'Cause that's rock, that's big, that's not just sending a dredge out there."

The essence of the conflict, as far as he was concerned, was that Louisiana's coastal program was really an engineering problem—one of organizing a project, preparing the drawings and technical reports, and then getting out there and doing something. The coastal program, though, was run by scientists—geologists and biologists who were more inclined to study problems than to act on them.

Let's back up, I said. What if they were to attack the problem from the other direction, the loss of sediment from leveeing the Mississippi?

Well, he said, a scientist at LSU had done a study that said that diverting 10 percent of the silt load now in the Mississippi River could maintain existing wetlands. The key word, Jones added, was "existing." Using sediment diversion to rebuild lost wetlands would take much more silt than just maintaining what was already there. But, he added, the Corps of Engineers had said such diversion was not worth it. The benefit to the areas receiving the water, according to them, was not worth the cost of construction on the civil works project.

But why? I asked. Had this diversion cost been compared to the cost of doing nothing at all? I had seen one draft report that had said that if nothing were done, the cost of wetland losses, in land value alone, could be as high as $1.1 billion by 2060. Had the cost of the project been compared to the long-term cost of what the state and parish were doing now? Had it been compared to other suggested programs?

Jones could not answer that. "Everything *I* look at says it is worth doing something when you start looking at the socioeconomic cost, not just the physical cost of the land that's being lost.

"Tomorrow the Department of Energy is going to come down and talk to us, and we are going to try to get them to give us two million dollars to go do work on the barrier islands. And why are they interested? If you ever take a boat ride, you see the little six-piling timber cribbings around the wells behind the barrier islands. Well, look at the structures out in front of the barrier islands. They are drastically concerned that these 'inland waterway oil wells' are going all of a sudden to be subjected to the Gulf of Mexico. Cost of production is different. Some people say it costs four times more just to bring a well in, let alone the type of well structure you would have to leave out in place. Behind the barrier islands, you are looking at something about half the size of this room for a wellhead." His office was barely fifteen feet square. "In front of the barrier islands, you are looking at forty-two-inch diameter casings, six of them, averaging a structure fifty to sixty feet up out of the water and who knows how the hell far down into the water, but all designed to withstand wave impact. What about that loss if we lose our barrier islands?"

Then there was the value of the fishing industry. "The second and fourth largest seafood landing ports in the country are right here in Terrebonne Parish. Probably if you look at some of the other of Louisiana's ports, you probably have three or four. And then when you look at the seafood that's caught in Florida, in Mississippi, and in Texas, and probably originates in the deltas of the Mississippi River, you've got a tremendous investment you're willing to write off. I'm not willing to write it off.

"A lot of people, particularly at the federal level, don't even really know what the magnitude of the problem is. What was really a minor hurricane—Hurricane Juan, one-in-ten-year, one-in-fifteen-year frequency—put more water in Terrebonne Parish than anything that preceded it, because it's open water everywhere south of Terrebonne Parish now rather than marshland. Hurricane Gilbert, which struck Mexico, put water over the southern levees. Every single one of those levees had water coming over the top of it from Gilbert, five hundred miles away.

"We can afford to protect ourselves against about a fifteen-year hurricane. No way we can afford to protect against a hundred-year hurricane. There are not enough physical improvements in Terrebonne Parish to warrant that level of expenditure, but if we look at the barrier islands as just another line in that defense, maybe we shouldn't allow permanent habitation on those islands.

"Now, I think you can provide protection for the people of Terrebonne Parish. You require them to elevate their houses and we could live down here, and we'd have to evacuate for the Gilberts and the Juans, but we can survive your everyday norther coming through. We can survive sustained southerly winds for fifteen days. We may have to move out once every two years, or once every three years, but we can maintain a place to live down here, if we get real active about marsh management, because marshes grow. That's the good thing about marshes, they grow upward. You know, give them a little bit of sediment or a little bit of protection from salt water and they can keep up with sea level rises and subsidence. That's not a problem for them. We start concentrating on our marshes and we go out and do something with our barrier islands, and we look about trying to get some kind of diversion for some places like Terrebonne Parish."

That included stopping the Corps from extending an Atchafalaya River channeling levee ten or fifteen miles to the Gulf. The levee would save the Corps from having to dredge the river and would increase downstream protection from river flooding, but it would also stop sediment coming off the river from replenishing some of the parish's western marshes. "You talk about the Corps—the exact same lesson we had from the Mississippi River cutting off the water and the sediment, they're trying to repeat on the Atchafalaya." The Corps, he added, was monolithic. It had decided on this levee ten or fifteen years before and was not going to change its plans now.

Whatever the obstacles, the parish had to do something. That something was a mix of solutions: diversion where it was available, marsh management when the feds would agree, barrier island rebuilding as it was needed. Whatever they had to do, they would not give up, because to do so would be to give up the parish.

Anything they did was going to cost, whether or not state and federal agencies saw such expenditure as cost effective. "You can't think of coastal erosion as a one-time project. It's ongoing. You've got to think of it as an automobile—you've got to do maintenance every year. You could look at the cost of coastal protection for Louisiana, and you compare that to the cost of one B-2 bomber, or whatever the hell it is, and there is no comparison. Just take one Stealth bomber not constructed and save coastal Louisiana. That is what it comes down to."

Even so, I said, if they kept building up the islands as the coast subsided, eventually they would have these artificial islands sitting out in deep water. They would be less and less stable and would call for more and more sand.

"By that point," Jones answered, "I'm not going to disagree that we might not be out on the barrier islands. But you've got to do these kinds of things now to give the big diversion projects that are going to take fifteen and twenty-five years a chance to come into play. You have to think in military terms. Occasionally you have to drop off a sniper to snipe at the enemy just to slow them down to give you time to retrench farther up the coast.

"We might not be talking about saving Terrebonne Parish forever and ever. We might just be talking about saving it for the next two or three generations. But that might give the people we have down here time to assimilate the fact that they're going to have to change."

———

Jim Sothern had written a book about Isles Dernieres. *Last Island* told the story of the island's use from its first mention as a temporary fishing camp in 1819 to its last days as a resort in 1856. By the 1850s the island had become a popular haven for southern Louisiana planters. A writer in the August 25, 1854, New Orleans *Daily Delta* had spoken of it as "a location of unequaled advantages as a marine resort . . . similar to that of Cape May [on the Jersey shore, where all this coming-to-the-beach seems to have started] with all the other essentials of a summer and sea-side residence." In later years many have spoken of the island as the "Newport of the South," yet at its peak only about twenty unpretentious cottages and one small hotel, the Muggah Billiard-House, stood on the island's western end. There were plans, though, to build a new hotel to accommodate some four hundred to five hundred guests. The Trade Wind Hotel was to be some twelve hundred feet long.

Then, on Sunday, August 10, 1856, a hurricane hit. Its storm tide engulfed almost the whole island, destroying all but five cottages. Just how many people died is unknown, perhaps about a hundred fifty, with a couple of hundred surviving. After that, all talk of the island's "unequaled advantages as a marine resort" stopped, and the settlement quickly deteriorated. (The story of Louisiana's barrier island settlement, according to the coastal geographer Don Davis of LSU, "hinges on hurricanes." After big storms, people simply abandoned the islands—most of the populations being transient, anyway—and today only Grand Isle has a permanent community.)

In 1950, as a young man, Sothern had rowed out to Isles Dernieres. He had been disappointed at what he saw. "A bleak, lonely sand bank revealed itself," he wrote, "with sparse, weather-bent shrubs, amid dunes partially covering huge pieces of driftwood." He had considered swimming across Whiskey Pass, which the sea had cut through the island, but decided against the swim. Just as well, considering the currents. He spent five days on the island, spearing flounders, picking oysters, and catching shrimp, crabs, and fish with a small trawl. He found no trace of the village.

Sothern now lived in Houma, in a house shaded by a rich growth of banana trees and looking as if it sat in the middle of the swamps. He too was a busy man. But with Sothern it was because he had promised to take his son to his camp in Cocodrie to let their dogs run and do a bit of fishing. He had hemmed and hawed when I called him. Still, he wanted to talk to me about the islands and would give me some time. He had charts of the coast before the islands started to disappear. He told me to read his book and then come over that afternoon.

He greeted me at the door, a day's growth of beard on his chin, a pungent cigar stub clamped in his teeth exuding the sweet, deep scent of Spanish market tobacco. His face and hands were tanned, his hair graying and lank. He wore half-glasses, the kind I imagined on book-sellers. One finger sported an ancient college ring, the details of college name and degree and year eroded from its gold. He looked me over, smiled, and motioned for me to come in.

The house was dark inside. We stood at a dining table covered with books, papers, and maps. The adjoining kitchen was dim and filled with dishes. As we spoke, a young woman (his daughter?) repeatedly prowled through to get something from the refrigerator. She said nothing. In another room with red shades down over the windows stood a drawing table covered with papers. In the background a TV droned—an Italian chef cooking pasta and singing.

Sothern paced as he talked, and after a while a slight Cajun sound began to reveal itself in his speech. Maybe I had not been aware of it at first, or maybe he let down his guard as we talked. He became more ex-cited about his ideas concerning the delta and the loss of the islands. He grew passionate, talking faster, throwing in more ideas, expressing his confidence more firmly that he knew what should be done and how to do it.

He had taught geology, Earth Science 101 and 102, though he did not say where. "I taught," he added, "but I was also in construction, so I know what I'm talking about. I surveyed a while, walking the marsh. It's rough. The bugs eat you alive. They were a tougher breed of men than you have today."

He showed me a recent photograph of Isles Dernieres and shook his head in dismay. "I'm trying to tell them the island is sinking, but no one listens," he said. The whole eastern end of the island was gone. "Village Bayou [the creek behind the original settlement] is now foreshore. The houses would now be out in the Gulf. There are some stumps and bricks on the eastern end." The island, he said, had subsided two to three feet, and the coast itself three feet, since 1850.

"Whiskey Pass is four miles wide. Have you been out there? There's nothing there. In 1950 Whiskey Pass was a thousand feet wide. Coupe Caillou you could almost jump across. Now there's about five miles of island missing. You better take a look at it pretty quick. I went down this summer—hadn't been there in two years. Goddamn, you couldn't even see across Whiskey Pass. It's a shame. The birds are all crowding in; so much of their nesting grounds are gone. The roseate spoonbill was coming back."

The problem, as far as Sothern was concerned, was oil wells. The island had changed very little between 1850 and 1930 (when, coincidentally, eustatic sea level began to rise rapidly) and did not start breaking up until the 1950s. "In the 1970s everybody started panicking—it looks like erosion and subsidence are accelerating. In 1929, 1930, they began drilling wells. Texaco has about five hundred wells in the area since 1940. The island would have sunk anyway, but it has accelerated since the 1950s, about twenty years after they started sinking these wells. Louisiana barriers have twelve-foot subsidence in areas. If we're going to have twelve-foot subsidence here, then my house is under water. Have you had any geology?"

I nodded.

"Then you know."

A cigar ash fell onto the 1853 Isles Dernieres chart he was pointing at. He swept it away. "This is a damned good chart. This guy must have known what he was doing. For 1853 this was damned good.

"These were beautiful islands before they let them go to pot. They could save them; I know what to do. Between you and me, with a drag line and a suction dredge, I could put you an island anywhere you want out there. But now you can't—there are too many people. And the federal government is in on it. The mentality is not there. The scientists are the worst. They want to make studies.

"An old man in his eighties told me how to do it, told me in French. They need to get rid of the computers and get a couple of people from Brown and Root [the Houston-based construction company] who know what they're doing. These environmentalists—I'm an environmentalist, too—they went down there and stepped on a couple of seagull eggs and ran the surveyors off. Nothing's been done.

"If you're going to build something, first you need a set of plans.

Then you see what it's going to cost. Then you build it. They haven't even got that far. Everybody's got to have a study. The islands have been studied under water. They haven't even decided whether they can be saved. Those islands can be restored. It's going to take a lot of money, but we just gave seventy million dollars to Mexico; we could do it for a fraction of that.

"All over the world the barriers are going. Whatever happened to the uniformity principle, 'One place is tearing down while another builds up'? I'm beginning to doubt all the geology I learned. It's entropy. Sea level hasn't risen that much—what, a foot?—in the last century. That isn't enough to do this." There was a bit of panic in his voice, the sound of a geologist no longer sure of the ground under his feet.

"And the sand was deposited quickly," he continued, shifting his focus to the deltas. "There are no bedding planes in these natural levees. This stuff was dumped quickly. If I didn't know otherwise, I'd say there was a Flood." He laughed at his notion. "The Mississippi must have been really big. The Bayou Terrebonne used to be very big; steamboats used to come here. Now it's no wider than this room. It's all filling in. This stuff doesn't last long, not nearly as long as people think."

It was time for him to go. His son had loaded the truck with rods and tackle and was waiting with the dogs.

I asked him about the graveyards I had seen.

"Yeah," he said, "they have to be buried above ground. We had a flood and all these coffins were floating around. You dig a hole, and before you can put the coffin in, it's full of water."

With the destruction of Isles Dernieres, Grand Isle was now the only inhabited barrier island. I headed east from Houma into Lafourche Parish, then turned south along the Bayou Lafourche levee toward the island. Out past the man-made levee at Golden Meadow, it was suddenly obvious how low the ground was: salt marsh only a foot or two above sea level for the next twenty-five miles to the island. From the high-rise bridge crossing the bayou at Leeville I could see the landscape, much of it already submerged several miles from the open Gulf. Three times I saw a car in the water beside the road, only part of the roof exposed. I doubted that this was one of Shea Penland's scorned marsh restoration projects.

There was also a heavy oil-company presence on these marshes, with Texaco and Chevron tanks near the road, helicopters coming and going, crew boats moving down the channel along with big shrimpers.

Grand Isle itself was extremely low, maybe a couple of feet high. It had a single dune line, which they called a levee, maybe six feet high. The dune ridge was almost continuous—I wondered if it were not artificial—with some sections lacking dunes at all. All those miles of Louisiana's barrier islands were reduced to this seven-mile strip of still-occupied land.

The island has seen long use, for being so young. A plantation sometime before 1840, it soon became a popular retreat. By the 1850s New Orleanians were coming here regularly for the summer sea breezes, and before long it had its own horse-drawn trolley, put in by one of the hotel owners. A hurricane hit the Louisiana coast in 1893, killing about a thousand people, and, as Don Davis had told me, people started leaving the islands alone. Grand Isle escaped the storm, but its popularity declined among the wealthy of New Orleans. It continued to have a small year-round population and to draw seasonal visitors, but on a less grand scale.

Today the island is heavily developed. Here on its eastern end, I could see small houses and camps extending from just behind the dunes all the way to the back marsh. There was not much room for more. Toward the center the island became wide, and along the lagoon side stood large Exxon and Conoco refining facilities and storage tanks. A seaplane sat by an oil-company building; later I heard its engine scream and saw it lifting out of the lagoon. And there were the oil-company helicopters, the ubiquitous yellow-and-white jobs coming and going.

East, past the oil companies, the houses were less modest. Soon look-alike condos appeared, two stories high, with a canal system dug in from the lagoon to accommodate a large and expensive collection of pleasure boats. The eastern end of the island had been hardened with riprap stone strung along its edge.

Across the pass I could see Grand Terre, a flash of red—what looked like an exposed red-dirt embankment was actually a brick wall from Fort Livingston's remains.

I crossed a walkway out over the levee. What I saw was a shock.

There was virtually no beach, maybe only forty feet of it, and the walkway itself extended to water. The line between levee and dune was sharply eroded, half of it gone, with a four- or six-foot scarp. This stuff was headed back to sea. And it was indeed artificial. Looking at the eroded dune, the levels of deposition were clearly visible, layers of sand interspersed with layers of shell in white streaks, exactly as they had been dumped. *So this is what they call a successful dune replenishment program*, I thought. In reaching dynamic equilibrium, the waves had already carried much of the beach and dune out into the deeper water. Groins extended into the water in either direction, at least eight of them, but they seemed to have trapped little sand. They looked as if they had been lengthened on their landward side to maintain contact with the retreating island. Where the dunes were gone, the houses were already out on the beach, some only thirty feet from the surf.

There was no question about what was happening. The geologists were right: as the island moved inland to keep up with sea level rise, it was dissolving.

I had one more thing to do in Louisiana. I wanted to travel down the birdfoot to the mouth of the Mississippi. Down past the citrus groves, down along the levee mile after mile to get to land's end to see the active Mississippi delta, the source of all this sediment and the father of barrier islands. Past trailers, past massive moss-encrusted live oaks, past a pudgy teenage girl in her yard facing the road, working through her cheerleading routine, her face furrowed, her mind not on the delta.

A second levee appeared on the other side of the road, to the west. The whole area was now low enough that it needed protection from the sea as well as from the river. This was dead delta, killed by the artificial levee. Bulldozers and cranes stood on top, ready to refresh it. I did not stop to climb the levee. I wanted to see the Mississippi open into the Gulf of Mexico. Past road-kill armadillos, past refineries flaring gas, past sulfur carriers docked against the artificial bank, past all the oil-company helicopters, through Venice to the end of the road where the two levees joined, protecting the outermost town on the river. Below lay a large industrial marina—tugs and tankers and work boats—but no glimpse of the river itself.

I drove down a narrow lane out onto the salt marsh. This, finally, was active delta and very wet, more water than land. Great and snowy egrets stood unmoving in the marsh by the road, dozens upon dozens of them. Some stood, their necks extended into kinked lines, peering into the water. Others bent their necks back into gentle curves, staring up. But none of the white birds moved.

Down to the fish harbor, with a couple of hundred shrimpers and a tangle of bayous and channels. Trees and brush grew to the water edges, and I had no clear view of the Mississippi.

The light was almost gone. I returned to the levee at the edge of town. Atop it, at last I could see the brown river sliding by, water slapping against the banks, carrying out the silt that would eventually become another series of barrier islands. The river was wide and carried much.

Odd Men Out

I had two missions in Ocean Springs, Mississippi: first to see the geologist Ervin Otvos, and then to talk to the family of Walter Anderson. Both had been more or less rejected by their communities—Otvos as a geologist who held loyally to an out-of-fashion theory, Anderson as a painter whose audience never understood him.

I was curious to meet Otvos, because Orrin Pilkey had mentioned his championing of De Beaumont's theory that barrier islands developed from submarine bars that had risen above water level. Otvos, who works out of the University of Mississippi's Gulf Coast Research Laboratory, is so strongly associated with the theory that Shea Penland had added his name to it, calling it the De Beaumont–Otvos theory. (Penland had also implied that this shoal aggradation theory developed backward, based on "model-driven" observations, as he put it: "You have a model in your mind and then you look at the data to fit your model, where it should be that you look at your data and then you develop a model.")

On my way to meet Otvos, I stopped at a restaurant for breakfast. As I got out of the jeep, a man from a nearby car saw my license plate and commented that it was a long drive from Maine.

"And a long drive back," I said. He nodded in understanding.

We saw each other again inside. He was a large man, with a florid face. He smiled and started the conversation again, inviting me to join his wife and him while we ate. (They were having biscuits and gravy.) He introduced himself.

He asked if I minded if they said grace first. He thanked the Lord for the food and for the chance to eat with me. They asked about Maine, about how far it was from Newfoundland. They did not travel much, he said, except to Houston or Atlanta, where their kids lived. Then it was always a long drive back. He used to be a truck driver, but he never got as far as Maine. Now they lived inland a bit, but had a fishing camp in the marsh. When he retired they had sold their house, remodeled their camp, and moved in. All he did now was fish—a regular swamp rat, he said. He would be there now, fishing, except he had to go to the Veteran's Administration hospital this morning. He felt the pain already, a whole day without fishing.

I saw people all over Louisiana fishing, I said, in the smallest bayous. Yeah, he said, yesterday he was fishing in a creek so small he had to choke up on his rod. What kind of fish do they catch in Maine? He caught brim mostly, though the other day he had hooked a big drum on the brim line. It took him a half-hour, but he landed him. They were going to bake him that night. He never thought he'd like baked fish.

We fish in the brackish water too, his wife said. Drum and speckled trout and redfish.

Yeah, he said, we got a little sixteen-foot boat; we don't go out too far. "Well, we're late," he said, getting up. "I hated to see you eat alone and I wanted to learn about Maine."

"Yes," she said, "it gets lonely out on your own."

I, too, had to hurry. Otvos planned to take me on a field trip today. We were headed to Dauphin Island, about forty miles east, just across the Alabama border and guarding the entrance to Mobile Bay, where he wanted to collect some sand samples. The island is about fifteen miles long, and its eastern end has a Pleistocene core, an older, pre-Holocene island against which the current island coalesced. At this core the island is quite fat, maybe a quarter of a mile across, with a dense maritime forest. Then it stretches to the west some fifteen miles in a sort of guppy shape, thinning westward with the trailing littoral drift. According to Penland, it is this littoral sand, not an offshore source, that is the sand supply. (The littoral drift is strong enough that the islands are moving west quite rapidly, as sand is carried off their up-current eastern edges and deposited to the west, extending their down-current ends. In fact, much of Petit Bois Island, about five miles west of Dauphin, was in Alabama two hundred years ago. For now, it is entirely in Mississippi.)

Driving east, Otvos told me something about himself. He was born in Hungary and left there in 1960. He worked for Mobil Oil, then taught at the University of New Orleans before joining the lab in 1970. He had become interested in coastal geology just because he was always fascinated by the coast—by the shore, not the open water. He had a strong proprietary feeling about the geologic research on these islands, he said, because they had been ignored until he started writing about them.

He seemed aware of the criticism of his work, though he never spoke of it directly other than to ask me what Shea Penland had told me about him—a query I avoided answering. In a way, Otvos countered the questions raised about his theories by questioning his detractors' theories in return. He would say: "Some people claim that barrier islands moved ashore, like tank treads. I don't know. Probably this is not the case. I'm probably in the minority. I don't see where they can prove this." And: "Louisiana is sinking like crazy, about three feet per century. The Derniere Islands in the nineteenth century were part of the mainland. They predict that in about twenty years they won't be left. At LSU people use this as an example of barrier island formation. But this is an unusual situation, because of the Mississippi River."

As we drove onto the eastern end of Dauphin Island, Otvos pointed out riprap that had been run into the water in parallel ridges to trap passing sand. "You can see how much sand they catch," he said.

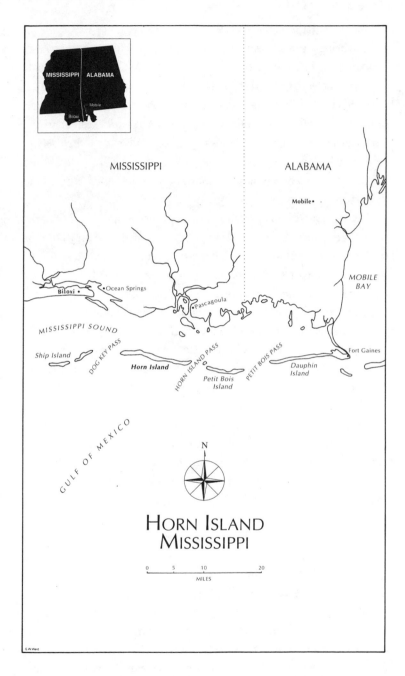

MISSISSIPPI

ALABAMA

Mobile•

MOBILE
BAY

•Ocean Springs

Biloxi •

•Pascagoula

MISSISSIPPI SOUND

Ship Island

DOG KEY PASS

Horn Island

HORN ISLAND PASS

Petit Bois
Island

PETIT BOIS PASS

Dauphin
Island

Fort Gaines

GULF OF MEXICO

N

Horn Island
Mississippi

0   5   10   20

MILES

"They're out in the water. I think they increase erosion." For all the attention being given Louisiana, these islands were falling apart too.

Dauphin's Pleistocene core was exposed here along the oceanside where the newer sand had eroded away. The old material stuck out of the sand above the shore and rose in sandstone stacks on the beach itself, along with the trunks of old trees. The trees were, it seemed to me, strong evidence that these islands did indeed roll over on themselves, since they had to have grown on the island well away from the shore's salt spray. Their remains had eventually been left stranded as the island moved out from under them.

Otvos pointed farther offshore, to a lighthouse standing out of the water at the inlet's ebb-tidal delta. That had once been an island, he said. It was there that Admiral Farragut had exclaimed, "Damn the torpedoes!" Otvos said, "This is one of the shoals—Pelican Island. I don't know if it's one island now, or two. It's proof that the islands can build up from sea level." Big, spewing surf was breaking on the shoal. In the nineteenth century two islands had existed there, he added.

Otvos has written that ebb-tidal deltas are one of the two settings in which islands can rise from the sea. These islands here at the mouth of Mobile Bay have a long history of emergence and destruction. Sand and Pelican islands at one time were two to three and a half miles long.

Otvos' other setting, coastwise barrier platforms (shallow, sandy-bottom areas parallel to the shore and adjacent to current or former barrier islands), is exemplified by the Chandeleur island chain, part of the Mississippi delta system. He cites the reappearance of islands on that chain after being broken up by hurricanes as evidence for the emergence process.

Where, I asked, did all this sand come from?

The Appalachians, during the last sixty million years, he answered. It had been worked and reworked in the intervening thousands of millennia, but that was where it originated. The minerals in the sand could tell you where it came from. "Quartz occurs the most, 90 percent. There are no so-called easily reworked soft minerals, or they occur only in small amounts. The rivers in Louisiana or Texas have lots more rivers draining a lot of glacial terrain, but they didn't have millions and

millions of years to weather the minerals." The result of all this re-
working is that the sand on these islands has been, as one writer ex-
pressed it, "ground fine as sugar."

As we traveled west, the island narrowed to a few hundred yards.
Behind it Mississippi Sound was large. Only Pamlico, behind the
Outer Banks, is larger. Shrimpers worked its shallow water as we
walked its edge. The shore was irregular, scooped out, eroding. There
was a beach on this side, only three yards across. The marsh was visible
under the sand, the deposit a thin veneer. The marsh used to be much
better developed, Otvos said. The sand was bluish gray with a heavy
mineral concentration. He slid his finger through it to cut a miniscarp.
The blue sand lay up to an inch thick over white sand. "It's sometimes
in layers," he said. "It can be very useful in reading the island." The
color came from titanium and zircon. "They were talking about min-
ing Ship Island [offshore from Ocean Springs] after the war. It would
have destroyed the island. At that time the island was in one piece." Today it is two islands, cut in half most recently in 1969 by Hurricane
Camille.

As we walked along the back shore, heads down to the sand, Otvos
came back to Penland. Had Penland given me any good information?
I had the sense that the question really was whether Penland had said
something about *him*, not about Gulf Coast geology. I grunted
vaguely. After a while he got quiet.

We crossed back to the ocean side, where we started to gather sand
from the small, round, isolated haystack dunes near the beach. We
carefully scraped thin layers of sand from their surface and put it into
small bags. Otvos was working on the sand, he said, because he was
trying to find out if it would be possible to distinguish dune sand from
beach sand by its characteristics. It would be valuable when looking at
old coastal sands to help figure out whether the sand had been at,
above, or below sea level. This study was an old one. People had been
working on it for quite a while. He had taken hundreds, maybe thousands, of sand samples and would take hundreds more. It would be a
few years before he had any results, he said, and he did not think it
would come to anything.

Later, as we drove back east along the island, he pointed to the off-shore shoals again, the evidence—the vindication—for his theory.

Folklorist friends of mine in North Carolina had told me about Walter Anderson, that he had survived a hurricane while tied to a tree on a barrier island—reason enough for me to seek him out. When Hurricane Betsy hit New Orleans in October 1965, it grazed Horn Island and drowned it. Caught there, Anderson managed to find a tree on high ground and held out till the storm had passed. Only when a pilot reported seeing a solitary man walking the Horn Island beach with an easel over his shoulder the next day did his family know he had survived.

Such an adventure had evidently been a long-standing ambition of his. But Anderson was more than just an adventurer. He was an artist, perhaps the greatest painter the South has produced. He loved Horn Island, finding in its undisturbed sand, marshes, freshwater pools, and forest the muse that drove his art.

That someone could be so drawn to such an isolated place, could feel such containment and independence alone on a minimal strip of sand surrounded by ocean—that idea appealed to me. I wanted to know more about such a person—what he was like, what his experience had been. That experience represented, I felt, the state in which we all lived our lives more or less, though we tended not to think such things aloud. Anderson's had been a way of living that was true to some part of our nature, at least symbolically. It was also a way, I had to admit to myself, that I was still not completely ready for. I loved islands and found them strengthening—I lived on one—but, as I had realized on Padre, I was not ready to be the farthest out, to be completely alone. Anderson had been. And for that, beyond his art, I admired him.

He would row and sail out to the island in his skiff (his last one a ten-foot wreck he had found on the beach and rebuilt), sometimes taking as long as three days in rough seas and unfavorable winds to travel the twelve miles across Mississippi Sound from his Ocean Springs home to the island. Once there, he lived simply; he slept under the overturned skiff on the sand behind the first dune line, a small fire beside him. In rain he sat under the skiff's shelter to paint his "realizations," as he called his watercolors. Otherwise he lived outside, walking the fourteen-mile island, examining the details of its plant and animal life, becoming intimate with this strip of sand and marsh.

His focus was intense. He devoted his entire life to art, letting everything else—the world, his family, everything—fall away. Looking back at him now in the almost thirty years since his death, he is almost mythological in his intense devotion to life as art, to art as something to be lived.

Anderson called himself "the Islander." His output during those years of discovering Horn Island was prodigious. After his death his family discovered thousands of watercolors painted on typing paper. Obviously they had known of his painting, yet they had had no idea of the volume. These realizations were, after all, Anderson's private work, painted for himself with no intention of having anyone else see them.

His art did have a public side, the linoleum prints, murals, sculpture, and pottery—the public art he created as part of what he saw as his responsibility to the outside world. That, in turn, earned him the right to create his own private art. It was a distinction that admits to the difference between the experience of creating art and that of viewing, of consuming, it. The creating needs no audience or acknowledgment. It exists only for the artist, and then only in the act itself.

Ironically, what he did for an audience is not nearly so powerful as his private work. These personal pieces were what eventually brought the world to his door, a perverse fate, given the public's initial dislike of his art. (In 1951 he contracted with the town of Ocean Springs to paint, inside its new community center, a mural of the flora and fauna of the Gulf Coast. His fee was one dollar. When he finished the three-thousand-square-foot work fifteen months later, townspeople so disliked it that there was talk of repainting the walls. Anderson withdrew even further into his private painting.)

As the years passed, he had spent more and more of his time on Horn Island. Maybe the rejection of his work had something to do with that, but it is more likely that the island simply drew him in, and the extended periods of solitude made it harder and harder for him to be around others. In a way Horn became more of a home to him than

Ocean Springs. Eventually he became almost a stranger to his family. Gone for weeks at a time, he would see them briefly when he came ashore to work at the family pottery to earn enough money for art supplies. (His quota was to decorate ten pieces per week, for which he was paid ten dollars. He lived on that income for the rest of his life.) Then he would fill a garbage can with art supplies and food, load it aboard his skiff, and sail off again for Horn Island. He continued to spend his time on his island until he died in 1965 at age sixty-two.

Anderson was the Islander in other senses, too. His Ocean Springs home was an island of sorts, a compound where his mother and his brothers and their wives and children lived and worked at their Shearwater Pottery, secure against the world. More, Anderson was himself a kind of island, closing away the world. During most of his adult years he suffered from mental illness, and that further separated him from his family.

The intensity with which he approached life certainly made it difficult for him to be around people. While at Shearwater, he isolated himself physically, even from family. He managed to free himself of the daily human contact and routines that could be so distracting from his work. In a way Anderson lived on an island within an island—often adrift within himself, most of the time alone on Horn Island, and otherwise insulated in his studio.

But the true island of Walter Anderson's being was not internal or metaphorical; it was a real island—Horn Island, where he spent most of the last eighteen years of his life. Here he painted his greatest work, and here he kept his logs, the records of his thoughts and doings out on the island. "Such a sky—such water, and Horn Island between with me walking it—the back of Moby Dick, the white whale, the magic carpet, surrounded by inhabited space—strange—inhabited? space," he wrote one January day in 1959. That was his island.

Anderson had not always been so insular. Especially in his earlier years he traveled and participated in the lives around him. Born in 1903 and raised in New Orleans, he had started early to be a painter. He studied at the Parsons Institute of Design in New York and then at the Pennsylvania Academy of the Fine Arts, where he won an award for his animal drawings and eventually a travel grant that allowed him to study in France.

In 1922 his family moved to Ocean Springs, where his parents in 1918 had bought a twenty-six-acre summer retreat. Fairhaven, as they named it then, served as the elder Andersons' retirement home, as well as an occasional art colony. There Walter's older brother, Peter, founded Shearwater Pottery in 1928 (Shearwater soon taking over as the estate's name), and on his return from France at age twenty-six, Walter began working there as a designer and decorator, along with his younger brother, James. He soon met and fell in love with Agnes Grinstead, whose sister, Patricia, was engaged to Peter. Agnes and Patricia were the daughters of a Pittsburgh family that owned Oldfields, an antebellum pecan plantation fifteen miles away in Gautier. Walter and Agnes married in 1933.

In 1937 he had his first nervous breakdown, brought on in part by the conflict he felt over having to work so many hours at the pottery that he had almost no time for his own painting. No formal diagnosis was ever made, but he was unable to work for the next three years and spent much of that time in institutions.

In 1940 he and Agnes with their two young children went to live with Agnes' father at Oldfields. There Walter became happily absorbed in his own painting, working at it full-time. Almost ten thousand drawings survive from this seven-year period alone. As he became increasingly preoccupied with his work, the presence of other people disturbed him more and more. At the end of 1946 he moved back to Shearwater to live alone in a cottage beside the pottery and devote himself entirely to his art. Within a year he was sailing regularly to Horn Island. Though his wife and children soon returned to Shearwater, he continued to live by himself in his studio, visiting them in one of the compound's other houses as he needed.

During this period he began to travel again. He occasionally pedaled his bicycle the ninety miles to New Orleans to buy art supplies. Once he bicycled to the east coast of Florida, and another time to Pennsylvania and Virginia. In 1949 he journeyed to China with the intention of crossing to Tibet, to him a spiritual mecca. Within sight of the mountains of Tibet, guerrillas attacked the camp where he was sleeping. They took everything—his money, passport, and supplies, his paintings, drawings, and notes. He remained where he was for a long time, gazing at the mountains that he now could not attain. Then he turned around and walked back across China. He begged for food on the way. Having no bowl like other beggars, he would hold out his cupped hands to receive the alms of strangers.

When he returned to Mississippi, Horn Island would occupy more and more of his time till he called the island, not Shearwater, home.

Something happened in his painting at about this time. His early work had been precise, his hand accurate from thousands upon thousands of renderings. He was long a master of form and line, and his early work shows his exquisite draftsmanship. But now his palette exploded. His paintings of Horn Island's maritime forest capture not only the shape of its pines and tangled live oaks, but also its spirit. There is a power in the brush stroke and its colors—blues, golds, greens, reds, purples, yellows—a mass of three-dimensional color that seems to have a life beyond the rendering of the subject. His shrimp and crayfish are as much color as shape, becoming almost kaleidoscopic. Turtles and shells are vibrant. Mallard ducks are alive. He reached the point, one critic observed, of delineating spaces and not just objects.

If there was a significance to his work, another wrote, it was in "his perception of fundamental reality: the interconnectedness of the world . . . the knowledge that man is a participant in nature rather than an observer." This, perhaps, is why Anderson called his pieces realizations. They were the rare moments when he realized, made real, in his work a unity between himself and his environment. Anderson once said to his wife that few people were better qualified than he to paint the appearance of things. But, he added, that was not what he wanted. He wanted to find the heart of things, to mingle his heart with that heart. He wanted to become one with what he saw.

Eighty-five volumes of his island logs survive. Of these, some have been published as *The Horn Island Logs of Walter Anderson*. In them Anderson talks of details, of rowing the boat or sleeping under the skiff, of fighting mosquitoes, of the magnificence of thistles bursting into bloom. He talks about the animals he saw and painted with which he shared his island. He talks about how fast life moved and how interesting it was. He talks about the senses, about poetry and music. And he talks about the light and about color and the reason for art.

Back in 1944, on one of his earliest visits to Horn Island, Anderson wrote: "I left the boat and carried my bedding and a can of sauerkraut and salmon to the top of the dune and ate by the light of the moon, and ate by the light of the moon without the runcible spoon—I used my fingers. After supper I renewed my youth and went swimming. The foam made beautiful patterns on the surface of a wave after it had struck, and I went until I could barely touch the sand with one foot between each wave and danced by the light of the moon." These logs reveal a man who was alive.

In November 1965, six weeks after riding out Hurricane Betsy alone on Horn Island, Walter Anderson told his wife he was coughing up blood. The diagnosis was cancer. Within a few days he was dead.

The first stop on my way to learn more about Walter Anderson was at the Ocean Springs community center to see the mural the town had rejected in 1951, the rejection that had hurt Anderson so much. I collected a key from the Chamber of Commerce—clearly the townspeople had now changed their minds about him.

This was not just a painted wall; this was a painted room a hundred feet long. The images flooded in. The colors were muted, softened enough that the walls did not overwhelm the room. I could let the massive painting be background. Or I could look at any one piece of wall and be absorbed by the detail: Indians, white and brown pelicans, shearwaters, red-winged blackbirds, crows, chrysanthemums, frigate birds, terns, ducks, dolphins, French explorers, priests, turtles, stars, foxes, cats, opossums, owls, woodpeckers, magnolias, oaks, squirrels, blue herons, butterflies, parrots, stags, bears, countless indecipherable (to me) flowers and trees, blue jays, mushrooms, alligators, skates, the sun. Walter Anderson's icons encircled this great hall. I walked along the walls for some indeterminate time, looking at the details.

From here it was a short distance to Shearwater itself. It was a place filled with life. A rabbit crossed the narrow shell road as I drove in. Squirrels were everywhere, and all around me I heard the chirp and caw of birds, even the heavy croak of a heron. Towering over the compound, great trees enclosed it. This really was an island, a place where the outside world could not intrude. And like an island, it allowed its community, the family, to hold its members together.

Anderson's daughter Mary met me. An energetic, vivacious woman in her early fifties, she was the oldest of Anderson's four children. Her hair was dark with a bit of gray, her eyes deep grayish blue, her smile big. Mary lived at Shearwater with her husband and the extended Anderson family. She now administered her father's estate, which deepened her absorption into the facts of her father's life.

We walked through light drizzle to the cottage where Anderson had lived alone from 1947 until his death, a small building grown over with bushes and trees. Outside in the grass lay the skiff he had used for the last few trips to Horn Island. It was small—afloat its gunwales would have been mere inches above water. After Anderson salvaged it, he had built up the bow and stern to keep waves from washing in.

"He always traveled, when he went on the water, in fragile boats with the greatest skill," Mary said. "Frequently he had to use that talent to save himself because his little boat would get in storms."

In the cottage after his death the family had found a chest filled with two thousand paintings and watercolors, pieces he had apparently culled from the mass of his production. The cottage became a kind of shrine to Anderson, filled with his work—not only his paintings, but also carved figures. One of them was a deer, part of a great composite sculpture that had stood twelve feet high and represented Father Mississippi surrounded by animals. Its central figure had been painted blue, a giant with a golden beard and golden horns rising from his head. The antlers, Mary said, were not just antlers; they were tributaries of the Mississippi River. Part of the work broke while Anderson was carving it, and though he repaired the damage, he lost interest in finishing the sculpture. This solitary deer, a fragment of the greater work, was one of the few pieces the family still possessed.

There were other carvings—toys, articulated figures Anderson had made for his children when they were young. At one time he had carved them a rocking lion. Near the Father Mississippi fragment lay a boat maybe five feet long holding several Greek torsos (the helmets gave them away) set on pegs. Their arms were hinged, their hands open to receive oars. "Ulysses' boat," Mary said, "for his odyssey." It was fitted with a rough mast and square sail. Anderson had carved it for the children while reading the *Odyssey* to them. *Ever the journeyer,* I thought, though his greatness seemed to have been in his ability to stand still, as he had on Horn Island.

What had been the appeal of Horn Island to her father, I wondered aloud.

Its isolation, Mary said. "Some people from a research laboratory used to go out there and study the lagoons and the creatures in them. An occasional photographer would be out there, but really he had the island to himself. And in his writings he said that he went to the island to seek what he called the conditional: 'If something else doesn't eat me I have as much right to be here as somebody else, and I'm here on an equal footing. And I share this space with them and I'm not taking anything that belongs to anybody else. I'm on my own. It's conditional.'"

As Mary spoke, she would slide into quoting her father's writings—whole epigrams that she entered so naturally that at first I was not sure whether she was speaking for herself or for him.

"My father never went to the island to get away from work," she added. "He worked like a fiend. And it was not until his work had been effectively rejected by the public that he became so very reclusive." The community center mural had been his last public work. In response to its rejection, she said, Anderson had come home and put a padlock on the door to a room he had built onto the studio for Mary when she was a baby. No one knew what he worked on inside. "We didn't go into it until after he was dead," she said. "But what he did was paint a mural here that no one would ever see, and therefore it would not be judged or rejected."

She led me inside. Its four walls were painted, the room a realization in itself—an entire island encompassing creation. They called it *Creation at Sunrise*. The room was overwhelming. Bending close to look at the many details, a thrill went through me. I felt happy. This was an expression of life, of the power of life. Birds flew up; the whole work was filled with a stirring upward movement.

On the north wall was a female figure—his muse, Mary said, but also clearly Mary herself as a young girl-woman. She bore the same antlers swirling from her head as Father Mississippi; here they were more ephemeral, their tributaries-capillaries fading into the field of the image, as if conduits to something overhead, some kind of cosmic antennae. A duck sat at each shoulder. A deer bowed by the muse's side, as did a rabbit and a turtle below her.

That wall, Mary went on, represented night. The other walls represented, among other things, morning, noon, and afternoon-evening. Perhaps, I felt, this north wall represented more. Maybe it represented the deep mystery, the unseen and unexplainable threads of life connecting us—those swirling antlers.

We looked at the east wall, sunrise. " 'I felt strange things today and walked through fire,' " Mary said, quoting her father. " 'And most wonderful of all, I saw a minor prophet make an offering among the stars. I sought lily pads and found them and yellow daisies of strange new kinds. I saw the burning bush again and warmed my heart with its fire.' "

Here were the night creatures, the toad, the opossum. Here too were osprey and heron, and sandhill cranes flying toward the sun, and pitcher plants reflecting the new light.

"The plants of this wall are the plants that are growing immediately outside that window," she said, pointing at the magnolias. "That's the harbor right down there. The black skimmers come to the harbor." (Locally the black skimmer was called the shearwater.) "He loved zinnias, because they had such a spiral form—you know, his epitome of a spiral—and this was on the back of a drawing of a zinnia: 'Oh zinnias, most explosive and illuminating of flowers, a summation of all flowers, essence of ecstatic form, essence of concentric form.' " To Anderson the spiral represented the upward, aspiring cycle of life.

On the west wall huge moths collected, their patterns spreading beyond their wings. One moth was partly amorphous, completely abstracted. It was a cocoon, Mary explained, the changeover, a transformation. The moth's wing extended from the cocoon, and its pattern too extended beyond the wing, becoming less concrete, more designerly, as it swirled toward the ceiling in a great spiral.

"When we were children, he made a book for us called *Butterflies*," Mary said. "It was a linoleum block print book. The moths, though, were his special passion." She pointed to the swirling moth shape. "It was the closest he ever came to abstract. It's a spiral, without beginning and without end. And he said that all life was change and growth in a spiral." This life, he felt, was a stage in the process of becoming something else.

"Every time I come in, I get excited about it," she said of the room. "You go and sit on the floor in the center of that room if you're down sometimes, and it will fill you right up."

We left the cottage and walked to the main house, which Mary's husband had designed. Recently completed, it was formed by two side-by-side octagons—one large, one small—with a long ell along one side. In the hall stood a small mural, a series of wood panels of saints. Her father had painted these on the walls of a studio that he had built here himself. Hurricane Camille had destroyed the house, and they found the mural boards scattered behind the barn. She had decided to put them up in the new house as soon as it was completed, as close as possible to their original location.

From the second-floor deck, precarious exterior stairs led to an open tower room that looked out past Marsh Point to the southeast, toward Horn Island. From the height, we peered through the drizzle and fog.

I could see the island.

"You can't see it," Mary said. "It's navy blue if you could see it, but you can't. Some days you can see the white line of the beach and all, if it's clear."

We ate lunch in the kitchen, looking out a glass wall at the squirrels and birds among the trees. Mary's brother John, visiting from Florida, joined us. He was the youngest of the Anderson children, slender and red-haired, with a red beard, in his midforties. At one time a biologist, he was now a psychologist. He had just become more specialized, he said, moving from estuarine ecology to human ecology. He answered my questions about his father thoughtfully.

What, I wondered, did they remember most fondly about him?

"When I was a small child," Mary said, "he had an ability to give you his absolute attention. It was a concentrated energy that you could feel. I remember that and I remember his enthusiasm. Much that I find myself getting the most from today, like flowers or birds, I think that I got directly from him. I would make up poetry and he would write it down, like it was from God."

"I think most of what I got was indirect," John said. "We're still receiving the benefits. The people that come to us, everyone that comes, brings something. It's like gifts."

"I really don't think I knew my father until after his death," Mary added. "Because having access to his writing has given me an understanding, a knowledge of the man, that few people have of their fathers, even if they live right in the same house with them and see them every meal."

If they had minded growing up with a father who was almost never there, they did not admit to such feelings.

"You have to know how my mother was," Mary said, "because she brought us up accepting him; this was the way he was. It's very hard to understand. My mother recognized him for an artist. And she made me accept it. I thought there were other children in other places whose fathers were artists who lived like ours did."

"Look at this place," John said. "This place is a very large extended family. Our grandmother came here and established something that's a little bit different. Her three sons all made homes and lived in this relatively small area. There were all these kids, the two sisters that married two brothers each had four kids. There's a tremendous amount of flexibility for the individual members because other members of the extended family fill in whenever anyone's missing. You almost didn't notice when a member left for short periods."

"Especially when he'd been going the whole of Johnny's life," Mary said. "See, Johnny never knew him when he was not going to the island. Johnny was born in '47."

"The year of the '47 hurricane," he said. "We had so many brothers and sisters around, plus all of the other men, and all of the other husbands were around. There were tons of father figures to fall back on. I don't think it was that big a factor. He was very visible. We knew where he was."

"If we ever thought about it, we thought we would like to be on Horn Island, too. We certainly didn't fault him or blame him for going out there."

Had they ever gone out there?

Oh, yes, Mary said, many times. Their Uncle Peter would take them out in his boat—a great adventure, four or five hours on the water, the whole clan, while her mother told them stories. "Those were wonderful, wonderful trips," she said. They would fish and picnic and hunt shells and run and swim on the island.

There were times when they were there at the same time as their father. But I got the impression that even then they did not really see him, except maybe to leave him supplies and make sure he was all right.

Why, I asked, did he go? What drew him?

"You get a certain perspective from being on an island or in a place," John answered. "I don't think it has to be an island, really."

"Everybody sort of picks out their island," Mary said, "and you don't necessarily mean a physical island. But you mean a place where it can come together and you can be able to understand."

"People can create an island anywhere they want to," he agreed, "but it's easier to do it on an island that has those definitive borders."

"I read an interesting new quote in one of the unpublished logs just last week," Mary said. "He'd just arrived on the island and he said, 'I realize that I can be as lonely here on this island in the midst of nature as I am in the midst of a household made of women and small children. The difference is'—and I haven't got the exact words—'the difference is that here as soon as I begin to paint I become connected.'"

"So he used his island in a slightly different way than we were discussing," John said. "Rather than just as a locus for his perception, for his perspective. He became part of it."

Mary added, "He said—this is a little quote from his diary—he painted 'and later I did a watercolor under my boat while the rain poured. Such is the life of an artist, who prefers nature to art. He really should cultivate art more, but he feels that his love of art will take care of itself as long as it has things to feed upon.' So here on the island he had that continuous flow of energy that never ended and kept changing."

"It was on Horn Island his work really came into focus," John said. "On Horn Island he was able to see the eternity in the grain of sand. He was able to see the universal." The island had been his metaphor.

John himself had spent long periods on the island alone. This was after his father had died, while he was working as the first ranger for the new Gulf Islands National Seashore. "What I found was that living on the island was very comfortable and comforting. If you stayed out there you were fine, but if you went back and forth you ran into problems. My impression was that in interacting with other people, we form a kind of psychological filter to protect ourselves. But if you live by yourself for a while away from people, at least with me, the filter gradually fades away. And then when I came in from a trip to the island, the slightest little insult was like somebody hit me with a sledgehammer."

If that was what happened to his father, what had he gained in return from the island to make that pain worthwhile?

"Heightened sensitivity," John said. "Part of the perspective is heightened sensitivity. The filter protects us, but it also reduces our ability to experience the intensity of life. You're lowering the intensity to protect yourself from—"

"See, that's why when my father came home he smoked and drank," Mary cut in. "He never did on the island."

"I wonder. What do you think he came in for?" John asked.

"To decorate his pots," Mary said simply.

"I thought he came probably as part of his responsibility to be present."

A better question, I said, would be why did he go out?

"Right," John said. "What I read in some of his writing is he was really dreading coming in."

"He said, 'Land upon which to walk with infinite refreshment.' He never said that it would work for anybody else," Mary continued. "He said, in fact, 'Whether I could share this with other people I don't know.' He said people need different things. So he never presumed to say that what was good for him would be good for someone else."

Had they seen a change in him from being on the island so much during those years?

The main change, Mary felt, had been in the way he paid attention to her. As she had said, early on that attention had been complete. "Later he was never quite the same. He was always preoccupied."

"Even when he was here, he was still out on the island," John said. "His spirit stayed on the island. He never left the island later on. He didn't come back."

Sea Islands

I had been to the Sea Islands before. Some eight months earlier I had traveled out to Saint Helena, South Carolina. It was a place where for generations people had farmed and fished for their livelihood, and where for generations they had lived in isolation, dependent only on each other and on the land that had stood under them for so long.

Part of the reason for that isolation is the nature of the Sea Islands. They are separated from the mainland not by shallow bays but by marshland, which is often difficult to cross and usually miles wide. In South Carolina alone more than a half-million acres of marshland separate them from the mainland. These marshes are cut by small back-barrier lagoons or sometimes by nothing more than a network of tidal creeks.

There is another difference between sea islands and other barrier islands—their geology. Sea islands are Holocene barrier islands, sometimes only a few hundred or a few thousand years old, which have migrated shoreward and hit Pleistocene islands, thirty-five thousand to a hundred twenty thousand years old. Thus a sea island is really two islands in one. The younger sits on the ocean side; the older lies on the landward side. The newer island may actually rest against the older core, or it may be separated by marshes and creeks. For instance, two to three miles of marsh separate Saint Helena's Holocene barriers, Fripp and Hunting islands, from Saint Helena itself. The young outer island at Hilton Head, on the other hand, is welded onto the old core on its north end but is separated from it farther south. It is as if the island had hit the core at an angle when it arrived, leaving a marsh driving up through part of Hilton Head's center.

These sea islands behave differently from many other barrier islands. Tide-dominated barriers (tides here exceed six feet) tend to be more stable than wave-dominated islands. More important, perhaps, is the fact that only the Holocene island—the outer part of the sea island—is dynamic. The core, on the other hand, is relatively high (generally well over the expected surge of a hundred-year storm) and stable, covered by a thick soil that supports a climax maritime forest. But stability here is a conditional term; the shoreline areas are still moving, retreating with sea-level rise.

And these islands, despite the height and stability of their inner areas, are not completely safe from hurricanes. A storm hit the South Carolina coast in August 1893 with a storm surge that may have reached fifteen feet and waves reported as high as forty feet. According to local accounts, it may have killed as many as two thousand persons on Saint Helena, and three thousand in all, though most estimates put the number between one thousand and two thousand for the entire coast, including Charleston. Whatever the number of dead, Saint Helena was so isolated, physically and culturally, that at first no one on the mainland gave much thought to casualties or damage there. It was only when islanders came ashore in Beaufort and pleaded for help that the outside world began to realize what had happened.

The first time I drove onto Saint Helena I had seen a sign. In a grove of young live oaks and palmettos that opened onto a marsh, it read, "View preserved by Beaufort County Open Land Trust." It was an alarming sign. People were realizing that such open land was disappearing and that it needed to be saved. I did not disagree with recognizing such a need. But it said that these islands were already in grave danger.

There were other signs. Surely their irony was apparent to those who had driven them into the ground: "LOST ISLAND. Residential lots for sale," and another, "COASTAL CAROLINA FOR SALE." How true. These were on Ladies Island, which lay between Beaufort and Saint Helena. Here the connection to the creeping intrusion of mainstream American culture was already apparent. Route 21 from Beaufort was five lanes wide from the bridge and filled with strip malls, branch banks, and heavy traffic.

On this earlier trip I had stopped at the Penn Center, the physical (as well as emotional and cultural) heart of Saint Helena. The Penn Center, the first organized educational system for black South Carolinians, was established by Northerners after Union forces had occupied the Sea Islands in 1861. Once the state's public school system finally recognized its responsibility to its black citizens in the 1940s, the Penn School, as it was called then, evolved into a center to serve the needs of its island community as well as the larger African-American community. It was here that Martin Luther King, Jr., met with the white members of his staff in the 1960s to plan the march on Washington, perhaps the only place in the South where he could do so. Today the Penn Center continues to serve its communities, striving, among other things, to help islanders keep their lands and to preserve Sea Island history and culture.

At the center I had met Emory Campbell, its director, and asked to talk to him sometime about changes on the island. This tall, graceful man had given me a long look. "It seems to me," he said mildly, "that we pass all these laws protecting the trees and the environment. But we don't have any laws protecting the indigenous population, especially if they're poor and black." His voice had a slight lilt, as if there might be a bit of Gullah in it. "You going to put that in your book?" he asked.

I said yes.

"Well, then we'll be talking a lot."

I had gone to the center's museum to read about the community's history, stopping on my way out to talk to a woman who worked at the center. As we spoke, her housemate came by and gave her two keys. The house would be locked, she said, and then she gave me an uneasy glance.

"She's worried about crack dealers," the woman said to me. "She thinks anyone from off island is a crack dealer."

At the museum I met someone much friendlier—Joseph Stevens, who was volunteering his time there. In his late fifties, Stevens was a powerfully built man, with a close, graying black beard and hair, and an earring in one ear. Stevens' wife's family was from Warsaw Island, which lay between Ladies Island and Saint Helena, separated by nothing more than a narrow fringe of marsh. He had been born in the Carolina low country, not the Sea Islands. After many years of driving a bus in Brooklyn, New York, he had retired two years earlier to Saint Helena.

This was a place, he said, where people don't lock their doors, where everybody knows you. Soon after moving here, he had gone on a visit to New York and set timers to switch the house lights on and off. On his return, Stevens had said to someone that he should drop by. The person answered that he would have done so before, except that Stevens had been in New York. "Everyone knows everything," Stevens said. "It's like a very close family."

It was an interesting contradiction: to me, the doors appeared locked; to Stevens, they did not. Actually, it was no contradiction at all. Though not native, Stevens was now local and treated with openness. I was an outsider and treated as such. And my chat with Stevens had revealed another island trait: native islanders were reserved, unsure of outsiders, whereas newcomers were friendlier. That seemed to be generally true of the islands I knew. Maybe it was because the newcomers (the "come-heres" as opposed to the "been-heres," as some said on Saint Helena) had had to work at being accepted themselves. These newcomers also seemed to me to be more willing to speak about island life. It was not that native islanders did not think about the nature and problems of these islands, it was more that they seemed unlikely to talk about them to someone from the outside.

As I had driven from Penn Center into the open, rich farmland at the island's center, past pecan groves that stretched out to the marshes, I had gotten the impression that few people lived here. But the houses were there—down the narrow, sandy oak-arched lanes that sprouted from the paved road. Inviting as they looked, I had hesitated to explore any of them for fear of intruding.

This trip to Saint Helena, I was arriving only days after Hugo had ripped through Charleston, some forty miles to the north. Still, from what I had been told, Saint Helena and the islands to its south had survived well. Saint Helena was starting to melt away, anyhow—not so much from the sea's attack as from the loss of land to the developers and the loss of its way of life to the changing times. The outside world was invading.

On my way I stopped at Hilton Head Island, just south across Port Royal Sound from Saint Helena, and named for its headland overlooking the beaches and for Captain William Hilton. An American from Massachusetts, Hilton had explored this shore for a group of Barbados planters in 1662, when the Spanish still claimed it as part of Florida. Evidently his report had helped spur the first wave of Sea Island settlement from England.

Driving onto the island—across a high-rise bridge like so many other new bridges to the islands, and down a four-lane divided highway, the William Hilton Parkway—made me sad, as if I had lost something. This island seemed a place without a heart. Much of it was groomed; tall pines, palmettos, and plenty of alien oleanders lined the parkway approaches. But where were the oaks? I suspected that they had been cut down to open up the scenery. Much of the landscape seemed covered with golf courses. (What effect, I wondered, does a golf course have on the environment?) Where was the real stuff—the garage, the drug store, the grocery? Not too long ago it had been a black community, but it was now almost completely overrun by whites. I knew there were real people living here, with real stores, but the island seemed to be infested with multistory condos on the beach and developments with fancy names, all with the accompanying post-modern restaurants and trendy shops selling running shoes and books on the environment. This island was hardly an island anymore, but

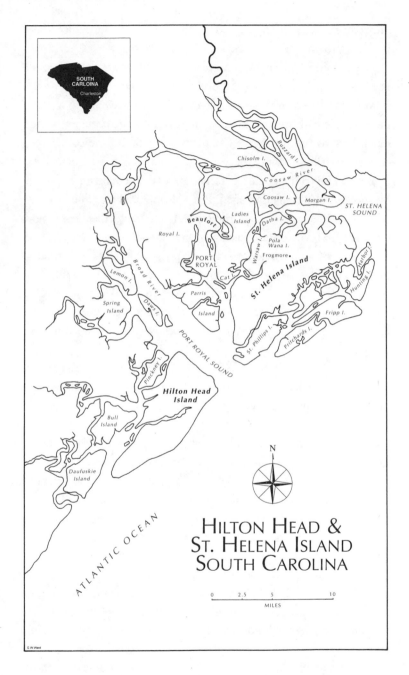

SOUTH CAROLOINA
Charleston

Buzzard I.

Chisolm I.

Coosaw River

Coosaw I.

Morgan I.

ST. HELENA SOUND

Ladies Island

Datha I.

Beaufort

Royal I.

Warsaw I.

Pola Wana I.

Frogmore

Harbor I.

PORT ROYAL

St. Helena Island

Hunting I.

Cat I.

Broad River

Lemon I.

Parris Island

Daws I.

Fripp I.

Spring Island

St. Phillips I.

Pritchards I.

PORT ROYAL SOUND

Pinckney I.

Hilton Head Island

Bull Island

N

Daufuskie Island

ATLANTIC OCEAN

Hilton Head & St. Helena Island South Carolina

| 0 | 2.5 | 5 | | 10 |

MILES

G. W. Ward

rather an extension of some middle American fantasy. It seemed like a warning to Saint Helena, so close by and so different.

About mid-island on Hilton Head itself, the beach dunes had all been cut down. Just to the north the shore had been hardened with a riprap seawall—clearly there was no beach at the seawall. No wonder these people had been worried as Hugo approached; there was not much here to protect them. The overwash would have come right down the parking lot, into the traffic circle, and down the avenue.

Before Hugo hit, people had talked about their concern that Hilton Head would be badly damaged. But Hilton Head was filled mostly with expensive second and third homes. Even though their loss would have hurt the owners, the houses were merely recreational. No one had been expressing much concern for the possible fate of the nonfancy homes—the first homes—here and on Saint Helena. After all, they were not worth a lot, and the numbers might not add up to much. But their loss would have meant a great deal more to the owners than the loss of some condos: to lose these homes would have been to lose everything.

Eventually they might be lost anyway. Development pressure was heavy on Hilton Head, and the original communities were disappearing before its onslaught. Each of Hilton Head's developments was a private community called a plantation—Sea Pines Plantation, Hilton Head Plantation, Shipyard Plantation, Something-or-Other Plantation—an unfortunate name symbolizing the entrenchment of wealth and a lack of imagination. The island's municipal government was organized in such a way that these plantations, not the town itself, supplied their members with essential services such as water and sewer. The relatively poor indigenous population—mostly black, those who had managed not to get squeezed out when the developers transformed their home into a playground, hidden here and there—was not provided with much. It was an ingenious way to limit the cost of owning recreational property on the island; wealthy neighborhoods would pay only for their own needs, while poor neighborhoods still paid high taxes.

The remaining islanders had watched their communities disappear as the soaring cost of living and the mainland newcomers squeezed them out of their homes. Whereas in 1950 nearly all Hilton Head residents were black, by 1980 whites outnumbered them five to one. It was becoming evident that on Hilton Head, as on many of the other Sea Islands, the original population was no longer welcome, if not because of their color then certainly because of their economic state. The island was too valuable. Those who managed to find work on Hilton Head often got menial jobs at the so-called plantations, raking the grounds or waiting tables. Worse yet in a way, many of these new enclaves encompassed the family cemeteries of those who remained. They had to suffer the indignity of asking special permission from plantation authorities to get past the guards, a pass to visit their own family graves.

It was a discomfiting echo of older days. I wondered if the new property owners saw the irony. It seemed that "plantation" was the right name after all.

When I arrived this time at Penn Center, several staff members were headed into Beaufort, on Port Royal Island, the most landward of the group of Sea Islands with Saint Helena at its center. Here Beaufort County would be holding a tax auction on the courthouse steps. *

The auction included land on both Saint Helena and Hilton Head, land whose owners had fallen behind on their taxes or for which no one could agree who should pay the assessment. Much was prime land, and the auction promised to draw both the poor who wished to redeem their land and opportunists who wished to grab it cheap.

The Penn Center people were trying to make sure that as much of Saint Helena as possible stayed in the hands of its owners. When the tax delinquency notices had appeared in the Beaufort *Gazette*, they had begun notifying as many of the debtors as they could find. Some

---

*A number of islands, more or less separated by marsh, make up "greater" Saint Helena. They include Port Royal, Ladies, Coosaw, Morgan, Cat, Datha, Warsaw, Pola Wana, Pine, Saint Helena, Saint Phillips, Harbor, Hunting, Fripp, and Pritchards islands—and probably more, depending on what one wants to call an island. The last four are the true Holocene barrier islands, lying along this group's seaward edge. In plantation days they were traditionally maintained as hunting grounds for islanders. Saint Helena, fifteen miles long and seven to eight miles wide, is the largest. About six thousand persons live on it, 75 percent of them black.

now lived in New York or Atlanta or other urban centers, while their grandparents remained on the land. Others, staff member Walter Mack said, just were not "the kind of people to buy the newspaper every day," and so might not know they were about to lose their land.

Mack and others from the center would attend the auction to see who bought tax-delinquent island land. The owners could still redeem it within a year by paying the tax plus 8 percent of the purchase price, which would go to the buyer. Either way, buyers stood to win.

I rode to Beaufort with Mack in his blue BMW 320i, for which, he admitted, he had to go to Charleston or Savannah to get a tuneup. Much of the land-loss problem, he said, stemmed from the growing complexity of the bureaucracy and the sophistication of developers wanting to get island land.

"People around here don't know how to deal with real estate people," he said. "They don't know what to do. And they've owned the land since slave days. One man paid two hundred dollars in taxes and suddenly the tax went up to fifteen hundred dollars. He's on a fixed income. We came in and helped him get that changed. You can put in trees and get your taxes reduced. I have three acres and had taxes about three hundred dollars. I put in trees and the tax went down to just over a dollar."

He pulled out a copy of the *Gazette*. In the back of the "Lifestyles" section ("Pasta—good for you") a Delinquent Tax Sale headline introduced four and three-quarter pages of property. Each line listed the owner's name, the location, acreage, and taxes due. The notice included more than fifteen hundred pieces of land. There were some good deals: a half-acre for sale for the $73.09 owed in taxes; four acres for $84.06; fifteen hundred acres for $342.03. The bidding would start at the value of the taxes. It would, of course, go up, depending on the perceived value of the land.

A tent had been set up in front of the courthouse, overlooking the marshes out toward Ladies Island. About a hundred people sat on folding chairs under the canvas or in the shade of the surrounding trees. This was such a classic southern scene—the corridors of mossy oaks, the tall palmettos, the old colonnaded homes peeping through the trees, the pleasant and relentless voice of the auctioneer, and the black faces and white faces watching it all, some to gain, some to lose.

It was quiet, not the carnival I had expected. Some people talked with low voices among themselves. Others studied papers, speaking out or nodding only to bid, a focal point of stillness and concentration as city traffic rushed by.

The auctioneer, standing behind a small podium, was already selling when we arrived. "Opening bid one ninety-eight thirty-nine. Two hundred. Two fifty. Two seventy. Three hundred. Three hundred. Three hundred. Three hundred once. Three-oh-five once. Three twenty-five. Three twenty-five once. Three twenty-five twice. Three twenty-five sold."

He started on the next one, first naming the delinquent. "Bernice Frasier Price and others. One hundred fifty. One seventy-five. One eighty-five. Two hundred. Two ten. Two twenty-five. Two thirty. Two fifty. Two sixty. Two sixty once. Two sixty-five. Two seventy-five. Two seventy-five once. Three hundred. Three hundred once. Three hundred twice. Three-oh-five. Three-oh-five once. Three-oh-five twice. Three-oh-five sold."

Price and others. *And others.* Therein lay part of the problem. Sometimes it just was not clear who held title to the land and who should be paying the taxes. The reasons for that confusion were old.

A new auctioneer arrived. He had white hair, steel-rimmed glasses, and a blue striped suit. His voice was firm, yet he managed to appear friendly and compassionate. His pace was fast and prices began to go up. The atmosphere became slightly frantic. Some people, it seemed, were passionate about certain parcels. Others were being left out in the rising pitch. The man sitting beside me, hesitating too long in the accelerating pace, was drowned out by the auctioneer's "Five hundred sold." Two women were working against each other, quickly raising their bids on one parcel from four hundred to eleven hundred dollars in twenty-five-dollar increments.

Then something new happened. As one piece of land came on the block, a man stood up and said, "I am the last surviving heir. I want to clear the title." The auctioneer answered that he, the auctioneer, could not himself tell that group that, but the man certainly could. He asked if he heard twenty-five hundred dollars. Only the man bid; no one countered. The auctioneer smiled. "Sold. Two thousand five hundred!" The group clapped.

Again—a couple, heirs to a delinquent owner, got the land for two hundred dollars. "They're just twenty-one years old, folks, and trying to get a start," the auctioneer said.

The auctioneer, who was also the country treasurer, Mack told me, was outspoken against high taxes and had criticized the county for wasting tax dollars and taking property when the owners could no longer afford to support its inefficiency. Word was that he would retire soon and then would run for county commissioner.

A man tried to pay the tax when his property came up for sale. No, the auctioneer said, he couldn't clear it now—he was not clearing an heir's claim. The man would have to pay next Wednesday; the auctioneer could not delay the bidding. The man apologized. The land sold for three hundred sixty dollars, from the forty-seven-dollar opening for taxes due. No doubt the knowledge that he would be paying off the taxes had driven the bidding up. Someone would made twenty-nine dollars—8 percent of that three sixty—by the end of the week.

It was a hard scene to watch.

The auctioneer moved to property on Hilton Head. The selling prices were high—$800, $1,000, $3,300, $6,500. The land was selling for more and climbing further past the value of the taxes due than the land on Saint Helena. *Big surprise*, I thought.

Hilton Head land belonging to Johanna Ford came up. A man stood and said that he could not get the family together to pay the $597.80 in taxes, so he wanted to bid on the property himself.

Who was the oldest member of the family? the auctioneer asked.

"Johanna Ford."

"Age?"

"Seventy-four."

Where did she live?

Hilton Head.

"And your relation?" The auctioneer placed his hand on the man's shoulder.

"I'm her son."

He turned to the others. "This is the son of the matriarch of the family. He would like to bid on the property." He got it for six hundred dollars.

The situation with the next parcel was similar. A man wanted to bid for his father's home, sitting on his grandfather's land. The auctioneer turned to the crowd. "The lawyers in Beaufort County can tell you, if you want to get into a sticky wicket, try tracing back some of the titles to this land." The man got his home for the taxes.

Obviously these people—scavengers, speculators, and those wanting their own land back—were very aware of the predicament of those trying to settle their families' titles. I had expected this to be a kind of sport, but it was not that at all. The people who gathered had been interested in buying land or making a profit. At least on this day, even though they were out for money, they were not out for blood.

Mack pointed out three men sitting in front of us. They had, he said, spent at least fifty-eight thousand dollars. Even if every one of the owners redeemed his or her land, an 8-percent return on their investment—$4,640—wouldn't be a bad profit. And if not all the land was redeemed, then they owned land that was escalating in value.

The afternoon wore on. The sales slowed as the crowd and the auctioneer tired. He recessed the sale until ten the next morning.

I had, I realized, watched something strange and unique to this part of the country—the sale of land to settle complex tax and ownership questions. To understand these questions, as well as the entire cultural challenge Saint Helena islanders were facing, I would have to understand some things about the history and way of life of these people and their island.

That history had begun with the abduction of black men and women in West Africa. It had started early. The first shipload of English colonists in 1670 brought black slaves to the state. In the hundred years before the Slave Trade Act of 1808 banned the further importation of slaves, more than one hundred thousand Africans had been carried to South Carolina and Georgia.

The slaves brought to the Sea Islands came almost entirely from the west coast, from Senegal to Angola. This was not mere circumstance.

The South Carolina coast was a hard place in which to live—a hot, humid climate infested with malaria and other undefined miasmas, much like that of the rice-growing Senegal-Gambia area. For the newly arrived African slave, the environment, if not the circumstances, would be familiar.

Madagascar rice was brought to Charleston in 1685, and by 1700 the Carolinas were producing more than they had ships to transport. Rice, though, was not a significant Sea Island crop; rather, it was cultivated on the inland swamps and at the freshwater ends of the tidal rivers. On islands like Saint Helena the cash crop was indigo, for which the British Crown paid a premium. The light and dry island soil produced the most valuable indigo. The colony produced more than a million pounds in 1775, before the Revolution destroyed the market for it.*

In indigo's place came a new crop, long-staple Sea Island cotton, introduced from the Bahamas. This cotton was stronger and of a finer grade than normal upland cotton, and it would eventually make Sea Island plantation owners very wealthy. While in 1790 the entire Sea Island cotton crop was about thirty bales, by 1801, only eleven years later, it had grown to about twenty-two thousand bales—eight and a half million pounds.

What made the Saint Helena (and other Sea Island) cotton crop so abundant was the discovery that salt-marsh mud and *Spartina* could serve as powerful fertilizers, especially when mixed with available manure and vegetable compost. Annual marshland production of *Spartina* grass is as high as eight thousand calories per square yard, and the planters had managed to tap that productivity. (It was a hard business, though; each acre of cotton took forty ox-cart loads of marsh mud, all dug by hand, often in the mosquito-infested summer heat.)

By the time the Civil War hit the Sea Islands, they had developed a culture that was unique. These islands were peopled with slaves of

---

*Indigo production, many believe, is the origin of the tradition still seen among some Sea Islanders of painting the doors and window frames of their houses blue. The color was available to them from the remnants in the dye pots. Whether the islanders considered the color to be protection from spirits was something I would never know.

common West African roots. And their extreme isolation allowed these roots to survive and flourish.

One of the ways they did so was in the development of Gullah, a language whose significance for a long time was not understood. Its genesis is still not clear, and pronouncements about it remain controversial. It was at one time not even considered a language, but rather the unintelligible attempts of these Africans to speak a kind of broken English, developed from the baby talk supposedly used by masters to command their slaves. (Actually, the opposite may be true. Many plantation owners evidently spoke to their slaves in fluent Gullah. These whites may have started learning Gullah from their black nurses before they spoke English, and that exposure and fluency may have helped shape the distinctive sound of Sea Island white speech.)

In fact, Gullah was a genuine creole language, a language that started as a pidgin and grew. A pidgin is any language developed by speakers of different languages whenever they must communicate with each other. It is usually quite simple. A trading pidgin had developed in West Africa, and it may have been carried to North America by the newly enslaved Africans. On the American coast it allowed people of different African backgrounds to communicate. A creole evolves from a pidgin. The children of pidgin speakers, if they are given no other native language of their own, will acquire their parents' pidgin and very quickly—within a generation sometimes—turn it into a full language of complexity and subtlety. That, evidently, is what happened with Gullah.

It is a language whose parentage lies primarily in several West African languages, including Wolof (of Senegal and Gambia, perhaps the single most important African source), Ewe (Togo and Dahomey), Kimbundu (Angola), Mandinka (Gambia), and Yoruba (southern Nigeria). Its words are taken both from these languages and from English, but its grammar, its structure, is almost entirely African. In some ways Gullah is more complex than English.

And it has, in turn, enriched English. When Southerners talk of goober peas, their speech echoes words used in Angola. *Guba*, Gullah for peanut, has its origins in the Kimbundu word *nguba* and Umbundu *olungupa*. Likewise, gumbo comes, by way of Gullah, from

Tshiluba (a Congo language) and Umbundu words for okra. When we samba, we do something done by generations before us, speaking a number of West African languages, including Hausa (northern Nigeria), Tshiluba, Kongo (Angola), and Bobangi (Congo). In these languages it carries a range of meanings having to do with dancing and worship. And then, having danced the samba, when we sit down to a meal of yams, we are eating something the Mende speakers of Sierra Leone (*yambi*) and Gᵃ speakers of the Gold Coast (*yamu*) enjoyed, too.

This language with its rich parentage held the people of these islands together from Georgetown, South Carolina, to the Florida border. Obviously it helped them communicate with each other and keep their identity, but it also helped them maintain their distance from strangers, maintain their separateness. (The Gullah people were, according to the linguist Lorenzo Turner, particularly suspicious of strangers, in whose hands they had suffered so badly.) The isolation of the islands only served to strengthen Gullah culture. As late as 1978 as many as one hundred thousand persons spoke some Gullah, of whom ten thousand spoke only Gullah, no English.

When the Civil War hit, it isolated the islands still further. In following years the former slaves, now owning much of the land, were left pretty much to themselves. Except for the period during and immediately after the war, few outsiders settled there. With minimal contact with or interference from whites, the indigenous culture deepened.

For the next hundred years or so the island would remain almost entirely black. (Until the bridge between Ladies Island and Beaufort was built in 1927, over the objections of some islanders, there was no direct access to the mainland. Even by the 1930s many islanders had never been off the island.) Their isolation allowed them to continue in their ways. Gullah survived, particularly on the islands. This culture remained coherent enough and close enough to its African origins that some years ago a Smithsonian curator mistakenly identified a Gullah rice basket as being from West Africa.

On the islands the land was of paramount value. While slaves, the islanders had been chained to it, forced to cultivate it for the gain of their masters. Once freed, for those fortunate enough to get land of their own, it was often the most substantial property they had. And it was always the most important, since they depended on it for their survival. It certainly represented their freedom.

Land deeded to a former slave tended to remain deeded to that person. That practice continued into the next century, as one writer reported in the late 1930s: "Deeds to practically all Negro-owned lands in Beaufort County are still recognized in the names of these ex-slaves; their children and grandchildren pay taxes in the names of the forefathers long since dead."

Soon, with several generations living on a single piece of "heirs property," just who had title became obscure. Putting a fine point on it really did not matter when brothers, sisters, cousins, aunts, and uncles were all living in this island community, and the outside world was leaving them alone. But as family members moved away, often to cities in hopes of jobs, and those who left continued to hold legal interest in the land, just who had the right to sell and who was responsible for the taxes started getting muddied. As taxes went up, ownership and responsibility became more of an issue. Sometimes one person paid the taxes for a while and eventually tired of it. Then no one did. The land could easily end up on the courthouse steps.

That had been the meaning behind "Bernice Frasier Price and others." The *and others* were hard to identify.

Additional problems tied into land ownership but still were distinct issues. The islands were slipping into the hands of developers. With the successful exploitation of adjacent Hilton Head, surely someone had gazed across the marshes from Beaufort and smelled money: if only Saint Helena and its contiguous islands could be developed. Surely this theoretical developer had contemplated a future of condos and time-sharing and tennis. Well, this person was not so theoretical. Development was increasing, and along with it, land values.

Escalating values were a temptation for islanders in that they offered a chance for some cash. And because figuring out who held title had become a mire to trap the landholder, those with the money to clear the title stood to flourish. It could take thousands of dollars. If someone living on the island wanted to develop his or her land, that cost alone could make it impossible. If an islander could not develop his own land, maybe he could sell it to someone who would be willing and able to untangle the title. Unfortunately such an act would leave the seller without a home—and sometimes without a connection to the island. As Mack had said to me, "When those people lose or sell their land, they have nowhere to move to."

The effects of such changes could be devastating to a community such as this, where, since the end of slavery, families had lived on the same piece of land within a coherent community. The situation of Hilton Head islanders clearly illustrated the problem. Those who did remain lost much of their connection to the land: witness having to get a pass to visit a burying ground. And without the land, many people found they had nothing—no home, no community, no culture.

The Land

Free of the courthouse auction and wanting to forget the issues of land loss, I went off in search of more of the island. I drove down Route 21, the main road from Beaufort, which cuts through the center of Saint Helena and out onto Harbor and Hunting islands. Lands End Road crossed this road, passing the Penn Center and extending the length of the island to its southern tip. Here I stopped at the tabby Chapel of Ease to enjoy the afternoon air. (Tabby is a cement made from a mixture of crushed oyster shells, sand, and lime. The Spanish evidently brought the technology to the New World, but its origins are African, traveling to Spain by way of the Arab countries. Kongo speakers call the material *ntaba*.)

The chapel was only a shell now, but during the plantation days it had served the community. It offered me no ease. The mosquitoes were so savage and swarmed so quickly that after ignoring them for two or three minutes I was overcome. I scratched one bite and all the others cried out. I walked away from the swarm, both hands busy.

Back on Route 21 I headed east, looking for a sea breeze. I crossed to Harbor Island. A dark blue Cadillac sedan was parked at the side of the road. A man in yacht visor, olive T-shirt, and flowery pants was casting a net. A woman in a pink bathing suit sat next to him, watching, sipping a beer.

Farther on was another of those signs: "Welcome to Harbor Island. A Private Oceanfront Community." I passed Harbor, onto Hunting Island along its marshes. A deer was feeding in the marsh in the late afternoon light. I stopped. She looked up and bounded into the trees. Here in the marshes was the life—red-wing blackbirds clinging onto the reeds, egrets picking their way through the shallows. In marshes like these the shrimpboats gathered, running up creeks that seemed too narrow and shallow to contain them. They were tied to the banks alone or in tight clusters that were all white hulls and tangle of raised outriggers, with only the wheelhouse and rig visible above the golden green marsh grasses.

I walked among the dense trees toward the beach. I saw no live oaks, just palmettos and the dramatic, eighty-foot loblolly pines; the air was filled with their scent. There had been much erosion here. The Hunting Island lighthouse told the story. It had first been completed in 1859. The beach eroded so fast that a new lighthouse had to be built sixteen years later. The erosion continued, and fourteen years after that the light had been moved to its present location. In the years since the construction of the 1859 lighthouse, parts of the beach had retreated as much as twenty-four hundred feet. The first two sites were long since under water.

I stepped onto the sand. The big trees came right up to the beach. I was used to seeing live oak maritime growth offering a shoulder to the sea; but here the trees stood full height at the beach line, their undersides exposed. Grayish white sand stretched away, smooth and clean, with a few shells scattered through it. This place looked like heaven.

But the beach was eroding and tree stumps stuck up in the sand, some as far out as the surf. There was virtually no dune line here; the few dunes were obscured by the growth. Their sides were crumbling rapidly, the erosional scars in the dune remnants fresh from recent ravages. Palmettos and pines lay in the sand where they had fallen. The palmetto roots were tight balls of root hairs around the tree base—not deep, not wide, not much for holding on in a blow. The destruction stretched as far as I could see in either direction.

I asked a man on the beach if this damage was from Hugo.

Yes, he said, it wouldn't have happened naturally.

I stood and stared. It was a scene of dramatic beauty and horror.

Development was a bigger threat to Saint Helena's islanders than any storm. In addition to the resort on Harbor Island, another had been established on Fripp, and one could not go onto the island without permission. Development was expanding on Cat and Gibbs islands, which are marshland fringes of Ladies Island. And just past Warsaw, Alcoa Properties had already broken ground for the Dawtaw Island marina. (The island still bore the name Datha on some maps, but somehow this development was helping to transform it.)

The Dawtaw marina would cost close to four million dollars and would eventually accommodate up to two hundred boats. This development, a company representative had said, would be "environmentally compatible" with the wetlands. I wondered. Already development had polluted the marshes enough that shrimp harvesting was severely restricted and oysters in any local restaurant were likely to have come from Louisiana. This pollution-caused loss of fishing had in turn undermined the economy of those who supplemented their incomes from the sea. Now many Saint Helena islanders made their living by working for the Hilton Head resorts.

When I had mentioned all this growth to Penn Center director Emory Campbell, himself a Hilton Head native who lived on the land where he was born, he said simply, "We're surrounded." He viewed the changes with dismay and had been quoted in a local paper as saying, "I can't see development helping blacks." They would share in little of the profit, would be unlikely to be able to use the new resorts, and would probably suffer from the potential degradation of their environment.

Just as profoundly, this development was going to change the way islanders lived. Campbell had already seen it on Hilton Head. "Everybody shored their boat, sold their horses and their plows, and went to work up on the hill," he said. "So that whole way of life has kind of changed. I mean it has changed life in so many ways that people are not even as interdependent on one another as they used to be. It's almost a kind of sin now to ask someone to borrow a sack of flour. Because everybody has become this rugged individualist, they're going to take care of themselves, they now have a job.

"We had nearly a hundred years of black people living on the land, and all of a sudden we have resort development coming in, and now many of our people have a very capitalistic idea about Beaufort County and couldn't care less about the poor who's been here, the poor who's on the land. Too much of the attitude is if you can't afford to do something with it, sell it."*

In response to this burst of development, the county was now zoning the island, and the state planned to expand Route 21 on Saint Helena. Ominously, that road was now called Sea Island Parkway. And, though zoning potentially could help by letting islanders control and even prevent development, instead it seemed to be serving the interests of developers. Many of those in charge of the zoning appeared, at best, indifferent to Saint Helena's concerns; at worst, they wanted development, perhaps for their own gain.

Islanders were struggling to set up a zoning system that would al-

---

*Interestingly, International Paper Company, whose real estate arm was developing a resort on Daufuskie Island, just south of Hilton Head, had recently given twenty-five hundred dollars to the Penn Center for its Academic and Cultural Enrichment Program. Talk was that this new development, which would envelop most of the island, and include nine hundred homes, two inns, two golf courses, and two tennis clubs, would in the next twenty years bring in ten thousand permanent and another ten thousand seasonal residents. At one time as many as twelve hundred persons had flourished on the island, until pollution from the Savannah River had killed off the fishing and oystering. By 1980 the population had been down to fifty-nine, forty-five of them black. The development was being called a playground for white people. In giving the money to Penn, the company was evidently making a bow to the tensions arising between such development and cultural preservation. One writer, speaking of Daufuskie, had remarked that at times on the island he would find himself thinking about ancient people who had "lost their history and died."

low them to continue to live much as they do now. But the planning board seemed very interested in zoning island areas, particularly along Route 21, as commercial or high-density residential, which allowed as many as eight residences per acre. The current density for the whole island is about eight acres per person, which might translate to thirty acres per residence, though of course much of that is locked up in farmland.

At a planning board meeting I attended an islander asked why the board was so insistent on this zoning for the island. A board member answered: "We feel we have to look for areas around the county where we could allow heavy development. We could have zoned the whole county for two or four, but that would not have been acceptable." The board, another member remarked, saw the intersection of Route 21 and Lands End Road as the "urban center" of Saint Helena—an inappropriate and telling term.

"There are people," Joe Stevens remarked to me, "who are going to benefit from development—but the wrong people. I'd love to see some of the people from Saint Helena benefit."

Some of this zoning smelled of potential conflict of interest. One member of the planning board (who resigned from the board the night after the tax sale) was an owner of the new Royal Frogmore Motel and the adjacent Klackers, a slick brick, fast-food chicken restaurant with a drive-through window, at the so-called urban center. His wife reportedly was a real estate broker. In relation to his connection with some proposed development on Saint Helena, Stevens had asked him about conflict of interest. Stevens told me, "He said, 'There's no conflict of interest. Don't worry, go home and get you a night's rest.'"

Meanwhile the proposed widening of Route 21 from two lanes to five would also bring development. The reason for the expansion, officials claimed, had nothing to do with Saint Helena. It had much to do with moving traffic from Ladies Island to Hunting Island, which is now a state park. Still, it was an odd coincidence that meanwhile developers were trying to get the Saint Helena land on either side of that road zoned commercial and were buying up as much of it as they could get.

The paper seemed filled with articles about the zoning controversy.

One planning board member was quoted as saying: "Development is going to come. The reason I am in favor of zoning, if we don't have zoning now, it's going to come in a very haphazard way." When someone was quoted as saying that, without zoning, a pig farm might be built next to a home, Joe Stevens had replied, "Everyone on the island, one way or another, has been associated with a pig farm, but no one has been connected to a condo."

Stevens invited me to his house to talk about the problems. It was a pleasant place off the road, hidden by a stand of trees and brush. Seven fishing rods leaned against his porch (a clear indication of his commitment to his retirement), and the trim lawn had recently been planted with young trees (a clear indication of his commitment to the future).

As we talked about zoning, I wondered why the board seemed so thoughtless about its responsibilities to the island. He asked, perhaps rhetorically, "Who do they serve?"

To that, I rephrased my question: "Are they simply thoughtless, or are they smarter than we think?"

He agreed that this was maybe a less naive way to look at the situation.

It was no surprise that he opposed the commercial zoning. "They say, 'Well, we want to zone it neighborhood commercial because we do not wish to disenfranchise the current landowners, black people, poor people. Because if there is any development, we want them to be able to get a part of the action,' meaning if you want to open up a business you don't have to go through a long process to get your land zoned commercial, because you have it commercial already. It takes a minimum of twenty thousand dollars to go into business, and it may take as much as sixty thousand, because you're going to have certain standards you're going to have to conform to. The average income on the island is seven thousand dollars. There are no black people that are going to go into business on that type of income."

Still, to Stevens' eye, zoning was not what the islanders needed to attack. That was just the monster's tail. They needed to go after the road expansion. That was the monster's head. And as far as he was concerned, saying that the road needed to be expanded to handle traffic was a diversion, a false issue. During what passed for Saint Helena's rush hour, he could drive the seven miles from his house to Beaufort in fifteen minutes. Once the road was widened, sewage lines would be next, and then "all they've got to do is put feeder lines onto it, and the island is gone; it's going to be another Hilton Head."

Was the island really doomed?

"Yes and no. Yes, if the people let it happen. And no, if the people don't want it to happen," he said. "Eventually if the people continue to sell or lose their land, yes it's doomed. But I don't know. It could be saved if the people worked to have better leadership."

Someone, I said, expects this island to become a very busy place soon.

"That's the question," he said. "That's the sixty-four-dollar question. Who? Who?"

I had already seen changes in the eight months since my previous visit. Across from the Royal Frogmore Motel at the corner of Route 21 and Lands End Road now stood the Island Plaza, a combination convenience store, deli, and laundromat with a gas station as its focus. (And why should we, many islanders might reasonably argue, be denied the convenience of such a store instead of having to drive into Beaufort?) When I had been on the island before, there had been nothing other than an old general store at this intersection.

The nearby motel and restaurant both sported blue trim, a promotional piece in the local paper had said, in recognition of the old beliefs of the islanders. The food would feature "local Frogmore cuisine" (this part of the island had at one time been named Frogmore, after one of its plantations). "The market we're shooting for is a tourist market," one of the owners was quoted as saying, the same man whose job it supposedly had been to zone the island in the interests of the islanders. The writer went on to say that the business partners hoped to promote the Frogmore area as a destination: "The fact that they are located halfway between Historic Beaufort and the beaches of Hunting and Fripp islands will attract tourists." I wondered again, was the board smarter than we thought?

When I had showed the article to Vanessa Thaxton, the center's museum curator, she laughed. "Have you eaten there?" she asked, mocking. She pointed at the line about blue colors. "They don't know anything about this," she said. "A lot of people around here do paint their houses to keep away bad luck. Maybe some of them do it now and don't even know why anymore. Just like you'll find a lot of bright yellow or pink houses. But these people don't know anything about that."

After staring all too long at the Royal Frogmore and the gasoline plaza, I went into Cormier's Grocery, an old colonnaded building near the intersection. Four men sat outside on the porch. One by one they went inside, returning to their seats with a cold beer in a paper sack. The store had twelve-foot tin ceilings and mostly empty wooden shelves.

A woman in her early twenties tended the register, a year-old baby in a pen behind her. She looked down at the postcard I had picked out.

"Doing a bit of visiting," I said.

"Yeah, he's from Maine," a man nearby said. He turned to me. "Your plate stuck out." He was her husband.

The store, they said, was dying because of the plaza and Klackers and the new Exxon station up the road. Nobody came in, except tourists and a few of the people who were still loyal. The owner had put it up for sale—he made only enough to pay her, the wife said.

He should wait another five years to sell, I said, after the boom starts.

Already, even for me, the island did not feel nearly as isolated, as insular and protected, as it had before. It was about to become part of the rest of the country, part of the uniformity of shopping malls and gas stations everywhere else. It was about to be lost. This corner was seven miles from Beaufort; it had seemed a world away. But the world was getting closer.

Emory Campbell had had a right to feel that the island's "indigenous population," as he put it, was endangered. After a biology degree from Savannah State College, he had gone off to Boston for six years, where in 1971 he had earned a master's in environmental health engineering. When he came home, Hilton Head had changed. He was lucky, though; his family still had its land and he had built himself a home there. Now he commuted in the direction opposite to most local Sea

Islanders. When we sat down to talk again, I reminded him of his earlier comment.

He was still worried about that, he said. Part of the problem was that often the increased land values were just too much of a temptation. "People are becoming—even though they are third or fourth generation on the land—they have become, some of them, land speculators. They have just left the land, sold and left the land, and moved into apartment buildings."

Even on Saint Helena, I wondered?

"No. But it's going to happen because I've seen a whole lot of activity in real estate sales. And they're sending out cards, they're putting things in mailboxes, sending people letters. They want you to know what your land is valued at. People are going to rush in, the land value's going to be higher and higher, and people are going to try to displace the people who are here.

"It can survive providing we educate the residents that are here. We educate their children, we find out what kind of lifestyle they want; if they decide on that and are really serious about it, I think we can survive. Otherwise, you know, people just remain ignorant of what's going on around them and they're going to get wiped out."

Here was, I said, an island whose way of life was unique, partly because of its isolation from the rest of the country. What was to be done? Did they try to bring the island into the twentieth century in a hurry, so that people would have lives that were materially improved and they would be better able to deal with the courthouse? If they did that, they threatened what was unique about the island. Or did they try to preserve the old Gullah culture and by doing that risk the island's survival, because people very likely would lose the land?

It had to be both, Campbell said. The center worked hard to improve the academic achievement of students so they would understand how government works and would know what they were up against when they dealt with fast-moving developers. At the same time, they tried to teach the islanders the importance of their history and their culture.

"We try to make people proud of their heritage and their way of life.

But that is a challenge, because if it's not functional for an individual family to go in the river anymore to catch fish—it's easier for them to go to the supermarket because they're on their way from Hilton Head and they've got some cash in their pocket—then we cannot force them to go back to the river. And so the river is taken over by recreational fishermen, people who are wealthy enough to stay all day and cast a net."

The island was caught in the middle between the old ways and the new. I thought of the man I had seen before, casting a net—the man with the dark blue Cadillac.

It was now late afternoon, and finally cool, or relatively so, after the ninety-degree heat. Back outside I could hear the loud chatter of a mockingbird and the heavy tapping of a female hairy woodpecker. She was right above me, somewhere in the oak. The wood was so dense that the sound had a heavy timbre and did not carry far, but I could catch glimpses of her.

The mosquitoes were out. They got to work on my ankles and fore-arms almost immediately, sharp, itchy little stings that would not go away. Campbell had said they were worse than they had ever been, a result of all the fresh water from Hurricane Hugo. The light was begin-ning to slant, and shining down on the trees it made the Spanish moss glow. A slight breeze picked up, and I began to hear the occasional snap and thump as an acorn fell out of the big oak beside me, rico-cheted off a limb, and embedded itself in the sandy ground.

Of all the islands I had been to, I had seen no lovelier place than Saint Helena. Looking at this island, I could see why so many South-erners felt tied to the land, felt an emotion for it that Northerners might never understand. It was a place where I would have wanted to have a piece of land and a small house of my own, an island where, away from the rest of the world, I could learn about the rhythm of life on a barrier island. But I was an outsider here and could never become part of this place. More than that, by moving here I would make Saint Helena's problems worse. As one more person squeezing out Camp-bell's endangered islanders, I would be part of the problem. Still, it did not keep me from fantasizing, sitting there among the live oaks and palmettos, feeling the warm air on my face and Saint Helena's sand under my feet, feeling the peace this island held.

It was a peace already disturbed—disturbed by growing traffic down the road, big engines whining, reminders that development and change and the outside world were only a few miles away and poised to come roaring down Sea Island Parkway.

As people on the island talked about what they might do to prepare for eventual development, I had wanted to call out, "They're here! They're here!" as in some cheap horror movie: the development blob is rolling over Ladies Island, and some sticky stuff has been spotted on Saint Helena. I had a sense that much had already been lost. And that more would soon be gone.

Sadly, I wondered if trying to save the island's unique culture might not be like replenishing the beaches or building a seawall—ultimately futile. No matter what you did, the sea kept encroaching and the shoreline continued to fall back. You kept having to pump sand at an accelerated rate to maintain the appearance of the status quo.

Earlier, when I had spoken with Joe Stevens, he talked about the island's life, away from the rest of the world, buffered by the marshes. It had been a world unto itself, he said, a community that had nourished and protected those who had come here from Sierra Leone with their rice and indigo culture, an island whose isolation had kept that community intact and allowed it to flourish. But Saint Helena was really no longer an island; it was connected to the mainland, and the development tide was inundating it from the land side.

The new people would give the area new names, some of which would be Something Island, because these new people, too, liked to think of themselves as being on an island. "There's a lot of islands popping up now and they're changing their names," Stevens had said. "Why? I guess it's the in thing to live on an island." These come-heres did not really want it to be an island, of course. Most people, when faced with it, do not really want to be on an island. They just want the idea. They want the word ISLAND emblazoned on their stationery. But they want the continental flood to hit here and support them. They want the conveniences—the delis, gas stations, boutiques—that keep their lives easy and connected to the mainland. They do not want an island. When Saint Helena had truly been an island, they wanted nothing to do with it.

If Saint Helena and the other islands continued to be developed, they would be only memories, ghosts preserved only in names retained or revived because of their charm. Pola Wana Island would not exist, but maybe there would be a Pola Wana branch of the Frogmore State Bank; there would be Warsaw Plantation condos, a Ladies Island Reserve restaurant, or some such nonsense to give the new islanders the illusion that they were participating in an ancient process, that they were connected to this island's past, and that this past had something to do with them.

But then, what had I expected? Dirt roads and quaint folks? What right did I have to want this place to stay locked outside time? Maybe this was just nostalgia for a way of life almost glimpsed in these places, a life I *imagined* people had, and that I envisioned as somehow more whole and connected and complete than the mainstream. I did not belong to this island. And I had no right to say, one way or another, what was a desirable future for these islanders. I had a right to demand what I wanted only for the island I lived on—that it be contained and whole and independent of the outside, wherever or whatever my island was. And this was not my island.

Maybe the question was not whether the islanders were going to lose their culture. That was up to them. Besides, all culture is continuous; it changes and evolves, and it dies if it does not change. The question really was whether they would lose their land. That is discontinuous. If they lost their land, they would lose the center of their lives. They would lose their grounding, their place—physically and metaphorically.

"I think the culture is going to have to be based on the land," Emory Campbell had said. "I think if people remain, if people keep the land, then people can remain here and change with the times; they can evolve as well. But they have to be given an opportunity to evolve."

When I had asked Joe Stevens what happens when islanders sell their land, he had said simply, "They're giving up everything. Everything."

Perhaps I had found the essence of this place's islandness after all. I had found it in its people's strong sense of themselves, in their struggle to keep their separate identity and to keep their land. And I had found it in the islanders' response to me as an outsider. There was no attempt to pretend I was one of them. I was not invited into anyone's house—except Joe's—and when I knocked on a door, sometimes the people inside did not answer. What had I expected? "Come by anytime you're around," Joe had said to me. "But call first." The islanders were polite and direct, but they were wary. Still, people here looked me in the eye, something that did not happen in many places. And when I looked back, they overcame their hesitation and insularity and waved a hand or smiled and said hello.

"Did you know that there was a different type of person that lives near the water?" Joe Stevens had said to me. "Inland they seem to be more intense, unfriendly, but near the water it's different."

Maybe so.

There was one more person I wanted to see, Marcus Bell. He had, I was told, two interesting skills—making casting nets, a West African craft he learned from his father at about the age of six; and the ability to multiply and divide Roman numerals, a process so clumsy and well-nigh impossible that we have good reason to bless those mathematicians on the Indian subcontinent who invented the Indo-Arabic numeral system, which eventually found its way west.

I had trouble finding him. His brother-in-law had given me directions to the house, but I could not tell one road from another. I finally found a trailer near where I thought his house was supposed to be. The woman who came to the door pointed at an overgrown road, a cut in the trees. "He lives in there," she said. "It looks like nothing, but he's in there."

The brush was thick, a barely penetrable tangle right up to the road. I pushed my way through the growth and there it was: a collapsed house, small once, now hardly anything; the walls fallen over; the roof, what there was of it, down almost to the ground. The walls had been patched with metal in small sheets, overlapped in places and rusted.

I hailed him as I approached, to let him know I was coming. As I rounded the side, I could see that the house was even less than it seemed. What small amount of roof survived had lost almost all its green asphalt shingles; only weathered boards remained. Two sides had almost no walls at all.

Bell answered me and came to the entrance, now a frame with a door and a small amount of wall around it that leaned out severely. He was dressed in blue pants and a long-sleeved shirt with a dark blue tie. His skin was glossy and dark, his beard and hair white with a slight yellowish cast. We stood in the doorway and talked. Past him, a fire smoldered on the dirt floor. Under the remaining roof sat a small frame bed, a cot high with blankets. A small suitcase lay open on it.

He had been in this house for sixteen years, ten years without a roof, he said. He had not had heat for ten years now—since the roof went. But they gave him blankets and he slept warm.

He mumbled, as if speaking more to himself than to me. When I asked a question, he answered almost unintelligibly, his voice trailing off as he spoke—but he kept on talking for a while, long after I stopped understanding what he was saying. Sometimes the words would become clear again, but I did not understand them. It was as if they were an entirely new language. His voice was low and gravelly, with a kind of smooth modulation over it, strangely soothing, almost a moan more than a set of discrete sounds. Sometimes the moan rose at the end of what must have been a word, as if he had tossed in a question. Sometimes I could hear laughter in his voice.

I thought of Walter Anderson and what his son said, that when you are alone on an island you move into your own world and it gets harder and harder to be with others—what might be the obverse of the otherwise positive self-containment of islandness.

How big were his nets? I asked.

"About five and a half feet," he said.

I repeated the words to be sure I had them right. What did he catch in them?

Fish, shrimp. His voice trailed off again, though I thought I heard the word "trout" in there.

How many had he made?

The words slid into each other. "I made one," mumble mumble.

"Then I made another one," mumble mumble. "South Carolina . . . forties . . ."

I could not follow him.

How long, I asked, had he been making nets?

"Since sometime in the nineteen forties—I'm not sure. I was only that tall." He held up his hand.

Did he have one?

No, not now.

Would he be making one soon?

He had been thinking of starting another, maybe in a week or so.

I asked how he learned.

He went inside the house and pulled one out of a barrel. He began to show me how his father taught him to start it. "This one is unfinished," he said.

Did he fish, himself, with a net?

"Yes . . . net . . . boat . . ."

What did he sell a net for?

"Twenty-five or thirty dollars."

I asked how many weights it would have when finished.

He counted out. "Eighty-three, eighty-four, ninety-seven. Ninety-seven."

Maybe he could show me sometime how he made them? And how he cast them?

"Yes. This one," he said, fingering the net, "is too big to catch shrimp." He got mullet in it.

As we talked, I began to swat mosquitoes and sweat and struggle with them as they stung me. I don't see how you can stand it, I said.

"Oh," he said, and then mumbled in amusement.

"Is this your garden?"

"No . . . a friend . . . water."

How did the hurricane affect him?

"Very little hit the island . . . quiet . . ." He laughed.

"A lot of changes here on the island."

"Yeah," he said very clearly, followed by a long mumble.

His family lived nearby, he said. He seemed to be saying that they were going to move away.

Would he go with them?

"Well," he said, "they have new laws now in the city. You can't live there unless you were born there."

What city are they going to?

He mumbled thoughtfully for a long time, his voice taking a serious tone.

Did he like living here by himself?

"I like living by myself, but in a better place."

"I'd like to come back," I said.

"Yes, that would be all right. I go to the grocery sometimes in the morning. But I am back by ten-thirty, eleven."

I left and he turned to the fire. He was talking quietly to himself as I retraced my steps down the overgrown road.

The next day I saw him walking toward Beaufort along Route 21 on Ladies Island, near Palmetto Federal Bank and the shopping malls. He was elegantly dressed, with a dark brown suit, dark tie, and white cap, and carrying a brown leather suitcase.

"Mr. Bell! Do you need a ride?" I called across the four lanes.

"I'm just going right here, anyway," he said. "Thanks." He pointed toward the bank. His voice was clear, no mumble. It had a beautiful tone—resonant, with clear articulation, almost studied. There was no Gullah in it. Even when he mumbled there was no Gullah in it.

I went back to his house a few days later. I smelled smoke as soon as I started down the old road. When I got there, I saw he had a fire going—larger this time—several sticks lined up, burning with a bright flame, a log on either end parallel to the sticks. He had put a two-pound coffee can on to boil. His smoke-blackened pots sat nearby.

"Is anybody here?"

"Yeah!" he called clearly. He invited me in. Though there was no wall, I went through the door anyway. I had to stoop when I entered; it opened in, so gravity kept it closed against the out-leaning frame.

Would he show the net to me?

He mumbled in response, but again I could not understand. Evidently he no longer had it.

I asked then about multiplying Roman numerals.

He smiled and started to show me. He scribbled some numbers in Roman notation, fractions that he was going to add. He began to multiply numbers in a series incomprehensible to me, writing down Roman numerals and mumbling the numbers as he worked. He covered a page:

$$\text{VII } \frac{IV}{VIII} = \frac{LX}{VIII}$$

$$\text{IX } \frac{VI}{VIII} = \frac{LXXVIII}{VIII}$$

$$\text{XVI } \frac{CXXXVII}{VIII}$$

$$\text{VIII} \sqrt{\frac{XVII}{CXXXVIII}}$$

$$\frac{XVI}{XXXIII \, ^{I}/_{IV}} \qquad \frac{II}{VIII} = \frac{I}{IV}$$

I could not follow.

"There," he said. "Add seven and four-eighths and nine and six-eighths, and you'll get seventeen and one-quarter."

I started to add them the quick Arabic way.

"No, you do it this way." He had me multiply the seven by eight the way he had in Roman. "Seven times eight," he said, "equals fifty-six, plus four equals sixty. Nine times eight equals seventy-two, plus six equals seventy-eight. Seventy-eight plus sixty equals one hundred thirty-eight, divided by eight equals seventeen, plus two, which is two-eighths, or one-quarter."

How, I asked, did he figure this out?

"Well, I learned I, V, X, and L in school, and then later learned C and M."

But how about the multiplication?

Oh, he just worked with it. He had a book, he said, with the Roman numerals in it, but he had thrown it away just the other day. It got wet. I looked around and saw only a book of Holy Scriptures.

How did he do this multiplication?

Bell pulled out a legal pad filled with multiplication tables. "First," he said, "you have to learn the tables. The tables run from II times I equals II, to XLIV times XII equals DXXVIII. Here, take this." He handed them to me. He could make himself another set.

"Thank you," I said. "This will keep me busy."

He laughed and mumbled for a moment.

The water was boiling. "I have to do the dishes," he said. I watched as he used a piece of paper to hold the pan of water and poured it into a dishpan. He pulled open a garbage can and rummaged through it (it held his supplies) till he found a bar of soap.

As I shook his hand to leave, he produced two Tampa Nuggets, offering me one with a conspiratorial mumble. He pulled a brand from the fire to light it.

"It's nice to smoke a cigar after doing a little math," I said.

He laughed again and coughed from the smoke.

"I'll be here again in November," I said. Would he be here?

"Well, I might be in the other house by then," he said, "over there." He motioned southeast across the fields.

I would find him, I said, and made my way back down the tangled path.

I had parked beside a house near the road to Bell's house. After my talk with him, I was sitting in my jeep writing some notes when a woman pulled into the drive. I waved as she passed. When I looked up again, she had stopped behind me.

"What's the problem?" she said, looking apprehensive.

"No problem," I said. "I was just talking to Marcus Bell and was making a couple of notes."

"He still here?"

"Well, he said he was going to be moving soon."

"That was a long time ago. Are you helping him move?"

"No."

"You brought him home?"

"No. I was told to see him about fishing nets."

"He going to make some for you?"

"I just wanted to see how he made them. But he doesn't have any. I'm sorry if I was trespassing."

She smiled. "I don't care about that. You can't take the land with you when you go. I'm not like some others around here who are selling. It's all right."

Hugo

I watched Hurricane Hugo on television. When it hit on September 21, 1989, I heard one Charleston resident say, "I think this is God's will, putting us in our places." That had been at nine at night, as the storm center approached the coast. By 10:00 P.M., Hugo's winds were reported at 135 mph; the storm was moving northwest at 22 mph, with a storm surge of 11 to 15 feet on top of the tide. This was a Category Four hurricane—an extremely dangerous storm.

At 10:20, as a network newsman was trying to interview a meteorologist in Charleston, the weatherman said, "It's difficult to hear you; the roof of this building is tearing off." Later, as he spoke of the potential for deaths from the storm, he said, "It's a shame that people won't heed our warning."

At 10:50, a newsman reported all of downtown Charleston under water. High tide was still two hours away.

At 11:45, a reporter in Florence, South Carolina, about a hundred miles north of Charleston, said, "In the distance I can see transformers exploding." One man, he reported, had called 911 to ask advice, because he lived in a trailer. He had been told not to worry.

By midnight, the eye of the storm had moved onshore.

Thirty hurricanes had hit South Carolina between 1878 and 1989, one every four years or so. Hugo was number thirty-one.

The next morning, the mayor of Charleston said the city had suffered "a degree of destruction unseen in anyone's memory." It had been the strongest storm in thirty-five years, with twenty-nine dead and, in Charleston alone, more than fifty thousand homeless. The city, someone reported, looked like a war zone.

Now, two weeks later, as I approached the city, I was starting to get some sense of the storm's power. In Ravenel, thirteen miles southwest of Charleston, thickets of pine had their tops sheared off twenty feet up. Other stands remained intact, if somewhat skewed, all the trees leaning uniformly thirty degrees from the vertical, as if a strong wind were still blowing. It was an eerie sight.

It got worse as I approached. Live oaks and pines two feet thick had been snapped off, others had been pulled out by their roots and laid down, as if by a great hand. Billboards looked as if they had exploded. Utility poles were down in a tangle of wire, in some neighborhoods every house had roof sections torn off, the ruptured windows of a glass storefront still littered the street.

Strangely, in the midst of this stood houses and groves that appeared completely untouched.

When I reached Charleston, one- and two-story frame buildings in a rundown part of the city looked as if they had simply been stepped on. One was a mass of splintered wood, less than half the roof and one gable end recognizable. These fragments sat on the ground on top of the rest of the debris. The metal roof was peeled back like the lid of a can, a section of it lying half a block away, another part twisted around a nearby palm tree. The house itself was more or less wrapped around a live oak. When that big foot had hit the house and collapsed it sideways, only the oak tree had kept it from smearing out across the street. Close up the wreckage exuded a smell of sewage and mildew. A woman nearby swung a broom handle idly and laughed to herself.

Yet here, too, were neat piles of debris—sawed-up oak stacked at the side of the road, building remnants cleared and heaped where someone had started to dig himself out and rebuild.

The houses by the battery—the great old three- and four-story mansions on the water—were surprisingly undamaged. Some facing the harbor directly had lost bricks on their facades; some had lost clapboards. Others had roof damage, sections of metal torn away, now replaced temporarily with plastic or composition roll-roofing.

One man here had found two cars in his back yard. Another, who had stayed for the storm and now swore he never would again, said the wind had hurled a telephone pole through his house like a javelin. It had missed him by a foot as it passed.

The people I was staying with, a block back from the harbor, had had a foot and a half of water on their first floor. The ground here was about seven feet above the harbor, and the floor itself three feet above that. My host said that when they had come back to Charleston after the storm, he had not expected to see his house standing. It had taken him thirty minutes to get through the debris in the yard to the door, a distance of less than thirty feet. But they had been very lucky: one chimney was down—it was in the swimming pool—and they had lost a little roofing. The rest appeared to be nothing more than water damage.

Others had not been so lucky, he said. In fact, he was just back from an insurance board meeting; companies were estimating Hugo's damage in South Carolina alone at almost four billion dollars.

The old battery, now a park with rows of decommissioned cannons facing the water about a block from his house, looked a bit odd. It was filled with live oaks and palmettos. The palms had done well, but the oaks had lost branches, mainly sections less than a foot thick. They had also lost most of their leaves to the wind, exposing a gnarled network of raw limbs. These were evergreens, and their shapes were usually hidden unless you were directly underneath. It was a denuded park. A section of metal roof hung tangled in an upper branch of one of the oaks.

Two men were climbing the trees to clean up the damaged limbs, removing the ripped edges with a chain saw. "I want to take that one and that one," one said. They resumed their cutting. "All right!" he exclaimed. "This place is looking good!" The debris lay in piles along the road to be picked up later.

A few pigeons, survivors, patrolled the grounds, approaching pedestrians in hope of a meal. A woman began to throw some bread; a group of the thinnest pigeons I had ever seen gathered. "There are not nearly so many as there were two weeks ago," she said. A gray squirrel hovered nearby, eying the bread, the fur missing from its left flank.

Everywhere crews from across the country were rebuilding. A convoy of power-company trucks had come from Florida to restore electricity, along with crews from as far north as Wilmington, Delaware, and as far west as Houston, Texas. The crews were working long shifts; a man I spoke to in the battery said it was his day off after six twelve-hour days.

I went off in search of a television station—the reporters and cameramen probably would have stayed through the storm. I found a crew at WCBD-TV, working out of a temporary newsroom, and joined them as they headed out to do a story on the city's rebuilding. We found a side street where earth-moving equipment was taking away a large downed oak.

While they set up their cameras, we talked. Newsman Terry Casey and a crew had been at the emergency operations center, a command post during the storm. Through the first part of the hurricane, as the roof slowly tore off, the building had been assaulted by the sound that had kept the weatherman from hearing his interviewer on the live national broadcast.

The sound, one man said, had been like "waves in the air. It started to pull the roof off in ripples. It was a hundred-and-fifty-mile-an-hour lawn mower. We jammed into this concrete hallway like sardines, and two offices. Just as we got into the offices, the dropped ceiling dropped, and the roof—all of a sudden we were looking up at the sky. So we huddled back into this real narrow hallway, all of us. And the ceiling that we were now under started to fall on our heads and water was coming down and we could hear the winds whipping at a hundred and thirty miles an hour above our heads. A rather humbling experience. I must say we were all on even ground at that point."

When the eye passed over, they evacuated the building. The eye, he

said, "was nothing. Except for some twisted metal and some rain pud-
dles, you couldn't tell a storm had passed. It was as calm and eerie as
people say it is. It was just like a balmy, humid evening."

Before dawn they were out to evaluate damage to the city. To one
man the strangest part of what he saw was "the fact that there didn't
seem to be a power pole standing where it should be. It was either tilted
over or broken off. And the trees. Everywhere you looked, it looked
like someone had taken a huge lawn mower and just mowed it, especially the pines."

The driver of a truck waiting to receive the tree remnants wandered
over to join the conversation. "I was down on Jones Island," he said. "It
was terrible."

"Metal poles were bent over as if they were clay," Casey said.
"Wooden poles were snapped off. There were live wires everywhere,
like snakes. We had to jump the median and dodge overturned trucks
in the middle of the road. There was nobody there. No one really expected what happened, the savagery of the storm. I think the whole
city is still in deep shock. You focus so singly that you just want to get
the story. You don't have time for the tears."

The entire crew seemed to have been deeply affected by the experience. One man, when I asked him how going through the storm had
changed him, thought for a moment and then said, "The most important thing is being with people." The others nodded.

"I have to think about the simplest things now," cameraman Jim
Alexander said. "My wife says, 'Put that glass in the sink,' and I have
to think about it."

"Yeah," another one said. "My wife came back and said, 'I thought
you'd have cleaned up more.' That cut to the quick. It wasn't important. It was important that I was alive. I've covered hurricanes before,
but, man, I've never seen anything like this."

I was starting to hear storm stories. One fellow, I had been told,
could not get off Sullivans Island, a heavily developed barrier-island
suburb of Charleston; he blew a tire just as police were closing the
road. He walked home, then got very drunk and passed out. He awak-
ened in the eye of the storm, thought it was over, and walked down to
the beach. There a big wave hit him and dragged him out. When a

truck floated by, he grabbed that and survived. I had no idea whether to believe the story.

When the storm hit the rotating bridge connecting Charleston with Sullivans Island, it moved the structure and broke its gears. For the rest of the storm, someone said, the bridge just spun like a carousel. There was talk around Charleston that the bridge keeper was aboard during the storm and had gotten very dizzy.

But nothing, I was told, was like what had happened to Mc-Clellanville, forty miles northeast of Charleston. There the storm surge—the actual water level—reached seventeen feet, with thirteen-foot waves on top of that. Thirty feet of water. The village of six hundred had been destroyed.

I wanted to see what had happened. It was quickly obvious, as I approached the town, that Hugo had been much more violent here than in Charleston. Thousands of acres of trees were broken off twenty or thirty feet up—not just a few, not half, but all of them, raw ripped and twisted ends sticking up. They had all been knocked in the direction opposite from those southwest of Charleston, the shattered tops swept to the west as the easterly winds had torn into them. Some looked as if they had been twisted till the wood fibers had simply given out.

I stopped the jeep and got out. I could see nothing but destruction. The few stumps that remained standing had been completely stripped of their leaves. A stillness covered everything. The effect was ghostly, a feeling of death. Now I knew what "chilling" meant—this was it. I shivered as I looked out at Hugo's remnants.

A nearby house appeared to have been peeled inside out. Another nearer the road looked as if it had been ground into pieces too small to be recognized and then just scattered like coarse powder across the grass.

The two roads into McClellanville from the state highway were patrolled by armed National Guardsmen. One smiled and waved as I drove by—this was not an army of occupation. I stopped at the roadblock. The guard said it was a mess in there, but I could go in if I came out the same way so he would know I had left.

The village was at the edge of the backbarrier marshes, three miles from open ocean. Even so, boats were strewn about like toys. One small shrimper lay on its side in a grove of live oaks near the highway, at the head of a creek too small to have ever carried it this far. The treetops were all gone. Nearby I saw debris, clearly a watermark, ten or fifteen feet up in a stand of trees. This area had been under water.

One pine tree about four feet thick had been twisted and snapped off five feet above the ground.

Several houses remained standing. Many of them looked relatively undamaged, but others looked askew, jolted from their foundations. Some small houses had been thrown together in a heap, carried off their foundations and jammed against each other, stopped by two stout oaks. Houses were strewn about, cars crushed into metal and glass splinters, brick houses looking as if a bomb had gone off.

Everywhere there was wreckage. Everywhere—between houses, in great piles along the road, in uncleared disarray on the road. Mats of marsh reeds and debris covered the ground and hung high in the trees. I picked through the rubble; it was a snarl of crab pots, bricks, lumber, pipe, wire rope, dock decking, netting.

People all over the village were cutting trees, sorting boxes of clothing outside the churches, or carrying supplies out of trucks. They looked tired. At the harbor itself, large shrimp boats seventy, eighty, ninety feet long were scattered about. Two lay against a house just above a dock. Two others, about seventy-five feet long, had been carried across the road and had come to rest neatly side by side against a sturdy live oak. At the dock a metal building still stood, but its sheathing was shredded like a cheap sardine can. Cranes were lifting the smaller boats onto flatbed trucks. Helicopters circled low overhead.

Robby D., *Silver Hill*, *Patricia Anne*, *Four C's*, *Marybelle*, *Abby Lane*, *Daddy's Girl*, *Mystic*, *Betty H.*, *Miss Kim*, *Regulus*, *Mary Margaret*—all dead. I counted twelve boats destroyed.

Two shrimpers, *Smiley* and *Patricia Anne*, had ridden out the storm with crews aboard—a captain and three crewmen on *Smiley*, captain and one on *Patricia Anne*. They had lashed themselves together. I spoke with Jeff, the crewman on *Patricia Anne*.

"Thunder," he said, "it howled, like a dog through a vacuum cleaner. It made my hair stand on end. 'What was that? Mother Nature is coming to get me!' "

Another sailor joined us. "You can't describe it, just a tidal surge," he said. "The captain was running the boat and the prop scarred some tree limbs on the tops of the trees."

Two weeks after the storm, these men were still anxious to talk about it, to get it off their chests, as if they still couldn't believe it had happened, though the memory remained all too real.

"We were up in the trees for a while," another said. "The water started dropping. We got back out in the creek, but we couldn't steer, so we went back into the trees. We ended up in somebody's yard. At five or six we were able to get off the boat. The wind kept pushing us— we thought we were going over the trees."

"It sounded like a freight train running right through you. They say it was a hundred and thirty, but it had to be much higher."

"It took about a minute to go from here up the creek, about half to three-quarters of a mile up. Houses were passing us by in the creek. The mayor's wife said she saw lights flashing by; she thought it was an airplane—it was *Smiley*."

"Our bow is missing, anchor, sampson post, two holes in the bow below the deck line, the rudder and prop bent."

"It was twelve thirty when the barge first hit us," *Smiley*'s skipper said. "The wind hit a hundred fifty or a hundred sixty. The barge was cartwheeling down the creek. We took some of the dock with us. I hit four boats in front of me. *Patricia Anne* took out the building." He motioned toward the large shredded metal building on the dock. "The barge hit the front of the bow and we went skidding down the ditch. We were probably going twenty knots going down the ditch in full reverse. We knocked all the superstructure loose. Then we hit another barge up in the creek. When we got knocked off the dock, we could see about three feet of the top of the metal building there." He pointed back to its roof peak, some twenty feet high.

"It was about five hours, six hours, till we were back on the ground. We were nearly on Route 17 when the eye hit. Then we were carried back out the creek. We almost ended up on top of a lady's house, but we pushed ourselves off with the engine and back into the trees, or we'd have been on top of her house. The water came in like a river. It wasn't a tidal wave or anything—just a fast river."

"I was out there looking back in at the destruction when a military helicopter came through," Jeff said. "It was like Vietnam again."

The next day I drove out to Sullivans Island with a property owner, across the now rebalanced bridge. This was the first day authorities were allowing people back onto the island. Damage on the barriers had been severe, much worse than in Charleston itself, and only residents and insurance people were being allowed to enter. National Guardsmen drove the roads in olive-drab-and-black all-terrain vehicles. Similarly camouflaged helicopters patrolled overhead.

The debris along the road was heavy: I counted a bookcase, a door, palm logs, utility poles, marsh reeds, floor timbers, plywood, stairs, a desk, dresser drawers, dock parts, pine cones—even a small sailboat, *Joey*, out of Wilmington, Delaware. Long streamers of fiberglass wall insulation dangled from a small tree.

A "Welcome Back" sign greeted us on Sullivans Island. The wind was blowing briskly onshore. One flag flew, a Texas flag raised on a flexible temporary pole above a house only moderately damaged. The sun was bright, the air warm. My guide looked around, taking in the changes. "There used to be a clock shop right there," she said, pointing. "This house was not there—I don't know where it came from. That house is just gone."

Some houses seemed all right. Others were in place, but stood askew, like someone with a game leg. Others looked firm, but sat in the middle of the street—one had been moved so gently that bottles still stood on the kitchen table. Many had been picked up and tossed around. Others had parts missing—the roof, a wall, a wing. Others were piles of rubble, some recognizable, some not. On one street all the houses were gone; all that remained was some debris. The trees were splinters. The palms, though, remained.

We drove east along the island. Parts of the shore road were washed away. The sand had moved back; three rows of houses away from the beach, several feet of fresh sand covered the road. Crews were removing sand from the roads and driveways, bulldozing it back toward the beach. Here was clear evidence that the island had retreated in the face of the storm. One house now sat on the beach edge, its foundation mostly undercut, the sand well inland.

People were walking around almost aimlessly, trying to figure out what had happened. They smiled and said hello, but they kept looking back at their houses as they talked to us.

My guide's house was in the first tier of houses facing the beach. The road alongside running toward the shore had become an overwash, funneling the sea and beach sand into the island. The dunes had been cut through in a deep channel, and the sea had then carried the sand right down the road. The asphalt had been lifted and pitched back slightly. The road's shoreward edge had collapsed down about three feet where the underlying sand washed away.

A woman, my guide's tenant, came out of the house. She was not sure whether she could talk, she said. She had held it in earlier, but she had been crying all day. "The dunes are just gone," she said. "The beach looks nothing like it did."

I walked away, toward the beach. What she was feeling right then, what she had to say, was none of my business. The two women went inside.

The house sat several hundred yards back from the beach, but except for a few dunes three or four feet high, the sand between house and beach was flat. Closer, I could see deep gullies, cut through where the encroaching water had run back out.

The shore itself was in chaos. It was pitted by gullies and blowouts where the wind had carried entire dunes away before the sea had done the rest. All the sand along the shoreface of the island had been leveled. A few sea oats were visible, but the taller grasses lay flat and brown.

A man in a tractor had become mired trying to push some of the remaining beach sand into a dune in front of a house. Down the beach large earthmoving scrapers were scooping sand off the beach to deposit it farther up. They filled up with sand, then raced down the beach and up toward the houses, where they dumped their loads.

A large sand ridge directly offshore from the washover was dark with brown pelicans, hundreds of them, standing facing the wind. The pelican population, I heard, had not fared well. This ridge might actually have been sand from the island, which the storm had deposited offshore. If so, then a period of mild weather was likely to return much of the sand reserve to the beach. Maybe, I speculated, as I watched the pelicans, I was seeing one of Ervin Otvos' emerging islands.

The next day I went back to the island on my own to take a closer look at what the scrapers had been doing on the beach. I drove past the police security check as if I belonged there. No one stopped me.

Four large bulldozers and two scrapers were building dunes. The dozers would back out into the water and push wet sand onto the beach from the surf. The scrapers headed west on the beach, where it was wide, loaded up with sand, and dumped it along the top of the growing dune. They worked fast.

I stopped a scraper driver and asked if this were an Army Corps of Engineers job.

"No," he said, "the city of Sullivans Island, through the Corps." They were building a dune seven and a half feet above the low tide mark. The lunar tide next week would be seven and a half feet, a foot or more above normal. They had, he said, till next Thursday to build a four-thousand-foot-long dune. Its center line was seventy-five feet out from the original dune line, the dune itself a hundred fifty feet wide. They were scraping sand out of the surf zone and then expecting the incoming tide to replenish it.

It was an iffy proposition. When, the previous night, I had mentioned to Orrin Pilkey on the phone that I had seen the big scrapers working the beach, he had said, "It's insane to try to rebuild the dunes with sand from the beach. The beaches will recover somewhat. But it will take months, years maybe, for the dunes. Nature will win."

Other geologists I talked to had agreed. The problem, one had said, was maintaining the equilibrium slope on the beach. Remove very small amounts of sand near the surf line and place them on the high beach, and you would be all right. But scrape large amounts and change the shape of the beach very quickly, which was what they appeared to be doing, and you were asking for trouble.

"I would guess it's going to last more than the tidal cycle," he said, "but I would sure agree with Orrin it's not going to be around in a year in any recognizable form." It sounded like an act of panic, a seat-of-the-pants move to calm people down, to let them think they were doing something to protect themselves.

As I spoke with the scraper driver, a man came over and asked if the scrapers would build up the sand around his house on the beach, to fill in where the sand was gone. He pointed toward some sand nearby. Could they scrape the beach right there?

"No," the driver said, "that sand has to stay there. But we will fill it in for you with some other sand." They would wait now till the tide dropped. If they kept going, they would lose an engine in the salt water.

The man concerned for his house was incredulous that I had managed to get onto the island. I asked if that upset him.

"It was very hard for us to get back on," he said, "and I see these people getting on who have no business here. People came by boat and went around the National Guard." Without taking a breath he added, "Look at this house."

It was forty years old, built of Italian marble and reinforced concrete. It had taken the full force. All the glass facing the sea, including big sliding doors, was gone. The roof was splinters. Evidently the concrete structure itself had survived the force of the sea. But the surging water must have broken through the doors and windows, and when the walls held up to its freight-train pressure, the surge would have gone right up through the roof and blown it out like a champagne cork.

Can it be rebuilt? I asked.

"I don't think they'll let me. With the new laws, it's not far enough back. And it needs to be raised. I can't raise this structure." Abruptly he turned away from me and went back inside.

He was right. I had no business here. It was as if I had walked in on a family funeral and was witnessing a very private grief.

I went back to the road. Immediately a highway patrolman stopped me. "Are you an island resident?" he asked.

No.

"Adjuster?"

"No," I said. "I'm here to see what happened to the island."

"Then," he said politely, "I wouldn't stay too much longer if I could help it. Thanks." He smiled and drove away.

King of
North Carolina

In North Carolina I joined Orrin Pilkey as he took two insurance men to Bogue Banks, just south of Beaufort. They wanted to learn about some development and insurance issues on the barrier islands. Bogue Banks was an enlightening place to start.

The twenty-eight-mile-long island had remained largely undeveloped until the 1950s, with at most a couple of hotels and beach houses at Atlantic Beach. In its earliest days, Rice Path and Salter Path were pretty much the only settlements. They consisted of descendants of those who had first settled in the eighteenth century, joined by shipwrecked sailors and eventually by a community of Shackleford Bankers who had seen how marginal life could be offshore and had abandoned their more exposed island after a hurricane.

These fishing villages had nestled on the back side of the island near the lagoon, where they knew from experience it was safest to build. In those days they built their houses to be dismantled, so they could move them as the island moved or if they decided to abandon it entirely. They had stayed away from the ocean side of the island, except to fish. When they needed to get there, they used paths (thus the path in Salter Path) through the heavy maritime forest.

Back then, I had been told, the maritime forest was magnificent. Today even its remnants are beautiful. But condos and hotels push up through it. Roads hacked into it expose the live oak branches and undersides. The trunks fork into multiple branches, and these, gnarled and twisted, thrust up into a finer and finer network to support the outer layer of leaves, which face the salt-laden Atlantic winds. The first time I had seen this exposed underside, it had reminded me of Walter Anderson's Horn Island realizations.

That time I had called a man who supposedly could tell me all about the island. "I'm not a native," he had said. "My roots are not in the Banks. On Bogue, the true Banker natives are getting squeezed out. There's a kind of insider-outsider mentality; the developers don't want outsiders telling them what to do. I've seen it go from Atlantic Beach and Salter Path and all the maritime forest to what it is now. A lot of maritime forest that you see is just lots that haven't been built on. That'll go. It's sad. There's some nice pieces of maritime forest—or there was about a week ago." That was all he wanted to say.

The island's dense development has destroyed more than the forest; it also has taken the protective foredunes. Today many buildings sit right at the beach edge, the dunes long since removed for a better view. Roads have been cut through to the shore, providing efficient channels for a storm surge to overwash the island. Bogue, one writer has said, is a fine example of how not to manage a barrier island.

Still, if you are determined to build on one, Bogue Banks is where to do it if you do so sensibly. It is the biggest of North Carolina's islands, the tallest and widest, and by far the largest in sand volume. And that makes for spots that are relatively safe. Relatively. Even Pilkey had to admit that, though he opposes development and advocates abandoning the islands.

One time at his home, far from the ocean in Durham, North Carolina—a rumpled, comfortable house full of books and dogs—I had asked what he would do about beach development if this were a perfect world.

" 'If I was king' is the way I used to put it," he had said. "If I was king of North Carolina, I would bulldoze down without the slightest hesitation—I wouldn't bulldoze them now, but as soon as buildings are threatened, they would be demolished. Which I hope is going to happen anyhow. And some developments, I think I would have to destroy the whole development. I think as king I'd have to recognize certain realities. People want to live on these islands. I'd probably have a revolution on my hands if I kicked everybody off the islands. But I think I would do everything I can to diminish the population on the islands, and maybe someday my son the prince would get everybody off the islands." It would be a formidable task—half of America's Atlantic barrier islands are now developed.

Among those with a vested interest in the barrier islands, this notion has not been particularly popular. One colonel in the Army Corps of Engineers Miami district responded to it, Pilkey told me, by saying "in effect that we're mighty engineers and we shouldn't throw up our hands and slink away from the shoreline."

There are plenty of people willing to take potshots at Pilkey for his views. One editorial writer, in a piece called "Orrin Take a Powder!", said, "It seems that Mr. Pilkey would like to see us abandon Topsail Island [south of Bogue, where we would be visiting the next day], scurrying inland in abject fear at his doomsday pronouncements." Another wrote that island residents resented Pilkey's "repeated public cries of doom and disaster."

But Pilkey's credentials as a geologist—his pedigree, as he says—are so strong that, whether or not you agree with his philosophy, you can hardly disagree with his geology. So people are starting to listen. The National Park Service, for instance, recently decided to move the

Cape Hatteras Light back from the encroaching sea instead of trying to defend it with a seawall, a philosophical victory for Pilkey and those others with like beliefs.

We drove onto Bogue Banks in his ancient brown Toyota, outfitted with a rear-view mirror that extended across the width of the windshield, an addition in deference to his neck's limited flexibility. He had broken it while diving from a shrimp boat's thirty-foot mast into six feet of water. Like many geologists I have known, Pilkey exhibits a strong mix of intellect and physicality. That time he had been trying to impress some junior high school students. "And I gave them a trip they'll never forget," he admitted with chagrin.

I asked him whether he owned any island property.

"No," he said. "I have to keep up my image." Then he added, "I'll show you the piece of land I'd own if I were going to own land on a barrier island—if I were stupid enough to live on a barrier island."

We drove to a house overlooking the lagoon. It sat on three acres, nestled behind and below Bogue's high center. It had been designed to withstand 200 mph winds. The wooded areas here, Pilkey said, were not even maritime forest; they were mainland forest, because salt spray did not reach this part of the island.

But that site was not what he was here to show us. We returned to the ocean side, where with some enthusiasm he tramped around in the sand, the insurance men listening carefully to what he had to say. (After they left at the end of the day, I asked Pilkey about doing such work; didn't he feel that he was compromising himself by consulting for special interests? No, he said, he didn't get any of the money himself; he was very careful about that. It would fund a graduate student who was doing barrier island research. Besides, he made sure he was not associated with either side. Whomever he talked to, he would tell them the truth, whether they liked what he said or not. "I've talked to a lot of bad environmentalists, too," he said.)

Pilkey turned to his attentive audience. "Most barrier islands are getting narrower," he said, "eroding on both sides—Shackleford, Core, the Banks. As it floods, the salt marsh marches in. One part of Shackleford is trying to become a sandbar. Two hundred to four hun-

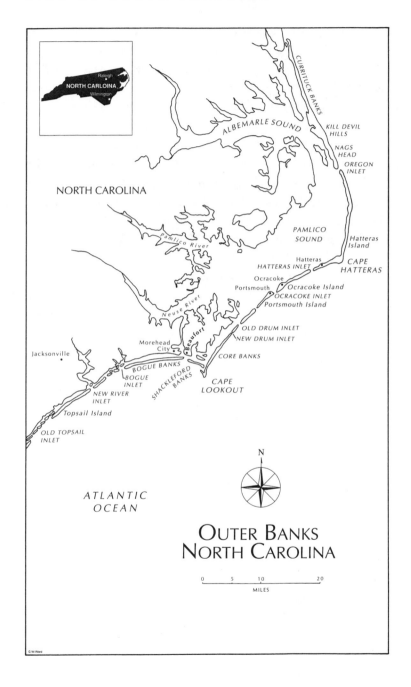

CURRITUCK BANKS

ALBEMARLE SOUND

KILL DEVIL HILLS

NAGS HEAD

OREGON INLET

NORTH CAROLINA

Raleigh
NORTH CARLOINA
Wilmington

Pamlico River

PAMLICO SOUND

Hatteras Island

Hatteras
HATTERAS INLET

CAPE HATTERAS

Ocracoke
Portsmouth

Ocracoke Island
OCRACOKE INLET
Portsmouth Island

Neuse River

OLD DRUM INLET
NEW DRUM INLET

Beaufort

Morehead City

CORE BANKS

Jacksonville

BOGUE BANKS

BOGUE INLET

SHACKLEFORD BANKS

CAPE LOOKOUT

NEW RIVER INLET

Topsail Island

OLD TOPSAIL INLET

ATLANTIC OCEAN

N

OUTER BANKS
NORTH CAROLINA

0   5   10   20

MILES

G. W. Ward

dred meters is the optimal width. The sea will overwash then. All the islands will be reduced to being sandbars as the sea level rises."

He looked around. "This clearly has had the dunes removed," he said. "On Bogue Bank flat areas like this just don't exist. Look at that dune removal. I don't think dunes should be allowed to be removed on *any* barrier island. Every speck of that sand is protection." He pointed at some nearby condos. "I wouldn't purchase one of those."

Then he stopped and looked at a building raised on piers, with breakaway material enclosing its ground level, a design that allowed the sea to surge through without necessarily carrying the house away. The trouble was that the breakaway material would hit something else. "I find that fantastic," he said. "That's what's going to destroy the next row of houses."

At the western tip of the island, we looked toward the inlet across a large expanse of small dunes and beach. Such areas are notoriously unstable, and this one in particular had been quite active recently. "There were forty lots here and a quarter-mile road," he said, pointing to the beach. "Within two years the inlet had moved here, a quarter-mile." He pointed to a spot close to his feet. "Now the inlet is moving out again. The Corps dredged this inlet recently, and the inlet ignored them. Within three years the channel had moved in along the shore."

He gestured at a nearby house. "The shore cut through right there," he said. The house had belonged to a state senator at the time, and he had started armoring his property to protect the house even though hard stabilization—the use of seawalls and jetties—was illegal in North Carolina. "Having a senator," Pilkey mused, "is probably worse than having a seawall."

To get here we had had to park illegally and walk; signs along the road had warned us not to stop. Reaching the beach was often a problem on islands. Any beach project with federal money attached—such as a Corps of Engineers beach replenishment—must maintain public access. But it is often given grudgingly. I asked if he ever had a problem getting onto beaches. "I have become fearless about trespassing," he answered. "The only way to see beaches around this country is to trespass and trespass and trespass." Once, in Florida, he had tried to park and walk to the beach, but a twenty-five-mile stretch of shore road prohibited parking, another way to keep away non–property owners. "You have to break the law to see the beach. I never have been run off, even with students. One time I was chewed out roundly by an old man in a golf cart. Right in front of the students. But he was right."

This time a police officer saw us. He parked by our cars and walked over. Pilkey identified himself and said we were here to look at some of the erosion. He knew who Pilkey was and joined the conversation. "I was raised on the coast and see these people who come from inland trying to solve these problems," he said. "If you solve the problems, let me know. Somebody asked me, 'How much erosion has taken place?' 'Since when?' I said."

"Topsail Island has the worst development in the state," Pilkey said the next day as we approached it. "It involves collusion with state government officials. It has *the* most dangerous development in North Carolina." He paused. "I have to be careful—I sound like a rabid environmentalist." This was the densest and highest-rise barrier island development in the state, Pilkey said. And it was on the north end of the island, where the federal government had tried to discourage building. It was, he had written, "a disaster waiting to happen," and it particularly upset him.

Topsail lies in the southern quarter of the state, about halfway between Cape Lookout (south of Cape Hatteras) and Cape Fear, the state's other great cape. Development of the twenty-two-mile island began in the late 1930s, and in 1954 Hurricane Hazel destroyed 210 of the island's 230 buildings. Much of the island had been submerged. Hazel generated floods of nine and a half feet; the island averages less than nine feet above sea level. The storm removed more than 850,000 cubic yards of sand from the beaches, much of which was redeposited as overwash; the island was moving back.

This time, instead of insurance men, Pilkey had brought some of his Duke University students to talk about barrier island formation and about development—his favorite combination. We crossed onto the island and immediately turned north along a narrow road toward North Topsail Shores, the development that he so disliked. The island was narrow here and low, hardly more than a large sand ridge in places. And it was eroding rapidly, about two feet per year. The dune line was only about five feet high and badly deteriorated from foot traffic.

"Here it is: Topsail Island," he said. "And the bulldozers. Right away. They're moving the road over there," he pointed inshore, "because they're going to develop here," pointing to the foreshore, "a very dangerous location. This is a very narrow island." He pointed inshore again. "There's the water right there. The island is a hundred yards wide there. Here it's sixty."

The new road would be lower than the old one. "That's madness," he said. "I can't imagine who designed the thing, what they were thinking of. It's lower. It's on the back side and it's lower, so it'll flood just as quickly." People here would become trapped by rising water long before any hurricane arrived. Though one of the developers contended that moving the road would protect it from overwash, the real reason for the move was probably not safety; more likely it was money. The move would open up enough oceanfront property for the developers to build thirteen hundred condominiums. At one time their plan called for eight towers up to twenty-five stories high along this four thousand feet of shoreline.

Pilkey looked north and paused. "Holy shit. That was not there when I was there last." We were looking at Villa Capriani, a massive three- and four-story condominium in a Southern-California-Italianate-Mediterranean-Spanish-Mission eclectic stucco style. It was under construction, almost completed. The road crossed in front of it, though not for long. Villa waited only for a new road to be built behind it and the old one to be torn up; then its front terraces could be connected to the boardwalk to the beach. Thus Villa Capriani would magically become beachfront property.

We drove past it into the heart of the development. There stood the next one, Topsail Villas. He counted the floors. "One, two, three, four, five." He sighed into his beard.

There was plenty of evidence of the sea's incursion here. A nearby pier had been damaged, its farthest-out pilings gone, its outermost remaining thirty-foot section dangling dangerously, ready to fall. Its land end had collapsed too, leaving it standing free in the water.

Much of the road was overwashed, with a steep dozer-made dune pushed up along its seaward edge, ready to slump. The road was damaged from crisscrossing treads cutting into the pavement. Bits of asphalt speckled the dune, and sections of the road had recently been repaved. Surely this road would flood—and the dunes wash out—with the slightest storm and tide rise. The same developer who had said the new road would be safer had also denied that erosion was a problem at all on the north end of the island. "We're talking about two hundred years from now, if it was to happen," he told a reporter. When I mentioned this to Pilkey, he answered, "Barrier islands are usually run by people who have no interest in the future, only an interest in profits."

Beside the road a large sign announced: "Coming Soon! Harbour Master, one of the finest resorts on the east coast. Luxury Resort, Sales Office, 17 stories, 400 units, on-site financing, 400 seat restaurant, 24,000 sq. ft. commercial area, 1 indoor—2 outdoor swimming pools, convention center, tennis courts, health club, ocean & sound views, covered atriam [*sic*], valet parking, 400 unit parking deck." The sign had been here a while; some of its painted letters were faded and hard to read. Maybe the developer had given up. Maybe it would never happen.

Pilkey looked around. "This is an artificial dune," he said. "This is why it's such a dangerous development. December 2, 1986, and January 1, 1987, this was all gone after the two storms. It was just flushed away."

About the next group of condos, Topsail Dunes, "These are the stack-a-shacks," he said. "They can be strong—though these aren't—but they're real firetraps because there's no way to keep the fire from going straight up. This is awful, just awful." The structure was seven stacks high, all wood, looking as if it had been erected quickly.

The development thickened as we moved closer to New River Inlet, at its end. Here the island widened, the sand in this seaward bulge part of the unstable inlet system: this sand could leave quickly. The next building was big, maybe a hundred fifty apartments in three- and four-story sections. There would be plenty of flying debris to damage other structures if this one ever broke up in a hurricane. Then came the Saint Regis, three five-story buildings, about two hundred fifty apartments in all. This stuff was massive, and it was right on the beach. It would have no protection at all.

Finally, at the inlet itself, we came on the New River Beach Club, the "exclusive" cluster of stucco houses with pink and lavender tiles. A large Corps of Engineers dredge was working the inlet, sucking sand off the channel bottom and pumping it into the shallows.

"For Sale" and "For Rent" signs were everywhere. These developers were selling the public a fancy dream—an island, the beach, a gate, an architect's design, exclusivity—all those things that island living can mean to those with cash. "It's a beautiful location," Pilkey said, "other than the fact that it's dangerous as hell."

I wondered how long these houses would last. Some, Pilkey said, had been flooded during their construction. Maybe this end of the island just needed a senator.

We walked through the property onto the beach. This time, fortunately, we met no policeman or irate golfer to upbraid us for our bold transgression. Pilkey had much to say and a considerable stretch of beach to travel, and it was best done without interruption. He was going to talk about sea level rise and sand, the combination that both created the barrier islands and made them move and change, the blessing and the curse.

"Barrier islands are found on all coastal plain coasts," he started. "In theory (I'm not sure about this), as sea level rises on a gentle slope, valleys flood and form estuaries. The ridges become headlands. They're vulnerable to erosion; they start forming a spit of sand from the ridge." Thus the first barrier island is born.

This sandy cosmology was vintage 1885 Gilbert, with no mention of the De Beaumont–Otvos theory, yet Pilkey was careful to admit his uncertainty about exactly what the process was. I had asked him about Otvos' theory earlier. He had given me a thoughtful answer typical of him: "I think he's absolutely correct that submarine bar formation is a means of either island regeneration or island formation to begin with. I don't find any problem with that. I think there are probably a thousand scenarios of island formation and island migration, and we're trying to do this usual bit of classifying. It becomes an argument that

Nature probably doesn't like us to have. If there is a Nature looking over us, Nature is probably unhappy that we're worrying about how many angels can dance on the head of a pin. It's probably sitting there and thinking 'God damn, can't you see that this is a complicated process that's different everywhere and it just doesn't fit into these nice little pigeonholes?' It's nice to have little categories, but it's stupid sometimes."

He continued: "Barrier islands form and they begin to migrate. This makes them a unique feature. Instead of being destroyed by sea level rise, they move up and back. Assateague [Maryland] has moved completely off itself since nineteen thirty-something. The surf zone is now behind where the lagoon edge was fifty years ago. They're doing something very sensible. They're not just standing there being beaten around the head and shoulders.

"If the sea is rising slowly, the islands get fat, like Bogue. If it's a rapid rise, they get narrow, like here—but here it's because of low sand supply. Given time and a lot of sand, this island would widen and get fatter. The islands are in an equilibrium between sea level rise and sand supply. Other factors are wave energy, big storms or little storms, wind. Waves bring sand ashore to the beach; the wind carries the sand from the beach onto the island."

Pilkey pointed to a big house close on the beach. "That building was flooded twice during construction. The builders were crazy. We'll see a lot more atrocities." An environmentalist had told me that one four-hundred-unit complex under construction here had collapsed in a northeaster. He had called the area a time bomb.

We were standing on the bulge in the beach, where it had widened. Pilkey pointed to waves breaking near the inlet and then back to the sand. "This wad of sand is very tenuous. It is likely to erode at a very rapid rate. I know from aerial photographs that this hasn't been here that long. When it goes, these houses will go. This is a very, very bad development. The developer—I don't want to talk about that. I get emotional."

He turned and started back down the beach, returning to his original point about future sea level rise and land loss.

"How flat is the coastal plain? Here it's [a ratio of] one to two thousand. A one-degree slope is one to ninety-five. You can't perceive a one-degree slope. The slope is about the same as on the continental slope."

Sea level began to rise rapidly again sometime around 1930. And the rate is expected to accelerate within twenty years. "The outlook is fuzzy," Pilkey said, regarding how much it would rise. "Maybe three to seven feet by the year 2100. Think of the shoreline retreat then. And think about this: the rate [of slope] is one to ten thousand in Pamlico Sound, and one to sixty thousand in some areas. On the mainland at Pamlico, a one-foot rise pushes the shoreline back two miles."

In areas with a slope of one to sixty thousand, that one-foot rise could mean a twelve-mile retreat. And with a sea level rise of seven feet, even Pamlico could see a retreat of almost fourteen miles. (The EPA goes a bit further, saying that though the sea is most likely to rise between four and seven feet by 2100, it may be as much as eleven feet, with correspondingly larger shoreline retreat.) Assuming a rise of five feet, scientists estimate an inundation of 1.24 million acres of North Carolina lowlands, displacing some 282,000 persons, with losses conservatively estimated at $1.86 billion. Farmers in coastal areas are already losing cropland to saltwater intrusion. Houses close to the shore would be inundated, no matter what we tried to do. And the barrier islands would move right out from under whatever we built on them. The prognosis sounded a bit like Louisiana's.

"And," Pilkey added, "this sea level rise is just a little blip, of little consequence." Of little consequence at least in the geologic time scale.

The dredge was now so close to the shore that it was dumping its spoil directly onto the beach.

Pilkey marched rapidly along, pausing now and again to point out a feature, this time a snow fence. "If I were living on this island, I'd tear this up. The beach is sacred. Nothing should be on it. But it's okay. A storm this winter will probably take this sand away. Building a beach is usually futile."

He held up an oyster shell. "Everybody knows what this is. How did this get here? Clearly, island migration! So we're standing in what was some years ago the lagoon." He held up a coquina shell. "This shows we have an offshore element. It was found in the ancient shoreline in the Pleistocene between now and a couple of million years ago. It was broken up and brought up."

We reached an area where the dunes were sharply eroded. A tall, steep scarp cut into them. He pointed at one part of the dune, then another. "Why is the sand brown here and gray there? It's bulldozed, an artificial dune. They have to do this at least once a year. The bulldozed sand disappears much more quickly. To be in equilibrium, the beach wants to be there"—he pointed inshore past the dune—"so it takes the dune away. The presence of shells in a dune is a dead giveaway; they can't get there."

He looked down the expanse of beach. "This is a very shady proposition. It's very discouraging to those of us trying to control shoreline development."

He went on. "On January 1, 1987, a number of people were trapped here." About two hundred fifty persons at the Saint Regis had been stranded in the winter storm. The next day, seas were still breaking across the road, though some people managed to leave. "Being trapped in a northeaster doesn't matter," he continued. "You just sit in your apartment and drink beer. But to get trapped in a hurricane is very different. I think there's more possibility of loss of life here in hurricanes than anywhere else in North Carolina. People don't move. And these people won't get off. They have shabbily constructed buildings—and I know they are—and it's a low-elevation island. In winds these buildings will blow apart and smash into buildings beside them.

"Can you imagine what a Class Five hurricane would do coming ashore in North Carolina? You will be paying for this for a very long time."

Pilkey had tried four times to get onto Topsail Island during that January storm. "I was stopped four miles from the greatest damage by the police," he said. "I pleaded with them. A friend just said he was with the Corps of Engineers and they let him through."

He paused and looked over the scene. "I wish the sea weren't so romantic," he said finally. "These people come here for the great adventure of the sea. And worse, they buy land and stay."

We began our march back to the inlet and our cars. "We're going to the Sea Vista Motel," Pilkey said, "almost at the south tip of the island.

One of the things that you'll see are trailer parks. They're held in by poles. They're virtually unsurvivable in a hurricane."

As we drove, he pointed out his favorite island features. He motioned to a tall building under construction. "This is 'the most environmentally sensitive development on the North Carolina coast,' according to the developer. You show me what way you can make a fifteen-story condo environmentally sensitive. We need one disaster badly on the East Coast."

Realistically, I asked, was there any way we could control the sea's incursion?

Pilkey laughed. "Nature always wins at the shoreline. In a geologic sense, the idea of controlling nature is outrageous, impossible, idiotic, insane."

I thought of a conversation I had had earlier with a former student of Pilkey's, now developing beach stabilization technology. He had dropped by Pilkey's house, and as the conversation about the problems of overdevelopment wore on, he had taken me aside, as if to conspire.

"It used to be," he said, "that we didn't have much of a problem on the islands, because even when someone built a summer place, it was just a little something in among the dunes. But now someone builds something, it's got to be five thousand square feet, and he has to landscape around it and take down dunes and put in a tennis court. He has to drop a piece of Long Island on it."

I agreed.

"You know what's different now?" He lowered his voice. "We can control Nature. We can do anything we want."

"That's been the problem from the beginning," I replied. "Ever since the Greeks came up with the notion that we're separate from Nature—you know, 'Man is the measure of all things.' We'd go out in these places that were dangerous or unstable and build in spite of that, because we thought we could control Nature. Every generation, we think we have some new way."

"That's right. But now we *can* control Nature." He had said it without humor.

Trouble is, I said to Pilkey as we drove on down Topsail Island, people see Nature's ways as challenges, not as lessons about the dangers of barrier island living.

"My God, yes." He pressed the steering wheel with his hands. "Patriotism comes out."

We begin to pass pastel pink, yellow, and blue houses, condos and townhouses on their stilts. "Cute" had come to the beach. The names of these developments all tried to evoke other places: Sea Oaks, Calinda Cay, Heron Cay, Portofino. It seemed that these islands were never seen for what they were; they were sold to off-islanders as fantasies.

Finally, as we moved southwest, the development became more traditionally middle class: modest apartments, houses on piers, and trailers, lots of trailers, Nature's battering rams, the first structures to disintegrate in a hurricane.

"Here's a lumberyard," Pilkey said with a strange glee. "I have to laugh when I see that. Amazing they have a lumberyard. Imagine the damage this'll cause in a storm."

We stopped at a three-story building on the beach edge, in front of the dune line. Its first floor was gone; only supports remained to hold up the second and third stories. This was the Sea Vista Motel.

"This is a very publicized case in coastal zone management history," Pilkey said. The fifty-unit motel had been built in 1971, two hundred feet from the ocean. The sea began to encroach almost immediately. By 1979 most of the beach was gone and the sea was flooding the motel regularly. "They put up sandbags almost to the second floor," Pilkey said. "The next storm took out most of the first floor. It was repaired, and it happened again. So they said to hell with it and took out the first floor." The motel closed in 1985 when storm waves destroyed its septic system but reopened the next year after the owners had cleared out the debris.

"What happened was that the inlet migrated south. As it migrated, the bulge moved with it. So there was rapid erosion here. It wasn't apparent: you had to look elsewhere to find the cause. So the problem here was inlet related." The inlet was a half-mile south. Its name, New Topsail Inlet, indirectly revealed the instability of the beaches here. Old Topsail Inlet was farther south.

We walked out onto the beach. Pilkey pointed at its scarp. "That's very unusual. You rarely see a scarp that sharp except on a replenished beach. And this is a replenished beach." That, too, was why the beach was now so wide. The sand had been taken from the inlet channel. It had not been an official replenishment project, Pilkey said. Instead, the Corps had dumped sand here while ostensibly clearing the channel. If this had been called a replenishment, the property owners would have been required to supply public access. There was none. We were trespassing again.

Pilkey had little good to say about the Corps of Engineers. There was talk now of a large Corps beach replenishment project on Topsail. It would involve one big pumping of sand, then a small amount each year for fifty years. Pilkey hated the idea. "They've vastly underestimated the amount of sand," he said. The evidence from replenishment on adjacent islands indicated they were off in their estimate by as much as 1,400 percent. "It's a major natural atrocity," he said. "It's unacceptable to our society. The Corps has a research lab, but it has little effect on the real-world Corps."

Maybe they were more interested in getting projects (their motto, the joke went, was "Keep Busy") than in scientific grounding. Pilkey has publicly called them "dishonest and incompetent" and has testified to a U.S. House of Representatives subcommittee that their "predictions of replenished beach durability are always wrong." According to him, they misrepresent geologic reality when they propose projects. For instance, they pretend that storms are not part of the natural system, that they are aberrations, something they cannot plan for in their engineering projects.

Pilkey had shown me three statements from the Corps. About the Miami Beach replenishment: "The beach should last forever—provided a major storm doesn't come by." About Jacksonville Beach, also Florida: "The beach has been eroding at double the rate of initial Corps projections, which engineers blame on storms." About dredging the Port Mansfield, Texas, channel: "One thing we had not counted on was that a major storm would occur just as the project was completed, so the experiment was not entirely successful."

But storms are very much a part of the system, in some ways among the most significant factors in barrier island dynamics. According to Pilkey, a hundred-year storm, for instance, might be more important in shaping certain islands than the intervening years of relative calm.

(In the same breath, though, he admits the danger of making such arm-waving generalities.)

"There is no excuse for their looking at storms as unusual. There's no excuse for that. Where else do storms occur but on the beach? And they must be taken into account. Nobody overlooks them, nobody but the Corps of Engineers. They say, 'Hey, God damn, we didn't know about those storms.' "

Back in reality, on the southern end of Topsail Island, we walked down the beach. Pilkey pointed to the beach edge. "We're seeing an exciting event here: we're seeing the beach widening. We're seeing a berm forming. That's a bar that's marched up onto the shore. How do we know that? We've been able to document that some of the bars that form off Shackleford Banks [between Bogue Banks and Cape Lookout] move ashore in about six weeks. They form just after a storm. It's different for each island. Some bars don't move as bars; they move grain by grain. They stay there and get smaller as the sand migrates in.

"The beach is a critical part of the barrier island," he concluded. "Basically everything on the barrier island comes across the beach. The beach is in dynamic equilibrium: wave energy, sand supply, sea level, the form of the beach. The beach is like a living thing. The whole barrier island is a living thing."

The next morning we regrouped at the Duke Marine Laboratory in Beaufort (which sits, itself, on a stranded thirty-four-thousand-year-old barrier island). We were headed out to Core Banks. Core extends northeast from Cape Lookout, the southernmost of the Outer Banks, depending on what you count as outer. Core is undeveloped and, as part of Cape Lookout National Seashore, essentially unspoiled. After the depredations on Topsail Island, we were getting the chance to see a barrier island in its natural state. A physicist from Duke University joined us for the trip.

Aboard *First Mate*, a lab research boat, we worked our way along the shallows of Back Sound, behind Shackleford Banks and around to Core Sound. Shackleford trended at almost a right angle to Core. Because of that, the two islands were very different—at Shackleford prevailing winds blew cross-island, but at Core they blew along it. The wind carried sand; thus Shackleford was wide, with large dunes, whereas Core was narrow and low.

We anchored off the marshes and ferried ashore in a small boat, wading the last fifty or seventy-five yards in water up to our knees or thighs. The bottom was soft, adding to the difficulty, and the ooze got softer as we approached the shore. We scrambled with some relief out of the water onto the marsh edge, only to see that we still had a distance to go—the marsh was intercut with creeks, and we had to cross two or three before we would be on relatively solid ground. One by one we eased ourselves back into the water. These creeks were actually deeper than the lagoon approach had been, and the shorter members of the group were in almost to the waist. One slipped and got a quick, brackish bath. Finally on firm ground, we waited to regroup.

"We're standing on an old tidal delta," Pilkey said. "At some time an inlet opened and sand poured through. After the inlet closed, a salt marsh was established." He pointed toward the water. "This is a sharp bluff, a sure sign of eroding.

"The growth here is *Spartina alterniflora*. This is a classic, beautiful salt marsh, really well developed. Low salt marsh has only one species. As soon as there are two or more species, it's high marsh. Low marsh floods every day. High is flooded at least once a month." He pointed to a small clump of bushes on a rise of sand a foot or less high. "High marsh gets its sand from the island," he said. "That is clearly an overwash event. It appeared when? A few years ago, less than a hundred years." Like a true geologist, wherever he looked, he saw the sand and the dynamic process by which the barrier island had formed.

"We're seeing two methods of island widening: incorporation of tidal deltas, which takes hundreds of years, and overwash, which is rapid. If sea level rises rapidly, delta incorporation becomes less important and overwash becomes more important.

"The island is narrowing. It needs to get narrower to become an overwash island, to save itself from sea level rise."

Again Pilkey had anthropomorphized the island, as he had so many other times, speaking as if it had a will. I asked him about that later. "Nobody sees an island the way I do," he answered. "I have just come to the point where I think just because it doesn't have certain organs to make it a living thing doesn't mean it's not a living thing. They behave like living things. They do sensible things, and there are ways that they can be made sick and there are ways they can be made well."

A student asked how *Spartina* spreads. "This is not a botanical trip," Pilkey said. "You're not supposed to ask about plants." He laughed and then said, "I'm very excited about this. I've never been on the back side of this island before. This is stuff I've been looking at for years with aerial photographs. This is a clearly defined island. The zones are clearly defined."

He pointed at a clump of plants that extended toward the lagoon. "This is undoubtedly, or most certainly, or very likely, an overwash fan. It looks like we have a big tongue of vegetation here. So we have a high overwash event, maybe during a hurricane. When an island gets low enough and narrow enough, it will become an overwash island and will overwash on even the smallest event."

We struggled on through the high marsh, *Juncus* rushes cutting our legs. Suddenly the growth thinned and we were walking on sand. "You get an impression that we're on a plain that's dipping landward," Pilkey said. "The elevation here must be as low as the berm on the beach. We're standing on an overwash apron. It probably happens twice a year. Where the overwash is fresh"—he bent down to look closely at the sand—"you see hardly any shells. Over time, the wind carries away the finer sand, leaving shell lag. I think the reason there's so little sand here has to do with something happening out there"—he gestured toward the sea—"but I don't know."

The island was narrow indeed. We were already overlooking the beach. We walked seaward through a twenty-yard band of scattered low dunes four or five feet high at most.

This would be a good island to camp on for a while next summer, I said.

"You can camp here," Pilkey answered, "but in the summer life is hell here because of the horseflies."

Evidently there was another reason life would be hell in the summer: people drove up and down the beach. The National Seashore allowed vehicles to be ferried over and left on the island, evidently a compromise it had made with local politicians while trying to acquire the island. "There were two big fish camps and lots of garbage," Pilkey said. "A lot of wrecked cars, a school bus full of beer cans. The island was being used obscenely. They now license eight hundred vehicles; they took off two thousand vehicles from the south end of the island. Vehicles now must be inspected each year. You rarely see more than a half-dozen. It's very disturbing, but it's the compromise you have to make."

Looking out to sea, we could see four dolphins surfing, running back and forth parallel to the shore, turning and riding the waves. The students yelped when they jumped out of the water.

"Development shouldn't occur on an island of this sort, by my view," Pilkey said as he turned to take in the island. "This is a wonderful place to see what a barrier island really is. If this doesn't get you excited, you ought to be in sociology."

The physicist bent down and peered intently at a dune.

"Looking for processes?" Pilkey asked.

"No," the physicist said. "Just looking to see if I can see anything move."

Bankers

Inside the North Carolina sounds there are days of deceiving sweetness, when the water is oily smooth, its blue color almost white with the brightness of the sky, when zephyrs blow lightly across your skin and barely riffle the water surface. Days when boats in the blue distance pull a thin wake behind them for miles, and the faraway guarding banks are a hard blue line on the horizon.

This was such a day. I was riding the car ferry from Cedar Island, a few miles from Beaufort, twenty miles across the southern reaches of Pamlico Sound to Ocracoke, just south of Hatteras Island. Middle-aged and aging men had taken to the deck on this placid crossing, strolling with determination and a certain casualness in the arm and torso. It was as if, like Ishmael, they had finally put to sea after too long a beaching, and here they were again, where they should have been all along, wanderers on a rolling deck, seeking the far horizon.

Ocracoke was the southernmost inhabited Outer Bank, unreachable by bridge. Perhaps because of that isolation, it had retained some of the feeling of the old-time Banker communities. South across Ocracoke Inlet sat Portsmouth, my eventual destination. The village was at the northern end of Core Banks, but an island in itself, separated from Core's southern end by New Drum Inlet. At other times other inlets have separated it from the rest of the thirty-six miles of Core Banks. Outer Banks inlets are notoriously unstable, and at least twenty-five different inlets are known to have existed along the islands at one time or another in the historic period. As many as eleven small inlets have been open at a time, and as few as three large ones.

The village of Portsmouth had been settled in 1753. But it had died, its population dwindling during its second hundred years until the last two inhabitants left in 1971. Today it sat abandoned, a National Park exhibit. From the ferry its southern parts were a faint, irregular line visible through field glasses. Its few dunes were dark, covered with vegetation. Occasionally I would see one that was strikingly white—bare sand. As I looked farther north, the island gradually faded out, too low to be visible above the horizon; I could see only water.

Friends in Beaufort had told me about acquaintances of theirs who sometimes camped on a ridge of sand in the sound, which usually remained exposed at high tide. Someone would drop them off and they would stay overnight. They'd have to be crazy, I had said; I'd never do that. But I suppose this was the same—Ocracoke, Portsmouth, Hatteras, and the rest were little different from that ridge, except that the ridge was in extremis, its vulnerability more apparent.

Ocracoke's white lighthouse and water tower appeared. The island slowly rose from the water, first the houses of the village, then the low-lying extended sand ridge that is the island itself. This was a very small island, very far out to sea. It was a good time to remember that tranquil days like this could change quickly, the wind coming up, the sea rising in indifference to any human presence or concern.

Drawing closer, I could see that the inlet was wide. Portsmouth was now visible to the naked eye, but even with the glasses I could not make out its edges. The first European explorers to come through that inlet thought they had found in Pamlico Sound a great sea, maybe even the passage to China. It was apparent why: the land lay so low, both the islands and the mainland, that the space seemed great. And here, forty-five minutes out from Cedar Island, an hour and twenty minutes short of Ocracoke, the islands barely visible, I could no longer see the mainland. Even with the glasses, three-quarters of the horizon was empty sea.

As we approached Ocracoke, Portsmouth fell back behind us, becoming almost indiscernible. I could see only a black shape silhouetted against the late afternoon sun, its ragged sand hills petering out toward the inlet and back down toward Cape Lookout.

Englishmen had first arrived on Ocracoke in 1585, when Sir Richard Grenville anchored on his way to Roanoke, fifty-five miles north. Its earliest English name, Wokokon, may have been an Indian word for fort. The name suffered many variations among English writers—among them Wococock, Wosoton, Okok, and Oacock—till they settled on Ocracoke. Along with its name, the island's shape also changed during its human use. The original 1585 map showed the island to be about eight miles long; the old Hatteras Inlet went through the center of the present island. That inlet closed in the 1730s, and Ocracoke was part of Hatteras Island until the new inlet opened during a hurricane in 1846, doubling the island's length. (The Outer Banks are disheartingly susceptible to storms. Since 1585, at least one hundred fifty-five hurricanes and uncounted extratropical storms have affected the islands.)

About six hundred sixty persons now lived at Ocracoke year round, in what at one time had been a maritime forest. There may already have been some small habitation here before 1715, the year the North Carolina colonial assembly passed an act settling pilots on the island to bring ships through the dangerous inlet. They had named this new community Pilot Town, though eventually it had taken the island's name.

The village sat well back from the beach, near the island's southern end along Silver Lake, a broad harbor with a narrow entrance opening into the sound. Once known as Cockle Creek, it had been dredged in

1931, its spoil serving to fill some of the low-lying land. Far from the dunes, this was a sensible site, the kind that barrier islanders traditionally built on.

Although the village had remained isolated until the time of World War II, tourism had begun in about 1885, when a group of businessmen had built the Ocracoke Hotel. But Ocracoke today was still a working harbor. There were plenty of motels, including two on the water, but the fishermen had not been squeezed out by pleasure boats and high-end development as on so much of the rest of the coast. Fiberglass boats, mostly twenty-five to thirty feet, were tied up along the small docks that ringed Silver Lake. Near the ferry landing, at the mouth of the harbor, a couple of sailboats and a shrimper were docked. Most of the boats, though, were small and rigged for sport fishing. (These were not likely to be squeezed out by yachts. On the ocean side, Diamond Shoals, off Cape Hatteras, is infamous among sailors; the entire length of the Outer Banks from Cape Henry, Virginia, to Cape Lookout is littered with wrecks—more than forty have been recorded on Ocracoke alone—and sailors tend to pass well offshore on their way to somewhere else.)

Nets were strung out or lying on the grass to dry along much of the harbor. There was a kind of slow-paced bustle. Men worked on the docks or gathered around boats to talk. The streets were relatively busy, mostly with trucks pulling boat trailers.

The town had changed over the years, and it would continue to do so as development moved down the coast. But the transition from an isolated, subsistence-level fishing village to a place connected to the rest of the world, making money from tourism, had been relatively gentle. Despite whatever struggles it had gone through, the community remained intact.

I found Alton Ballance working on the roof of his house. He had written a book about the island, and I had called him from Beaufort to set up a meeting. He was tall and slender, his dark brown hair close to his head. An Ocracoker who had gone away and eventually moved back, he now taught at the island school. Face to face he was not unfriendly, but he was distant. He did not offer his hand—he had paint on it, he said. Yes, he would talk to me. Come back later, he said, when I'm not busy.

He suggested that in the meantime I take a walk down Howard Street, a relic of the old Ocracoke. It was a short walk; nothing was far here. I found a narrow sand passage near the harbor, one wagon wide, with cedars and live oaks arching overhead. The peaceful, dark lane offered a sense of protection. It was an appealing path from a time before streets opened up, before vision expanded—secure and quiet, close and embraced by the trees. Even in this tiny community, the most contained of places, these houses, the oldest on the island, were held within their own fences—some fresh with sharp edges and white paint, some mossy and corrupt with time, their edges softened, their tops irregular with rot.

Among the trees I spotted a small graveyard. I had almost walked past it. Leaning against the base of a tree was a scribbled sign: "Please do not walk on graves." I saw stones with "Ballance" carved on them. Small family plots lay scattered here and there, some neatly fenced, some with their fences down. By one gravestone stood an arrangement of yellow plastic roses with plastic ferns; at an adjacent grave were yellow, orange, and white plastic zinnias, with sprigs of plastic holly. The flowers had been there for a while, the semipermanent memorializing the impermanent. These clusters of graves and faded flowers under the trees offered a touching scene. It had the poignancy of all graveyards, a reminder that this was a place of human habitation.

Coming out of the lane, I turned up Back Road and there saw an old woman in a garden. What, I asked, were those plants? I motioned toward a cluster of callas. She began to move through the garden, pointing out the plants: calla lily, juniper, cedar, live oak, palmetto, cypress, locust, red myrtle, crape myrtle, mulberry, pine, "olander," holly, crab apple, and pear. It was an impressive litany. I was grateful. She smiled a bright, white, dentured smile and disappeared down a shadowy path into a grove of gnarled live oaks.

I came back to Ballance's house. The air was warm, and the outside door was open to the living room. He was sitting in an overstuffed easy chair, a floor lamp shining over his shoulder, his left leg slung over the chair's arm. On the mantle behind him rested a small model ship. The stovepipe receiver below the mantle had been covered with a recent layer of off-white paper, and as the chimney backdrafted, the membrane flexed in and out. The room was comfortable and small, of a scale and feeling I had seen many times in New England, particularly on islands, a late-nineteenth-century house built to be informal and intimate.

Ballance was reading Mary Shelley's *Frankenstein*. I was impressed that he was reading a book about being responsible for the monsters we create. The ramifications on this little island were endless. But he admitted that the book was for his class.

I wanted to talk to him, I said, about development.

One problem, he said, was that new owners were driving land values up. An islander make ten thousand dollars a year. Someone offers him four hundred thousand dollars for his house, which has been in the family for a few generations. What does he do? "Hell, yeah, I'll sell it for four hundred thousand dollars," Ballance answered himself. "And there goes the ownership. I don't dislike people who are moving in. I don't hold that against them. It is sad, though, to see a culture that has developed for two hundred years turn upside down. And it's not the same, it's not the same fabric, the same identification, it's not the same language. People who move in, they're accustomed to lifestyles elsewhere, they're accustomed to services elsewhere, expectations. And sometimes they bring in beneficial things, and other times they're demanding.

"That's when you have the tension. People who have been here for a long time and people who have just moved in. You've known your neighbor all your life, and your parents have. And then it's a stranger who plays weird music and stands nude in the back yard and takes showers, who has fifty people to spend the weekend, who puts a fence up, who puts a sign up 'No Trespassing.' What that does to everybody else, it makes them more isolated, more protective or suspicious."

These newcomers were different, he said, from those who had come in earlier times when the travel was difficult. "People who came to Ocracoke fifty years ago, a hundred years ago, really wanted to get here. They didn't try to take advantage of the people here; they didn't try to buy the property. All they wanted to do was come down and get back in touch with nature." Those visitors, he said, respected the island. They did not need to *have* it, and that was what had protected the island. "It's an irony that the very thing that attracts them and that they must possess contributes to its destruction, so that it's really just another slice of suburbia in a way."

How was the island going to protect itself now?

"Well, like everything else, there has to be a balance, there has to be a compromise," he said. There had to be a way for islanders to keep their homes and jobs, to live their lives here. "As long as they don't sell, then you won't get the older houses torn down or modernized. You will keep more local people. The culture will perhaps pass on down.

"Is Ocracoke going to survive as a community? I don't mean a place that closes down after Labor Day. The strengths of the community are schools and churches and things like that that identify us. If you don't have those things, if you have all summer people, or a retired population and no kids, then you have a place that's not really a community but just a stopping point."

And him? Was he here for the duration?

"Oh, I don't know," he said. "I'd like to try."

He had warmed up as we talked, but now suddenly the conversation was over. "I have to go," he said and stood up.

I want to get over to Portsmouth, I said, apropos of nothing.

"Talk to Junius Austin," he said. "Even though he may not talk your head off, and he won't, he will talk to you a whole lot; but you can sense that this is somebody who has been—who has seen a lot. He's been across that inlet many times, and what he has to tell you nobody else can tell you."

There was a potluck supper at the school, I had been told. I should go to it. Yes, I had said, I probably would.

Later, as I sat in the school's parking lot, watching people arrive, I hesitated. They greeted each other by their cars and at the door. I had a wedge of cheese I had bought at the store. I watched and thought about going in.

No, I would not go. *Islanders turn their backs to the outside world,*

I thought to myself, and for a long moment I felt painfully like an outsider. But that was not the reason I did not go in; I could not bear the thought of walking in on a roomful of people who knew one another so well.

Instead I drove out the four-wheel-drive road to the island's ocean side. The beach there was wide, with a small zone of dunes six or eight feet high. Trucks lined the shore, with big tires and pole racks across their bows. Fishermen stood in the surf or sat in lawn chairs, overseeing their rods. The rod holders were jammed into the sand; the poles lined the beach, leaning out toward the water, their lures somewhere out there in the surf.

It was a balmy evening, with a red sunset setting fire to the tall clouds to the east. A pleasant twenty-mile breeze drifted in off the Atlantic. Still, the surf looked mean, breaking three or four feet high, a couple of hundred yards off the beach. By the time it hit the sand, it had already dissipated its energy on the bar fifty yards out. But it was breaking constantly.

To the southwest, toward the inlet's ebb-tidal delta, the surf was an incoherent mass of spume extending out for hundreds of yards. Portsmouth was a dark shape on the far side of the wild water. The island seemed tattered, broken up in the looming light, its low parts lifted from the water by a layer of shimmering light.

Unlike most Banker communities, Portsmouth had been planned. Ocracoke Inlet was, till the midnineteenth century, the only navigable entry into Pamlico Sound south of Roanoke. (It also appears to have been the only continuously open inlet in the Outer Banks in historic times.) And so in 1753 the assembly had established a transshipment port on the north end of Core Banks to handle this traffic. The fifty-acre town was to be called Portsmouth. Deep-draft ships would unload their cargoes into its warehouses; from there lighters would carry the goods to various ports on the Roanoke, Pamlico, and Neuse rivers.

It had been a sensible plan. But it soon ran into problems. The inlet, always shallow and difficult to cross, began to shoal as soon as the village was established. Within eighty years it was only ten feet deep. When the 1846 hurricane opened the new Hatteras and Oregon inlets at either end of Hatteras Island, sailors used them to get into Pamlico

Sound. With less water flushing through to clear the littoral sand cross-ing its mouth, Ocracoke Inlet continued to shoal. By 1883 commercial vessels could no longer get through, and the inlet became useless.

Till then, though, trade through the inlet had continued to grow, and by the time of the Revolution, Portsmouth and Ocracoke were the two largest communities on the Outer Banks. The heads of Ports-mouth families reportedly were all pilots. By 1790 wharves and ware-houses had been built on the sound side. When at the end of that cen-tury the shifting channels opened a new anchorage at Shell Castle Island behind Portsmouth, as many as four warehouses and two piers were built on that small oyster-shell island. The port was handling more than fourteen hundred ships per year by 1860, when the popu-lation reached its peak of 685, virtually the same number as Ocracoke today.

After the Civil War, though, things were never quite the same. The island had been evacuated in the face of Union forces, and only about half its people returned. Shipping continued to decline, and by 1880 none of the 222 remaining islanders were pilots.

During these years, of course, hurricanes continued to plague the is-land. They struck the community in 1769, 1795, 1806, 1827, 1835, 1839, 1846, 1899, 1933, and 1944. In the August 1839 storm most of the livestock and many houses were washed away. Some reported the water as high as twenty-seven feet, a figure that is hard to believe. Four vessels in the harbor sank and seven ran aground. It was, according to the old-timers on the island at the time, the worst blow since 1795. Only one person was killed, the skipper aboard one of the ships that sank. According to the islanders, in its more than two hundred years no one on Portsmouth itself ever died in a hurricane.

Even so, these storms did depopulate the island. After the 1899 hur-ricane, then after the August and September 1933 storms, and again after the 1944 storm, which islanders said was the worst in memory, people simply left. Soon Portsmouth had lost a certain critical mass; there were too few people to sustain life. One islander whose family left in 1940 remembered that there were about sixty islanders before the 1933 storm, but only thirty-five by the time he left. About twenty remained after 1944. "They didn't leave because of fright," he said.

"They left because they were tired of cleaning up after the storms. People just got fed up with it."

Its vulnerability to the sea concerned islanders. In 1962 Ben B. Salter sent a letter to the Carteret *News Times*: "The outer banks have taken the worst washing ever, sand dunes washed and blown away and new inlets cut out through the banks here and there. The outer banks cannot last much longer unless something is done by man; unless something is done and that pretty soon, there will be nothing left to build to. I hope and pray that something will be done and quickly. The outer banks certainly need immediate attention, and Portsmouth Island in particular. The storm-battered banks."

There were other reasons for leaving, including the problem islanders had burying their dead on such a low-lying island.

One man, in later years remembering life there, talked about the burials. At low tide, he said, the water was only two and a half feet below the sand. That was as far down as a grave could go. "We had to bury them and stand on the casket," he said. "With Ike, Henry's brother, we had to do that. Four of us had to stand on the casket to keep it down in the hole until we could get enough sand piled on top of it to hold it down. And then it washed out partially. Henry had to go there and recover it. That's another thing that caused some people to leave here. They detested that. They didn't want to be buried in that water."

Joseph Morgan's parents had left the island in 1905, when he was eleven years old. Asked, at age eighty-eight, how hard it had been to make a living on the island, he had answered, "Well, you could make an existence, but nobody could ever make what you would call a living on Portsmouth."

Steve Roberts, whose family had left in 1912, when he also was eleven, said in that same interview, "If there were fifty people living on Portsmouth today, I'd move back there."

"Damn if I would," Morgan had answered him. "I thank God many a time that my people took me away from there when I was young."

The village school closed in 1943, and by 1956 there were no children at all on the island. Of the seventeen remaining residents that year, the youngest was Henry Pigott, age sixty. Three years later the post office closed after a hundred nineteen years of service. After that, each day Pigott would meet the mail boat at the inlet in his skiff. He died in 1971. Marian Babb and Elma Dixon, the last two islanders, chose to leave instead of living on alone. The village was gone and, as one islander said to me, time stopped.

Winter arrived overnight. Rain fell for most of the night, and the temperature was fifty degrees at midmorning, with a low scudding overcast. The wind was blowing more than thirty miles an hour from the west, a cold, cutting blast tearing the tops off the waves crossing the inlet. The Ocracoke Coast Guard station flew a single red flag, a small-craft warning.

I met Junius Austin at the harbor. He had agreed the night before to take me across to Portsmouth, depending on the weather. This morning he said we could go, though it would be a slow, wet ride in his twenty-four-foot boat. He was ready for it, in boots, foul weather pants, and slicker, a baseball cap over his close-cropped white hair. We would have to go out along Ocracoke's back shore, he said, along Teach's Channel (named after pirate Edward Teach—Blackbeard— who had been killed on Ocracoke in 1718), then out past the beach at the inlet, wending our way among the channels.

Austin had come to Portsmouth from Hatteras in 1929 at age twelve with his father, a lighthouse keeper. (He called it "Hattras," like any good Banker from western England.) When his father retired and returned to Hatteras with the rest of the family, Austin stayed on Ocracoke. For twenty years he had worked on Portsmouth, and he knew the island better than anyone now living.

Ocracoke Inlet was at most a mile and a quarter wide, but the distance from dock to dock was about five miles. On a nautical chart Portsmouth looked like a drowned island. Unlike most land-based maps, the chart did not show it as a single island. Rather, it was a series of small islands, with a strip of beach on the ocean side maybe a half-mile seaward of these insular hummocks. The rest, what might show as solid ground on other maps, was either marsh or tidal flat connecting the island to the beach dunes; three or four inches of water would flood this flat when the wind was right.

We took more than twenty minutes to cross over to the island, following a route marked in part by limbs driven into the sandy bottom, the leaves still on their branches. The channel itself was fifteen feet deep, but once we crossed it, we were in four to five feet.

The water danced and broke on the flood-tidal delta inside the inlet. Aside from the telltale chop, the delta was clearly visible; its water was a brown even murkier than the surrounding water. Outside the inlet, the ebb-tidal delta was more obvious, even from this distance. The surf there broke straight up in big plumes. It was that way all the way across the inlet—spouts, not a continuous line of surf, but columns of water suddenly rising up, then falling back while a hundred more shot up. I would not have liked to cross that bar.

It was a ride almost without conversation. The wind was loud. Running into it as we were, we could barely talk against its force. And, as I had been warned, Austin was not talkative.

Did I intend to take a long time? he asked finally.

A few hours, I said.

Well, if I was going to be only an hour or so, he would wait for me instead of coming back across the inlet later in the day.

That was fine, I said. I'd take only a couple of hours if he would go ashore with me and tell me a little bit about the community.

He agreed. His mouth had a firm, down-set line at both edges—a man of determination who had had that mouth set for a long time. But, as I soon found, he laughed easily once we had talked a while. He spoke slowly. Sometimes a trace of Banker, the accent's distinctive *oi*, as in "Hattras Oiland," slipped through.

He pointed out two islands inshore of Portsmouth; one had been Shell Castle. "They used to come here on the menhaden boats until the channel began to fill in," he said. "That's what happened here, really. On those other islands, there used to be a fort on one of those islands. There used to be warehouses on Shell Castle. There used to be forty-five people living over there." Now the islands were nothing more than stands of high marsh in open water.

"It's not hardly large enough for the pelicans and seagulls to lay and hatch there. That's what happened. Erosion is what got in these Outer

Banks." He spoke as if erosion were some kind of infection, a kind of wet rot that nibbled away at the edges of island existence.

We landed at a small Park Service dock at Haulover Point, well past the inlet on the island's lagoon side. Water was flowing up the creek into the marshes—the wind was driving it in from the sound. We slogged over the soft ground.

"The island floods out easily," he said calmly.

A pelting rain started again, driving hard against us until we got off the marsh and in among some small cedars. Then the mosquitoes took over. I had been warned that on Portsmouth they were "beyond anything you have been told or can imagine." Even in this wind and cold they were waiting for their blood. But they did not vex Austin at all. They circled his face ineffectively.

At first the wind seemed to be the only sound. Then I began to hear the sea in the background, faint and deep-pitched, a far-far-away freight train. I could hear cricket sounds; a bird calling somewhere out in the marsh; the harsher crrakk-crrakk closer in, of two kingfishers squabbling. Even so, there was a stillness here, as in a hurricane's eye, where you hear the storm around you but the center, where you stand, holds still and firm.

"Do you want to see the cemeteries?"

"Yes."

We stopped at a small plot. There, a stone:

George Rodnal Babb
Born Oct 16, 1924
Died Oct 18, 1924
Our Darling Baby

"This baby lived two days."

"Yeah," he said, regret in his voice.

Two days old. Everywhere the story was the same in these small isolated communities—the sorrows of a hardscrabble life. "At Rest," one said. "Gone Home."

We walked to several other plots, Austin naming one person or another, telling me when he or she died. Some had lived long lives. For

Benjamin Dixon, who had lived to the age of eighty-four, was written, "An honest man is the noblest work of God." Here also was Henry Pigott's grave. When Pigott had become ill in 1970, Austin cared for him at his own home on Ocracoke. After his death the following January, Austin brought him back and buried him on Portsmouth, this little island that had been his home. On his stone was written, "Gone But Not Forgotten."

These cemeteries were small—six, eight, or ten graves—and scattered through the village, down little lanes into the cedars, wherever the family could find a spot high enough and dry enough to bury someone. How deep they were buried, Austin said, depended on the rainfall and the tide. "You see, the big tides, they come up through the ground. A lot of people don't realize that, but that's what happens."

He showed me another plot. Here, next to a marsh, was a grave with a foot-high cement bulwark around it. "This grave here, this is one of Henry's sisters," he said. "Rachel. We had to bring sand in here to cover her up with. With the tides and storms, you see how low it is around here."

Sand filled the space within the low wall. When he buried Rachel, he had not been able to dig the grave very deep and the top of the box stuck up above the ground. Unwilling to leave it that way, he came back and made this wall and then hauled sand from the beach to cover it.

Austin seemed pleased that I wanted to see these plots. He must have cared for these people to be concerned for their remains; he must have loved this island to come back and cover a grave properly. There was, I felt, much in our conversation that was being left unsaid.

Everywhere the ground was boggy. With the previous night's rain, water stood several inches deep.

A lot of people had lived down that way, he said, motioning vaguely.

Was that ground higher?

"No."

"Is the whole island this low?"

"Yeah, mostly." He pointed over to the highest spot on Portsmouth, a clump of small trees with two tall pines crowning out above them. The ground did not look higher than anywhere else.

We came into what might pass for the village center, a cluster of buildings, three small shingle-roofed houses next to a white church on a green. Some of the houses had been placed here by the Park Service, which had evidently had a problem deciding where to put them. Traditionally, islanders moved the village back as the island retreated, so no one was quite sure where they belonged. These houses, all held off the ground by brick pilings, were well-kept, a pale yellow with white trim and white columns on the porches. Two others nearby had been damaged—one was down, one was collapsing.

"I don't know if you noticed this building or not, how it's canted on the foundation," he said. "The 1944 storm done this." It was as if the islanders marked time by their hurricanes.

Austin walked fast through the village. He did not stop to reflect. But he had a lot to say about it, particularly about the Park Service's acquisition of property. He was bitter. He pointed at buildings and named names. This man had been paid eight thousand dollars for his land; this woman, twelve thousand dollars. Others had gotten much more. He barely looked at me as he talked about how it seemed to him that powerful people had done very well, while natives had not.

"They came over here and the people who didn't have nothing, they're the ones that didn't get nothing for their property," he said. "For instance, the school building down there, there was a lady owned it. She got about eighteen, twenty thousand dollars, because she had nothing. They were afraid it might go to court, so that's what they settled for. Then the guy that I brought over here was supposed to go over each building to see how much property there was and how big the building was, what kind of shape it was in. He didn't do it. Because there was some mosquitoes.

"That happened here. And people have never forgot it, either. The ones who lived here, they got shit. That's what they got." He looked directly at me and his pale blue eyes were angry. There was surprise, too—shock at his own words.

The old school he had spoken of was south across a marsh, on a little hummock of its own. "You can go," he said. "I'm going to go back to the boat. I don't want to leave it any longer." He would wait for me at the dock. I walked slowly out onto the marsh. It reached from the edge of the village compound to the sound, hundreds of acres of dark green-and-gray spikes of *Spartina*. The path to the school had been raised over the marsh, with eight-foot-wide ditches on either side to keep the walk drained.

The small schoolhouse was a single room deep, on posts, its ridge-pole sagging. It was not a very important building. But I was struck by what it represented—the fact of a small group of people making a life out on these Banks. How tenuous this life had been. Yet in building a school these people had promised that they were going to stay and raise families out on this piece of sand that lay in such delicate balance.

Austin had said something to me earlier as we approached Portsmouth across the wild water in the inlet. It seemed obvious at the time, not significant. Simple as it was, though, it was the answer to the question I had been asking myself on this journey. Now, standing here on this meager island, surrounded by the sea roaring in the distance, I understood what he meant.

"People lived here," he had said.

A c k n o w l e d g m e n t s

I have many people to thank for their help in my efforts to see these islands and write this book.

Orrin Pilkey, James B. Duke Professor of Geology at Duke University, not only gave me an informal course in coastal geology and the issues surrounding coastal development, but also took the time to show me his vision of the islands.

Folklorists Mike and Deborah Luster, on the North Carolina coast, received a phone call from a stranger and invited me into their home. They generously gave me their time and a friendly haven each time I came through their part of the country. Joe Stevens also invited me into his home, while sharing some of his understanding of Saint Helena. Archaeologist Herman Smith, of the Corpus Christi Museum of Science and History, taught me a bit of coastal Texas archaeology, then suggested we go and look for treasure. One of these days I'm going to take him up on that.

Many others gave their time: Terry Casey and the crew at WCBD-TV, Charleston; Don Davis, Louisiana State University; Kathie Dixon, Duke University; Ann Ehringhaus of Ocracoke; Casey Green, Rosenberg Library;

Connie Mason, North Carolina Maritime Museum; James M. McCloy, Texas A&M University; Todd Miller, North Carolina Coastal Federation; Robert Morton, University of Texas Bureau of Economic Geology; Sally and Edward Pritchard of Charleston; Gary Stanton, University of South Carolina; John Welles and Jesse McNinch, University of North Carolina Institute of Marine Sciences; and the National Park Service rangers all along the coast, particularly Bob Patten at Cape Lookout National Seashore.

Then, when I returned home, Emily Adams and Robin Lonski transcribed miles of taped interviews that often were barely audible.

And now some old friends. Folklorist Deborah Fant shared her enthusiasm for this book from its beginning and led me to people who knew the islands. Librarian Robert Pyle always managed to find a book I needed and forgave me when I was late in returning it. As for Lydia Lyman, Preston Kelly, and Steve Clyburn, I know how much they helped me, even if others may not.

It is hard to know how to express my gratitude to Maurine McElroy. From my first day in her English Renaissance Literature class at the University of Texas, she listened to what I had to say; and in the years since, she has shown a genuine interest in whatever I have been writing.

Britton, Joseph C., and Brian Morton. *Shore Ecology of the Gulf of Mexico*. Austin: University of Texas Press, 1989.

Dabbs, Edith M. *Sea Island Diary: A History of St. Helena Island*. Spartanburg, South Carolina: Reprint Company, 1983.

Davis, John L. *Treasure, People, Ships, and Dreams*. San Antonio: Texas Antiquities Committee and Institute of Texan Cultures, 1977.

Ehringhaus, Ann Sebrell. *Ocracoke Portrait*. Winston-Salem, North Carolina: John F. Blair, 1988.

Kelley, Joseph T., et al. *Living with the Louisiana Shore*. Durham, North Carolina: Duke University Press, 1984.

Komar, Paul D ed. *CRC Handbook of Coastal Processes and Erosion*. Boca Raton, Florida: CRC Press, 1983.

Leatherman, Stephen P. *Barrier Island Handbook*. Amherst: Environmental Institute, University of Massachusetts, 1979.

Ludlum, David M. *The American Weather Book*. Boston: Houghton Mifflin Company, 1982.

McComb, David G. *Galveston: A History.* Austin: University of Texas Press, 1986.

Pilkey, Orrin H., Jr., et al. *From Currituck to Calabash.* Durham, North Carolina: Duke University Press, 1978.

Rosengarten, Theodore. *Tombee: Portrait of a Cotton Planter.* New York: William Morrow and Company, 1986.

Schueler, Donald G. *Adventuring along the Gulf of Mexico.* San Francisco: Sierra Club Books, 1986.

Sugg, Redding S., Jr., ed. *The Horn Island Logs of Walter Inglis Anderson.* Jackson: University Press of Mississippi, 1985.

Teal, John, and Mildred Teal. *Life and Death of the Salt Marsh.* New York: Ballantine Books, 1990.

Turner, Lorenzo Dow. *Africanisms in the Gullah Dialect.* Ann Arbor: University of Michigan Press, 1973.

Weise, Bonnie R., and William A. White. *Padre Island National Seashore: A Guide to the Geology, Natural Environments, and History of a Texas Barrier Island.* Austin: Bureau of Economic Geology, University of Texas, 1980.